ENGLISH SOCIETY AND THE PRISON

This social history analyses a period in which the modern prison experienced some of its most serious challenges both on a practical and a philosophical level. These include the way in which prison was utilised to deal with poor, disaffected and political sections of society, and the failure to establish in the prison a legitimate means of punishment. English prisons have been the site of continued struggles over power, waged between prisoners, prison staff and prison authorities. These dynamics are examined from a perspective which emphasises the forms of disturbances that occurred within English prisons between 1850 and 1920 and the consequences of a custodial sentence for those subject to it. For many offenders, the taint of imprisonment closed down their choices and instituted a pattern of 'revolving door' custody for petty crimes. For some convicts, the physical and psychologically under-mining effects of penal servitude, and in some cases extreme acts of self-injury, could incapacitate them for life.

Alyson Brown is a lecturer in the history of crime at Edge Hill College of Higher Education, Lancashire.

ENGLISH SOCIETY AND THE PRISON

Time, Culture and Politics in the
Development of the Modern Prison,
1850–1920

Alyson Brown

THE BOYDELL PRESS

First published 2003
The Boydell Press, Woodbridge

Transferred to digital printing

ISBN 978–1–84383–017–7

The Boydell Press is an imprint of Boydell & Brewer Ltd
PO Box 9, Woodbridge, Suffolk IP12 3DF, UK
and of Boydell & Brewer Inc.
668 Mount Hope Ave, Rochester, NY 14620-2731, USA
website: www.boydellandbrewer.com

A CIP catalogue record for this book is available
from the British Library

Library of Congress Catalog Card Number 2003012673

Typeset by Keystroke, Jacaranda Lodge, Wolverhampton

This publication is printed on acid-free paper

Contents

Acknowledgements

It would not have been possible for me to undertake the research upon which this book is based without a bursary from the University of Hull. My thanks must therefore first go to that institution. My sincere thanks also to Keith Nield, who provided copious amounts of advice and guidance, and to the members of the then Department of Economic and Social History at the University of Hull. In addition, I extend my appreciation to Professor William Forsythe and Professor Victor Bailey for their encouragement. Last, but by no means least, my thanks to Nick for his sense of humour and his constancy. Errors and misjudgements remain my own.

It is important also to acknowledge here the invaluable help of staff at the variety of libraries, archives and records offices I visited during the course of this research. The institutions visited included: the British Library; the Public Record Office; Hull City Record Office; Beverley Local Studies Library; the Bodleian Library; the Prison Service Library; Chelmsford Record Office; the British Library of Social and Political Sciences and central libraries at Hull, Leeds and Manchester. The images in Figure 1 are reproduced courtesy of the East Riding of Yorkshire Archives Service, QAP/7/37. I would also like to thank Hebblethwaite & Sons, Kingston-upon-Hull, for their kind permission to reproduce the plan of Hull prison from c.1870 (Figure 2).

1

Introduction: prison disturbances

The rules and regulations of the prison define a standard of behaviour that is expected from prisoners. The discipline established within the context of prison rules and regulations enables prison staff to construct an internal authority and hierarchy to enforce required standards of behaviour. Prison discipline has to a large extent been determined by policy developed by several levels of prison officialdom from the Home Office to individual prison governors. In turn this policy has been influenced significantly by wider parliamentary, public and media opinion as well as by events within the prisons themselves. Within this multi-layered system of prison administration and management has been confined the prison inmate whose incarceration is legitimated by their being convicted of, or awaiting trial for, breaking the law. This is a very basic description of the prison system in England during the period covered by this publication (1850 to 1920) and indeed up to the present day. This description has been pared down to its bare minimum and yet the complexity of the prison system's structure, policy and relationships remains obvious. The picture becomes more complex when it is considered that experience and perceptions of the prison differ with regard to the position that an individual or group holds within the prison system. Crucially, internal obstacles and resistances that, to a large extent, were both a consequence of the organisation and structure of the prison and a determinant of them have affected the operation of the prison system, or more accurately, systems.

This book is an historical examination of English prisons from 1850 to 1920 which approaches the complexity of this institution from the perspective of the disturbances that occurred within it. The primary aim is not to analyse the form and extent of prison disturbances during this period, although this will be considered, but rather to concentrate upon the origins, causes and effects of these disturbances. English prison disturbances are examined on several inter-linking levels with regard to the structures, policies and relationships within the prison and the ways in which these interacted and produced disorder. Prison disturbances are also examined with reference to factors imported into the prison, embedded in the person and body of the prisoner, in particular political activism, but also factors such as mental instability. However, analysis of the separate categories of prisoners with regard to gender, age, and physical or mental disability will be limited, as this book is concerned with the prisoner largely in terms of position, status and reaction.

The reason for examining the prison from the perspective of its internal disturbances is that they often revealed a great deal about the policies, problems and coercive nature of the institution. Indeed, as Sykes has pointed out in his early sociological examination of the prison in America, power 'unexercised is seldom as visible as power that is challenged'.[1] Prison discipline was such an important environmental determinant of power relations that much of this book also entails consideration of its functions and influence. What remains clear is that in prisons of the past, as in prisons of the twenty-first century, the problem of maintaining discipline and order on a daily basis was, and is, never far removed from the problem of disorder.[2]

Discipline was the means of ensuring that the rules, regulations and routine of the prison were adhered to. Any activity by prisoners through which they attempted to assert their own will, or to determine the conditions of their own imprisonment in opposition to the rules and regulations, was liable to be punished. As the first female Inspector of Prisons in England stated, those who directed and implemented the prison system were 'not afraid to hurt, or injure, or cause him [the prisoner] to run risks, in order to master him'.[3] The behaviour of the prison staff was also restricted as they both administered discipline and were subject to it. Prison officers were also punished for infringements of the prison rules and regulations that applied to them; they could be fined, suspended, demoted or discharged. Discipline required a specific use of space which determined movement and overrode the self-determination of human action. It also influenced and, to a large extent, constructed the complex hierarchy of relationships in prison.

In *Discipline and Punish: The Birth of the Prison* (1977), Foucault interpreted prison discipline as a central feature of the prison and other institutions which developed in the emerging industrial societies of the late eighteenth and nineteenth centuries. Discipline, according to Foucault, was a normalising agent which was both based in and enabled the complete surveillance and control of prisoners, or whichever body of people the nature of the institution dictated. The mechanisms of discipline centre upon the distinct organisation of space, a strict regulation of activity and time, and upon classification and surveillance.[4] Through the mechanisms of discipline, knowledge and power are created in a way that Foucault most clearly describes in his discussion of 'panopticism'. Foucault's concept of panopticism follows an analysis of the means by which the panopticon (literally meaning,

---

[1] G.M. Sykes, *Society of Captives: A Study of a Maximum Security Prison* (New Jersey: Princeton University Press, 1958), p. 53.
[2] This view was expressed with regard to modern prisons in R. Sparks, A.E. Bottoms and W. Hay, *Prisons and the Problem of Order* (Oxford: Clarendon Press, 1996), p. 3.
[3] M. Gordon, *Prison Discipline* (London: Routledge & Sons, 1922), p. x.
[4] M. Foucault, *Discipline and Punish: The Birth of the Prison* (Harmondsworth: Penguin, 1977), pp. 135–94.

the all-seeing eye) prison, invented by Jeremy Bentham, the founder of Utilitarianism, and his brother, in the late eighteenth century, enabled the few to see the many. Through a system of blinds anyone in the central rotunda of Bentham's prison could view the prisoners in the cells built in a circle around the rotunda without being seen themselves. The prisoners can, therefore, never be sure whether they are being observed or not and so become the agents of their own surveillance, 'authority could exercise a constant surveillance while remaining itself invisible'.[5] The visibility of the panopticon becomes a trap which 'objectifies' the prisoner, ensuring his self-control and 'the automatic functioning of power'.[6] Foucault described the panopticon as constructing 'a machine for creating and sustaining a power relation independent of the person who exercises it; in short, that the inmates should be caught up in a power situation of which they themselves are the bearers'.[7]

It has been suggested that Foucault provides little theoretical basis for the possibility of resistance within his vision of a total institution.[8] Garland concurs with this view and states that 'the resistance of prisoners to the disciplinary process, and the failure of the prison to effect their reform, raise serious theoretical problems for Foucault's account'.[9] Yet Foucault asserted that 'there always remains the possibilities of resistance, disobedience, and oppositional groups',[10] and the history of the prison institution clearly shows this to have been the case. Taylor insists that Foucault does allow for the existence of revolt or resistance, but states that, according to Foucault, such action cannot bring about liberty since it will only substitute one system of power relations for another within a regime; there is no way out.[11]

Despite the insights that Foucault offers, he discounts the existence of individual human agency which is not wholly determined by discipline and power and which is an important causal element of prison disturbances. As Garland has asserted, Foucault makes assumptions about the effects of penalties which leave little or no space for a consideration of moral or emotional aspects of punishment.[12] Certainly the moral and subjective

---

[5] J. Semple, *Bentham's Prison: A Study of the Panopticon Penitentiary* (Oxford: Clarendon Press, 1993), p. 116.

[6] Foucault, *Discipline and Punish*, pp. 200–1.

[7] Ibid., p. 201.

[8] R. Sparks *et al.*, *Prisons and Order*, p. 67.

[9] D. Garland, *Punishment and Modern Society: A Study in Social Theory* (Oxford: Clarendon Press, 1990), p. 171.

[10] M. Foucault, *The Foucault Reader: An Introduction to Foucault's Thought*, ed. P. Rabinow (Harmondsworth: Penguin, 1991), p. 245.

[11] C. Taylor, 'Foucault on Freedom and Truth', *Political Theory* 12, No. 2 (May 1984): p. 176.

[12] Garland, *Punishment and Modern Society*, p. 132.

aspects of the causes of prison disturbances compose an important part of the analysis here.

Analysis of prison disturbances committed by prisoners and prison staff is facilitated by the use of historical works and also texts in criminology, sociology and philosophy. The use of a measured interdisciplinary approach enables an emphasis upon particular fundamental themes which were important determinants in producing disorder not only at the particular historical point in which they are highlighted but also over the longer term. This will also provide a more theoretical foundation for issues which have been broached in existing texts, such as the problem of legitimacy for an essentially coercive institution. The purpose of a thematic approach to the subject of prison disturbances is, therefore, to highlight particular factors that influenced specific prison disturbances and also to analyse broad themes that have been decisive in affecting the stability of the prison throughout its modern history.

Large-scale, combined disturbances were not part of the normal daily routine in prison, but minor offences against prison rules and regulations were. Therefore, all kinds of infractions of the prison rules and regulations will be considered. Indeed, the fact that actions that were liable to be punished in prison were so wide-ranging and all-encompassing emphasises the coercive nature of the prison and the importance of considering small resistances. To whistle or sing in prison were actions as liable to punishment as to commit an assault upon another prisoner or a prison officer.

The nature and form of prison disturbances varied considerably. They could be a conscious protest or an unconscious or impulsive reaction. They could be passive or active – for instance, refusing to work or destroying prison property. Prison disturbances could also be a planned combination by prisoners, an individual cry for help or an indication of depression or stress, such as the practice of self-injury by prisoners. Such actions have been as much a part of the prison establishment as the systems of discipline but are much more revealing about the subjective experience of the prison.

In his study of peasant resistance in a small Malaysian village during the years 1978 to 1980, Scott emphasised the importance of analysing not only the more dramatic revolts but also the everyday, often individual and unplanned struggles. He states that the smaller resistances are important because 'they make use of implicit understandings and informal networks; they often represent a form of individual self-help; they typically avoid any direct symbolic confrontation with authority'.[13] To an extent this was also true of prison offences, although in the highly structured prison way of life even small actions could represent direct confrontation with authority.

[13] J.C. Scott, *Weapons of the Weak: Everyday Forms of Peasant Resistances* (New Haven: Yale University Press, 1985), p. xvi.

In such a social context the smallest actions by prisoners could be endowed with considerable meaning.

The majority of offences were minor infringements of the prison rules and regulations but these were often committed in large numbers. In the second half of the nineteenth century the number of prison offences committed annually in each of the large public works prisons in England often amounted to over two thousand. For example, between the years 1865 and 1875 the annual total of prison offences committed in Portland Convict Prison fell below two thousand in only one year and was over four thousand in four years. The daily average number of convicts in Portland Prison during this period remained fairly stable and was usually between 1550 and 1575.[14] The task of detecting, processing and adjudicating on these offences was a major administrative undertaking. The large number of minor offences that were punished in English prisons during this period must also be under-stood in the context of a large degree of discretion which operated within the prison system. For instance, individual prisons varied with regard to the effectiveness of the supervision and the priority placed upon punishment in the operation of discipline by prison administrators. These are important factors in assessing the detection, punishment and recording of prison offences.

Therefore, the broad range of prison disturbances is considered here because of the significance that could be attached to even the smallest actions and the problems these posed for prison management. One impor-tant factor to note, however, is that in many cases the most detailed and extensive historical evidence available concerns the larger-scale, combined disturbances which more directly and seriously threatened the discipline and order of the prisons. These were also the forms of prison disturbance which were the most vigorously put down. Thus, where such evidence has been particularly useful in examining the origins and causes of prison disorder, the large disturbances have been concentrated upon. Hence, Chapter 3 examines the causes and consequences of a major riot in Chatham Convict Prison in 1861 in which over 800 convicts were implicated.

Aside from the effects of the level of supervision and organisation in individual prisons, some offences, which were accepted as occurring by both prisoners and prison staff, were rarely detected or recorded. The incidence of sexual relations between prisoners or between prisoners and prison staff of the same gender is probably the best example of such an offence. One of the few pieces of specific evidence, as opposed to general comments, regarding such activities concerns an investigation carried out by the Home Office in 1883. This investigation was instigated when a boy, George Hawkins, accused a fellow prisoner, George Williams, of 'attempting to commit an

---

[14] *Reports of the Directors of Convict Prisons*, British Parliamentary Papers (henceforth BPP), 1866–1876.

unnatural offence upon him'.[15] No charge was brought as a result of this investigation because it was thought that the evidence was insufficient to secure a conviction. This is an aspect of the experience of imprisonment which, due to the scarcity of information, cannot be examined in any depth.[16]

Chapter 2 explores the concept of time in relation to the experience of a long-term prison sentence. The distortion of perceptions of time in prison composed an additional burden for prisoners and increased the likelihood of disorder. Discharged prisoners who published accounts of their experience refer repeatedly to an extended sense of the present that was brought about by the highly regulated and monotonous prison way of life. The experience of time in prison was dominated less by the clock than by the momentum of institutional regulation and also in purely personal terms as inmates were driven back upon their inner resources during the long hours spent in their cells. Examination of time in prison also highlights the inadequacy of a single conception of time which takes no account of the nature or intensity of the way time is experienced.[17]

Chapter 3 considers a theme that has attracted much attention in criminological work. An important inquiry into prison disturbances in England was held following the riot in Strangeways Prison in Manchester and disturbances in several other prisons in April 1990. The report referred to these disturbances as the 'worst series of prison riots in the history of the British penal system'.[18] The voluminous report produced by Lord Justice Woolf and Judge Tumin, published in 1991, instigated further research into the subject of prison disturbances and, according to Cavadino and Dignan, has become established as 'a historical and classically liberal account of what is wrong with English prisons, what causes prison riots and what should be done to prevent them'.[19]

The Woolf Report highlighted problems in prisons with regard to over-crowding, bad conditions, under-staffing, poor security and a 'toxic mix' of prisoners. However, the Report's emphasis upon the need for the upholding of justice in prison has been perceived as being of particular importance.[20]

---

[15] Public Records Office (henceforth PRO) Home Office papers (henceforth HO) 144/468/X83.

[16] Some efforts are made to examine this largely hidden issue in L. Zedner, *Women, Crime and Custody in Victorian England* (Oxford: Clarendon Press, 1991).

[17] Also see A.B rown '"Doing Time": The Extended Present of the Long-term Prisoner', *Time and Society* 7, No. 1 (March 1998): pp. 93–103.

[18] H. Woolf and S. Tumin, *Prison Disturbances April 1990* (London: HMSO, 1991), Cm 1456.1. Disturbances at five prisons, other than Manchester, were investigated specifically. These were: Glen Parva, Dartmoor, Cardiff, Bristol and Pucklechurch.

[19] M. Cavadino and J. Dignan, *The Penal System: An Introduction*, 3rd edn (London: Sage Publications, 2002), p. 23.

[20] Ibid., pp. 10–18 and pp. 23–4.

Woolf and Tumin asserted that the three requirements for a stable prison system were security, control and justice. They believed that the requirement of justice meant that the prison service had an obligation to 'treat prisoners with humanity and fairness'.[21] Cavadino and Dignan maintain that such statements amount to a concern with the legitimacy of the prison and that 'Woolf believed that genuine injustice contributes to a lack of legitimacy which in turn makes disorder more likely.'[22]

With reference to the problem of the legitimacy of the prison institution, Chapter 3 examines the circumstances surrounding one particular historical disturbance. The riot in Chatham Convict Prison in 1861 is one of the largest and best-documented disturbances in nineteenth century English prison history. Over 800 men were initially implicated in this large-scale disturbance, which necessitated military intervention to regain control of the prison. Chapter 3 is, in essence, an examination of the moral base upon which the prison was operated and the way in which the unfairness of the discipline resulted in a legitimacy deficit and increased the dissatisfaction of convicts. In the context of the several major disturbances that occurred in the public works convict prisons during this period, the Chatham riot highlighted to contemporaries the deficiencies of the discipline in these institutions and was instrumental in bringing about a change in penal philosophy towards deterrence.

Chapter 4 links the problem of legitimacy to the persistence of informal and unofficial accommodations and compromises within the prison. These accommodations and compromises were an important aspect of inmate subcultures. This chapter also examines the nature and speed of reforms in local prisons prior to nationalisation but with particular reference to the United Gaol and House of Correction at Kingston-upon-Hull. Integral to this is a consideration of the debate regarding the evolution of disciplinary mechanisms in modern institutions which Foucault instigated with the publication of *Discipline and Punish: The Birth of the Prison* (1977).

Analysis of a local prison highlights the difference between the rhetoric surrounding national policy-making and its practical implementation, and also indicates the inter-connections between prison discipline, inmate subcultures and the level of prison offences and punishments in individual prison establishments. Inmate subcultures persisted despite increased uniformity and regulation during the nineteenth century and the nationalisation of local prisons following legislation in 1877. Inmate subcultures did not

---

[21] Woolf and Tumin, *Prison Disturbances*, paras 9.19–20.
[22] Cavadino and Dignan, *The Penal System*, pp. 23–4. This aspect of the Woolf Report is also highlighted by R. Sparks, 'Can Prisons be Legitimate? Penal Politics, Privatization, and the Timelessness of an Old Idea', *British Journal of Criminology* 34 (Special Issue 1994), pp. 20–1; J.R. Sparks, 'Legitimacy and Order in Prisons', *British Journal of Sociology* 46, No. 1 (March 1995), pp. 45–7; Sparks *et al.*, *Prisons and Order*, pp. 303–6.

necessarily work to undermine order; indeed a degree of order could constitute the organisational framework for their existence. At the same time, however, an important aspect of prison offences was that they reflected the point at which inmate subcultures pressed against prison discipline to obtain more power.[23]

Chapter 5 analyses the basis for describing the period between the mid-1860s and 1895 as the most deterrent in English prison history. This period witnessed the further development of methods of segregation and a more meticulous system of progressive stages, which utilised a continuum of rewards and punishments to control the behaviour of prisoners. Fundamentally this constituted an increase in the intensity of the punishment of penal servitude, the subject of this chapter, which was reflected in the extreme forms of self-injury performed by a minority of convicts. This chapter also examines the philosophy of deterrence and explores the extent to which effective checks existed to prevent excessive severity during this period. Certainly, the level of independence enjoyed by the Prison Commissioners and Directors in their administration of the prisons and in their investigations into the petitions of prisoners did little to mitigate unfairness or abuse.

Deterrence in prison policy was based upon a classical liberal ideology which related the level of punishment to the seriousness of the offence and adhered to the belief that criminal activity was based on rational or moral choice. This reasoning contributed towards the particularly harsh treatment of convicts in the second half of the nineteenth century. David Garland has claimed, however, that the primacy of classical ideology in penal philosophy was seriously challenged during the period 1895 to 1914 by newer positivist and neo-Darwinist theories about the nature of criminality, which brought about the evolution of modern penal policy.[24]

Chapter 6 examines the seriousness of this challenge to classical ideology in penal policy during the late nineteenth and early twentieth centuries, initially from the perspective of an incident in Wormwood Scrubs Prison in 1907. During this disturbance a number of prison officers entered one cell after another in one of the halls in Wormwood Scrubs Prison and assaulted the inmates. This account develops into an analysis of the extent to which such violence on the part of prison officers can be seen as expressive of their frustration at being excluded from the change in the direction of penal policy. Chapter 6 also explores what this disturbance reveals about the obstacles to change that had become entrenched in the organisation of the prison by the late nineteenth century. The chapter then goes on to examine the contention of Victor Bailey that, although this period did witness some

---

[23] Zedner, *Women, Crime, and Custody*, p. 160.
[24] D. Garland, *Punishment and Welfare: A History of Penal Strategies* (Aldershot: Gower, 1985).

amelioration in prison discipline, this was not far-reaching and was not dictated predominantly by a shift to a more positivist ideology under which criminal behaviour was perceived as being 'determined by factors and processes that could be discovered by observation, measurement, and inductive reasoning'.[25]

Chapter 7 examines the presence of political prisoners in English prisons as a specific root of disorder during the years 1850 to 1920. Throughout the period, political prisoners challenged the classical principles that related the level of punishment principally to the seriousness of the offence. Political interest groups, whose members experienced imprisonment, claimed that the motivation for an offence which broke the law should be taken into account and that politically motivated offenders should not be subject to imprisonment on the same terms as ordinary criminals. The main groups of political prisoners during this period were Irish nationalists, suffragettes and conscientious objectors to compulsory conscription during the First World War. These groups, among others, posed fundamental questions about the role and purpose of the prison, and were able to exploit weaknesses in discipline and administration to a much greater extent than ordinary prisoners. Thus political prisoners were able to create disorder within the prisons that confined them and, in some cases, caused a breakdown in discipline.

The fundamental themes of this publication constitute an analysis of the facets of the prison that caused disorder during the period 1850 to 1920, but also highlight some issues which have resonance for order in prisons into the twenty-first century. The extreme monotony of prison regimes, legitimacy problems and the unpredictability of inmate subcultures are all elements which have affected the stability of English prisons. A tendency of prison authorities to rely on deterrence in the face of internal problems or public criticism, and an in-built structural resistance to change in an institution that often composes the last resort in dealing with social problems, to a significant extent remains. The activities of political interest groups whose members or followers break the law have been among the most contentious of the social problems that have been reflected in the prison.

There is no doubt that the prisons of 1920 were very different from those which existed in 1850. In 1850 many of the basic elements of prison architecture and classification had already been established, but it was in the years between 1850 and 1920 that the establishment and formulation of the modern prison system can be identified. This can be seen in several characteristics of the prison, including classification, segregation and a convincing degree of uniformity. This enabled the full sophistication of prison timetabling and routine to be implemented. In addition, this period

---

[25] V. Bailey, 'English Prisons, Penal Culture, and the Abatement of Imprisonment, 1895–1922', *Journal of British Studies* 36 (July 1997), pp. 323 and 290.

witnessed the evolution of the centralised prison system. This was brought about by the establishment of the Directorate of the Convict Prisons in 1850, the nationalisation of the local prisons in 1877, and the formal combining of the offices of the Prison Commissioners and the Directorate of the Convict Prisons in 1898, although the titles of both bodies were retained.

The term modern must, however, be used with caution as the term often lends a false image of progression to a modern static model. This is clearly not the case; new or modified methods of organisation and control continue to be implemented in English prisons. Following the publication of the *Report of the Inquiry into Prison Escapes and Security* in 1966, for example, all convicted prisoners were classified into four categories, A to D, according to their perceived dangerousness and likelihood of attempting escape.[26] In the 1990s, a system of incentives and earned privileges was introduced into prison as an encouragement to behavioural reform.[27] Among the most notable innovations in English prisons, with respect to the shape of future prison development, has been the increased use of closed-circuit television and other technology and also the contracting out of the management of a small number of prisons to the private sector from 1991.[28]

The expansion of surveillance technology in prisons, and indeed in wider society, has been viewed as further evidence of the perceptiveness of Foucault's panoptic model. Mathiesen has, for example, examined Foucault's panopticism in conjunction with his own theory of synopticism. Synopticism refers to, what Mathiesen sees as, the expansion of the media and technology so that the many can see the few at the same time as in Foucault's panopticism the few can see the many. According to Mathiesen, both of these processes resulted in the extension of a disciplined society.[29]

It should be noted that the siting of the period covered by this publication as 1850 to 1920 serves largely as an indication of the period of time to which the core material relates; comment will also be made with regard to periods both before and following this time. The year 1850 was chosen in part because this was the year in which the Directorate of the Convict Prisons was established, but largely because it marks the beginning of the first full decade of the birth of the modern prison as theorised by Foucault. The end date of this thesis, 1920, was chosen partly because this enabled the fortunes

---

[26] Cmnd 3175 (London: HMSO, 1966). Also see M. Fitzgerald, *Prisoners in Revolt* (Exeter: University of Exeter Press, 1977), pp. 49–51.

[27] See A. Leibling, G. Muir, G. Rose and A. Bottoms, *Incentives and Earned Privileges for Prisoners – An Evaluation*, Home Office Research Findings No. 87 (London: Home Office Research and Statistics Directorate, 1999).

[28] See A. James and K. Bottomly, 'Prison Privatisation and the Remand Population: Principle Versus Pragmatism?' *Howard Journal of Criminal Justice* 37, No. 3 (1998), pp. 223–33.

[29] T. Mathiesen, 'The Viewer Society, Michel Foucault's "Panopticon" revisited', *Theoretical Criminology* 1 (1997), pp. 218–19.

of the political prisoners confined as a consequence of the war to be followed to their final release. In addition, this allowed for consideration of the pressures faced by the prison system during wartime. Furthermore, this facilitated consideration of Garland's thesis, which, in disagreement with the timing suggested by Foucault, cites the period from 1895 to 1914 as pivotal in the transition to the modern penal system. The start and end dates chosen for this thesis are not hard and fast cut-off dates but denote the period with which this thesis is primarily concerned.

The bulk of historical evidence regarding English prisons has been generated and controlled by central or local government – bodies which have been sensitive to criticism as well as zealous in restricting media and public access to the prisons. The publication of officially generated evidence was designed to present a view of the prison that did not discredit the prison authorities. Hobhouse and Brockway, who edited *English Prisons Today*, which was the report of an inquiry instigated by the Labour Research Department and was published in 1922, commented on the secrecy which surrounded the prison system and stated that it was 'practically impossible' for the public to gain access to prisons. They were also critical of the seclusion of the Prison Commission and their unhelpful stance towards the inquiry. Certainly, the prison rules and regulations stipulated that prison staff were not allowed to communicate without authority on any matters regarding the prison for public use.[30]

The broad range of British Parliamentary Papers composes most of the published official documentation available regarding the prison, and includes Sessional Papers, Hansard's *Parliamentary Debates*, Parliamentary Acts and the reports of investigatory official inspectorates, committees or commissions. Parliamentary Papers in their various forms provide an enormous quantity of invaluable evidence. Most of the unpublished official records used were material relating to the administration of the prisons generated by the Home Office and the Prison Commission, which is held at the Public Record Office. In addition, local official records regarding the United Gaol and House of Correction at Kingston-upon-Hull, which are held at the Hull City Record Office, were consulted, as was a small selection of national and local newspapers, most notably *The Times* and *The Hull Advertiser*. Newspapers and contemporary journals proved to be an enlightening source of information for the opinions of influential individuals both inside and outside the prison administration. It should, however, be borne in mind that all such evidence may have been subject to bias, selective editing or even censorship.[31]

---

[30] S. Hobhouse and A. Fenner Brockway, *English Prisons Today: Being the Report of the Prison System Enquiry Committee* (London: Longman, Green & Co., 1922), p. vi.
[31] For greater consideration of the value of historical records appertaining to local prisons, see A. Brown, 'A Disciplined Environment: Penal Reform in the East Riding House of Correction', *Family and Community History* 4 (2) (November 2001), pp. 99–110.

The papers of a number of individuals who had been influential in English prisons during this period were also examined. The first of these figures was Lord Carnarvon, a local prison reformer and head of the Select Committee of the House of Lords on Gaol Discipline which resulted in the Prison Act of 1865.[32] Two further important figures whose papers were consulted were Joshua Jebb, who headed the Directorate of the Convict Prisons from 1850 to 1863, and Edmund Du Cane, Chairman of the Directorate of the Convict Prisons from 1869 to 1895 and of the Prison Commissioners from 1877 to 1895.[33] Also consulted were the personal papers of Evelyn Ruggles-Brise, who was chairman of the Commissioners of Prisons and Directors of Convict Prisons between 1895 and 1921.[34]

The published accounts of discharged prisoners and of individuals from the prison service have also been used extensively. These have been invaluable as they relate, on a personal level, the experience of the prison by those who were subject to it and who worked within it. Significant detail was also obtained from these sources with regard to how prisoners adapted to or conflicted with prison discipline. The use of this type of historical source shows the extent to which conflict has been an everyday feature of the prison. As Sparks, Bottoms and Hay have commented with regard to modern prisons, 'In reality prisons quite commonly seethe and boil with human agency, passion, and conflict – in ways that are not infrequently magnified and rendered more intense precisely by the restraints and frustrations encountered there.'[35]

[32] BPP, 1863(499), IX.1. Prison Act 1865: 28 & 29 Vict., c.126. The Carnarvon Papers are held at the British Library.
[33] The Jebb Papers are held at the British Library of Social and Political Science and the Du Cane Papers are held at the Bodleian Library.
[34] The Ruggles-Brise Papers are held at Chelmsford Record Office.
[35] Sparks et al., Prisons and Order, p. 68.

2

'Doing time': prisoners' perceptions and experience of time

During the past forty years there has been an increased academic interest in how prisoners perceive and deal with their experience of prison.[1] These studies have often been made in conjunction with attempts by criminologists to understand the dynamics of prison disturbances. In the majority of such studies prisoners' perceptions of time have attracted little more than a few sentences. One of the exceptions to this is a book by Stanley Cohen and Laurie Taylor published in 1972 and entitled *Psychological Survival: The Experience of Long-Term Imprisonment*. This publication dedicates a chapter to the consideration of the problem of time and raises important issues which have been apparent to prisoners since at least the development of model prisons in the nineteenth century. These issues concern the fundamental nature of prison as a punishment as well as the practical consequences of prison discipline on human behaviour. Cohen and Taylor found that the most useful way to make sense of the observations that they made during their study of men confined in the maximum security block in Durham Prison was to interpret the men's behaviour as 'attempts to survive'.[2] It is contended here that the distortions in time perceptions recorded by long-term prisoners in the past can be seen partly in this light but also as a consequence of their highly disciplined and routinised environment.

Examination of time perceptions in prison emphasises, as Sparks, Bottoms and Hay have pointed out, that prisoners do not passively undergo or submit to their imprisonment but rather that they live it in each minute of each

[1] For example, *Prison Violence*, ed. A.K. Cohen, G.F. Cole and R.G. Bailey (Lexington, Mass.: D.C. Heath, 1976); *The Prison: Studies in Institutional Organization and Change*, ed. D.R. Cressey (New York: Holt, Rinehart & Winston, 1966); *Theoretical Studies in Social Organisation of the Prison*, ed. R.A. Cloward and G.H. Grosser (New York: Social Science Research Council, 1960); G.M. Sykes, *Society of Captives: The Study of a Maximum Security Prison* (Princeton: Princeton University Press, 1958); D. Clemmer, *The Prison Community* (New York: Holt, Rinehart and Winston, 1958); P. Carlen (ed.) with J. Hicks, J. O'Dwyer, D. Christina, C. Tchaikovsky, *Criminal Women: Autobiographical Accounts* (Cambridge: Polity Press, 1985). R. Sparks, A.E. Bottoms and W. Hay, *Prisons and the Problem of Order* (Oxford: Clarendon Press, 1996).
[2] S. Cohen and L. Taylor, *Psychological Survival: The Experience of Long-Term Imprisonment* (Harmondsworth: Penguin, 1972), p. 9.

day.[3] More specifically, the added burden produced by the distortion of time during a long prison sentence has been an important cause of prison disturbances. Imprisoning offenders necessitated the establishment of administrative and disciplinary systems that ensured an ordered and dependent existence for inmates. This affected the way in which those subject to it perceived and related to the prison environment. Perceptions of time became distorted. An extended sense of the present assumed proportions which required formidable efforts on the part of prisoners to develop coping strategies. The routine of the prison produced a standardised way of living to the extent that any action that disrupted this routine could be defined as disorder or disturbances committed by troublesome and disobedient prisoners.

This chapter uses historical evidence in the form of autobiographical accounts of prisoners incarcerated between 1850 and 1920 to examine the way in which long custodial sentences distorted the time perceptions of inmates. Prison autobiographies provide a useful source for historians of the prison. As Morgan has suggested, prison autobiographies 'constitute a small but persistent *genre* within a wider discourse of criminal justice'.[4] The tendency for imprisonment to distort and extend the prisoner's sense of the present is one of the ways in which power reaches 'into the very grain of individuals, touches their bodies and inserts itself into their actions and attitudes' and is one of the most enduring facets of the prison experience.[5] In addition, of course, this amounted to a distortion of the past and future. According to autobiographical evidence, it appears to have been a conscious priority for prisoners to develop strategies with which to cope with such distortions. The alternative could be an increased tendency towards disruptive behaviour, resulting in higher punishment rates and disciplinary problems within the prisons.

Prison and the experience of prisoners who have served long sentences are also areas which highlight the inadequacy of a single conception of time measured by the clock. In the past, historians have written about the complexities of the perception and use of time with regard to the choice that workers have faced between work or leisure time. Concentration was on time as a quantity open to measurement as a means of gauging progress in the battle over working hours between workers and employers.[6] But the prison

---

[3] Sparks *et al.*, *Prisons and Order*, p. 53. They also state, however, that they believe the behavioural picture offered by Cohen and Taylor is too specific to the high security wing at Durham to be accepted as a general model.

[4] S. Morgan, 'Prison Lives: Critical Issues in Reading Prisoner Autobiography', *Howard Journal* 38, No. 3 (1999), pp. 328–40.

[5] M. Foucault, 'Prison Talk', in *Michel Foucault: Power/Knowledge, Selected Interviews and Other Writings*, ed. C. Gordon (Brighton: Harvester Press, 1980), p. 39.

[6] E.P. Thompson, 'Time, Work Discipline and Industrial Capitalism', *Past and Present* 38 (1967), pp. 56–97; S. Pollard, 'Factory Discipline in the Industrial Revolution', *Economic*

as a coercive and relatively closed community offers perhaps one of the best representations of the way in which values of time depend 'not only on their absolute length but also on the nature and intensity of their qualities'.[7]

The perceived loss of control, threat to identity and curtailing of outside contact by the convict made a sentence of penal servitude, in particular, an exceptionally harsh punishment. Penal servitude referred to those sentenced for longer terms (usually two years or over) to incarceration in a convict prison, as opposed to a local prison, which held prisoners serving shorter prison terms. The prison rules with regard to the amount of communication that inmates were allowed with relatives and friends outside varied over time, but remained quite strict during this period. Prison rules published in 1903 stated, for example, that a convict,

> after two months of the term of his sentence have expired, shall, provided his conduct and industry have been satisfactory, be allowed to communicate with his relatives and respectable friends by letter and be visited by them in prison, and this privilege shall be gradually increased according to his conduct and industry until the interval be reduced to one month.[8]

Autonomous time was a liberty, it was also one of the rights of citizenship that was taken from an offender in much the same way as his right to free speech or movement.[9] The time of the prison sentence was time lost to the prisoner. A view which suggests an alien feel to prison time is that of Cohen and Taylor who state that prisoners 'have been given someone else's time. Their own time has been abstracted by the courts.'[10] Offenders were given prison time which had no individuality, was outside their control and was therefore unfamiliar.

For the prisoners who left accounts of their experiences in the second half of the nineteenth and early twentieth centuries the past and future increasingly became merely the parameters defining a present that seemed to be extended considerably. The recorded memories of the internal and external conflicts of prison inmates with their environment emphasise the

---

History Review 16, Sr 2 (1963), pp. 254–71. According to Pollard, the factory meant an 'economy of time' which required efficiency, avoidance of the waste of materials or time, consistency, fixed hours and scrupulousness, pp. 257–8.

[7] P. Sorokin and R. Merton, 'Social Time: A Methodological and Functional Analysis' (1937), in *The Sociology of Time*, ed. J. Hassard (London: Macmillan, 1990), p. 61.

[8] C.R. Henderson, *Modern Prison Systems: Their Organization and Regulation in Various Countries of Europe and America* (Washington: Government Printing Office, 1903), p. 127.

[9] G. Cross, *A Quest for Time: The Reduction of Work in Britain and France, 1840–1940* (Los Angeles: California Press, 1989), p. 11.

[10] Cohen and Taylor, *Psychological Survival*, p. 89. Also see R. Matthews, *Doing Time: An Introduction to the Sociology of Imprisonment* (London: Ashgate, 1999).

need for a more qualitative examination of time in order to describe what imprisonment, both in local and in convict prisons, actually meant for those subject to it. These sources provide a subjective perception of the prison that is lacking in official sources.[11] As the author of an article in *The Daily Chronicle* on 16 November 1898 observed, 'In these official documents the prisoner is a dim and shadowy figure, who is never for a moment permitted to stand before us as a man.'[12]

Publications by educated or politically motivated offenders, such as Irish nationalists and conscientious objectors, outnumber by far those left by more ordinary offenders. Among the best examples of such publications from this period are Thomas Clarke's *Glimpses of an Irish Felon's Prison Life* (1922) and A. Fenner Brockway's *Inside the Left: Thirty Years of Platform, Press, Prison and Parliament* (1947). Thomas Clarke, an Irish nationalist, not only served over fifteen years' penal servitude in England from 1883 to 1898 but was later shot because of his involvement in the Easter Rising of 1916.

Because of the prominence of accounts by educated or political prisoners there is a risk that the impressions given by prison autobiographies may not accurately reflect the experiences of the more ordinary type of offender. Many educated prisoners, for example, maintained that access to the prison library was of vital importance to their ability to endure prison life. One convict asserted that 'Books have saved many a convict from madness.'[13] 'Prison, my boy', wrote another convict to a friend outside, 'is the place where one really appreciates literature.'[14] Yet another later claimed that convicts 'wanted life from literature; and this was natural, for we are dead men in prison, so that any book which lives gives us for a brief space a sort of resurrection'.[15] For the large numbers of illiterate or near illiterate prisoners during this period, literature was a resource that was largely closed to them, although many prisons did hold picture books and basic reading books in their libraries to cater for them to some degree. At the same time, the contrast between prison life and life outside, at least in material terms, would no doubt have been more extreme for a prisoner from a comparatively wealthy background than for one from the poorer background from which the majority of prisoners originated.

A further consideration which needs to be taken into account is the fact that imprisoned political offenders often exploited their prison experiences to

---

[11] Morgan, 'Prison Lives'.

[12] From cuttings collated in an album held at the Prison Service Library, Wakefield (now transferred to Rugby).

[13] S. Scott, *The Human Side of Crook and Convict Life* (London: Hurst & Blackett, 1924), p. 140.

[14] E.W. Mason, *Made Free in Prison* (London: George Allen & Unwin, 1918), p. 176.

[15] W. Macartney, *Walls Have Mouths: A Record of Ten Years' Penal Servitude* (London: Gollancz, 1936), p. 205.

gain publicity for their causes, and therefore may have represented their suffering in a more dramatic manner.[16] Other prison writers also had agendas of their own, whether this was to assert their innocence and the injustice of their sentence or to raise money. For example, one of the primary motives for Susan Willis Fletcher, a medium convicted for obtaining jewellery and clothes under false pretences, in writing about her prison experiences was to assert her innocence.[17] Constance Lytton, on the other hand, wrote her account to both promote a political cause and highlight the plight of ordinary women prisoners.[18] Michael Davitt famously wrote to campaign for prison reform.[19] Having said this, the effects of the differing social and political backgrounds of the prisoners are mitigated to an extent because it is only prisoners perceptions of time that are dealt with in this chapter and not, for instance, their perceptions of material conditions. Furthermore, while acknowledging the limitations of autobiographical sources with regard to the selectivity and fallibility of memory and also the diverse motivations behind writing such accounts, analysis of a broad array of autobiographies reveals a consistency of experience that lends credibility to the use of such material for an examination of the impact of the prison on the person.

Using up the past

Autobiographical sources show that time in prison became something simply to pass, to be lived according to the direction of others. Prisoners developed various strategies to cope with what one woman convict described as 'the voiceless solitude, the hopeless monotony, the long vista of tomorrow, tomorrow, tomorrow'.[20] Some prisoners were reluctant to dwell on the slow passage of time and enveloped themselves in a kind of mental numbness or indifference.[21] For many, fatalism was their dominant reaction to a long prison sentence. One view of this was given in an article in *The Cornhill Magazine* in 1864 which stated that,

> Satisfied, after a time, that what is cannot be helped, that no anxiety on their part can undo the past or affect the future, they put aside all thought of past and future,

---

[16] See Chapter 7 of this publication.
[17] S. Willis Fletcher, *Twelve Months in an English Prison* (Boston: Lee & Shepherd, 1884), pp. 1–2.
[18] C. Lytton, *Prisons and Prisoners* (London: Heinemann, 1914).
[19] M. Davitt, *Leaves from a Prison Diary, or Lectures to a 'Solitary' Audience* (Shannon: Irish University Press, 1972).
[20] F.E. Maybrick, *My Fifteen Years Lost* (New York: Funk & Wagnalls, 1905), p. 75. Also see *The Evening News*, 16 December 1897, 'Story of a Gaol Bird'.
[21] Scott, *Human Side of Convict Life*, p. 13; Maybrick, *Fifteen Years Lost*, p. 177.

and live only for the present . . . fed, clothed, lodged, without need of care on their part, they come to lead the life of children.[22]

Comparisons with the extended sense of the present and the lack of autonomy that children possess occur repeatedly in prisoners' accounts.[23] For the prisoner, adult experiences and independence were suffocated within the kind of coercive paternalism provided by the prison. A possible consequence of this was the tendency of some long-term prisoners to revert back to the mentality and outlook of childhood.[24] In a sense, adult memories and experiences were used up during a long imprisonment, leaving behind the simplified reality of childhood perceptions.

One vivid account described a process in which long-term prisoners became increasingly remote from the past, that is, the events, knowledge and emotions of their previous lives. Thomas Clarke maintained that the past was a kind of protective resource rapidly used up by long-term prisoners. The past held a wealth of experience to ponder upon, but the opportunities to develop it with interesting or constructive material while in prison were limited. An educated man, Clarke suggested, would manage quite well during the early years of his imprisonment 'whilst his memory furnishes him with subject after subject to give his mind pleasurable occupation'. However, once this process had been gone through innumerable times,

> it is found that some of the ideas and memories have no further interest; the mind is sick of them; they have been turned over so much that they are too stale to arouse any further interest . . . Finally there comes a time when by this process of elimination there remains not a single idea of the original stock that has not been quite 'played out' and has now become hateful.[25]

The value of the past as a guardian of identity and evidence of an individuality that was threatened by the prison was gradually reduced and became less useful as a barrier against the relentless monotony and silence of prison existence. Certainly, the thought of mental decay, which was often

---

[22] Anon. [S.Roe], 'A Convict's Views of Penal Discipline', *The Cornhill Magazine* 10 (July–December 1864), p. 723.

[23] For example, J.S. Balfour, *My Prison Life* (London: Chapman & Hall, 1907), p. 70. A study published in 1963 also remarked on the regressive effects of long-term imprisonment but pointed out that 'unlike the child, a prisoner is expected to have a highly developed sense of right and wrong'. See T. Morris and P. Morris, *Pentonville: A Sociological Study of an English Prisons*, International Library of Sociology and Social Reconstruction (London: Routledge & Kegan Paul, 1963), p. 167.

[24] S. Hobhouse and A. Fenner Brockway, *English Prisons Today: Being the Report of the Prison System Enquiry Committee* (London: Longman, Green & Co., 1922), p. 495.

[25] T. Clarke, *Glimpses of an Irish Felon's Prison Life* (Dublin: Maunsel & Roberts, 1922), pp. 93–4.

thought to follow submission to such an existence, was repellent, especially to educated prisoners. Stephen Hobhouse, imprisoned for his conscientious objection to compulsory military service during the First World War, referred to this in an article in *The Quarterly Review*. He dreaded 'the occasional appearance of a spell of dazed vacancy of mind, of indifference to everything; for this seemed to be the prelude to the decay of mind and will, which, as I had been told by a prison chaplain, is a not uncommon result of long imprisonments'.[26]

Thomas Clarke, in common with other prisoners, felt that to preserve his sanity he must distract his mind from contemplation of the future. However, the attempts to distract attention from the future that are evident in prisoners' accounts also sometimes led to an obsession with their surroundings. This was partly a consequence of long hours spent alone in their cells with no occupation. In the public works convict prisons in 1885, for example, the hours taken up by daily routine on weekdays from 16 February to 31 October were from 5 a.m. to 6.50 p.m. The working hours within this time were spent labouring on public works projects, such as the dockyard constructions at Chatham and the building of Wormwood Scrubs Prison. After 6.50 p.m., prisoners were allowed fifty-five minutes before they had to make up their hammocks and lights were turned off. Prisoners were therefore in their cells, usually alone, for over ten hours of the day. For those inmates in other convict prisons who were in the initial solitary stage of their sentence, or who worked in their cells, this could be as much as twenty-two hours a day.[27]

To distract himself Clarke made endless calculations. He calculated the number and weight of bricks in the prison, the number of bolts in all the doors and perforations in the ventilators, the number of buttons on all the uniforms in the prison, and that over six feet of hair had been cut from his head in thirteen years.[28] The situation regarding the limited amount of time that prisoners spent out of their cells seems to have improved little by the early twentieth century. At that time, as Jabez Balfour, a renowned fraud,[29] pointed out, the inmates of Portland Prison spent from 5.15 p.m. to 6.55 a.m. in their cells.[30] In 1912, the convict prison timetable showed that on weekdays adult prisoners would be in their cells for upwards of sixteen hours a day, although some of this time was taken up with cell labour.[31]

---

[26] S. Hobhouse, 'An English Prison from Within', *The Quarterly Review* 230 (July 1918), pp. 33–4.
[27] 'Details of Duties in Public Works Convict Prisons throughout the Year', *Report of the Directors of the Convict Prisons*, BPP, 1886(C.4833), XXXV, pp. 492–3.
[28] Clarke, *Irish Felon's Prison Life*, pp. 68–9.
[29] H. Kingsmill, 'The Gigantic Frauds of Jabez Balfour', in *The Fifty Most Amazing Crimes of the Last 100 Years* (London: Odhams Press Ltd, 1936).
[30] Balfour, *My Prison Life*, p. 67.
[31] PRO PCom7/191, revised copy of the Standing Orders, Appendix 8, p. 452.

Not all prisoners felt that it was dangerous to dwell upon the future. Michael Davitt felt that prisoners often escaped from the present into a more attractive invented future, 'hiding the worst features of the objective present behind a picture of a pleasant and happy, if imaginary, future'. Prison, he remarked, 'is the paradise of castle-builders'.[32] Cohen and Taylor in their 1972 study of prisoners serving long sentences witnessed prisoners' extended perceptions of the present. They also noted that because the future in prison was unthinkable prisoners relied upon ideas about a future life outside to sustain them.

There is a sense in which the using up of the past resulted for some in a shifting of emphasis to the future, even if this constructed future was largely a delusion. Until the desire for a future outside the prison was satisfied, the compulsion to imagine it continued. In this light the horror of dying in prison is understandable. As one convict related, 'To be ill whilst a convict is sad, to die a convict is terrible.'[33] Cohen and Taylor point out that what 'appears to be totally unacceptable is the idea that one's life is experienced in prison. One may be serving life, but one is not serving "my life".'[34] It was unacceptable that 'life' could mean life and therefore some future outside of the prison was created no matter how unlikely this was. In fact the probability of dying in prison was quite low. Even in the nineteenth century prisoners were usually released on compassionate grounds if they were near death.[35] This also reflected well on the prison, keeping the numbers of recorded deaths in prison to a low level. Yet prisoners continued to present death as an analogy of prison existence. Comments that imprisonment was 'a living death' or that 'We are dead men in prison' were expressions of the time-lessness and isolation of prison life.[36] Such a life was, however, endurable for these inmates only if there was a life to be lived afterwards.

---

[32] Davitt, *Leaves from a Prison Diary*, p. 180.

[33] R. Bentley, *Five Years' Penal Servitude by One Who Has Endured It* (London, 1877), p. 117. Another prisoner wrote that deaths in prison were 'woeful affairs. There is something unutterably lonesome and sad about the idea of dying in a gaol', Macartney, *Walls Have Mouths*, p. 301.

[34] Cohen and Taylor, *Psychological Survival*, p. 93.

[35] Another aspect of the fear of dying in prison was that as late as the mid-nineteenth century the authorities sometimes laid claim to the body of the prisoner and, in some cases, the bodies went to anatomy schools for medical research. Sim has commented regarding this that 'Breaking the bond of incarceration was, for many, impossible even in death. The penal ties bound them to the gaolers for eternity.' J. Sim, *Medical Power in Prison: The Prison Medical Service in England 1774–1989* (Milton Keynes: Open University Press, 1990), p. 33.

[36] See Balfour, *My Prison Life*, p. 110; Macartney, *Walls have Mouths*, p. 205; D. Figgis, *A Second Chronicle of Jails* (Dublin: Talbot Press, 1919), p. 79; Mason, *Made Free in Prison*, p. 187. Mason, a conscientious objector, commented that 'I have a horror of dying in prison. I have seen four men die there, and it was terrible. No one cared.' Also see *The Evening News*, 15 December 1897, 'Story of a Gaol Bird'.

Many of the effects of long-term imprisonment upon offenders were revealed by interviews and questionnaires collected as part of an investigation into the prison system set up by the Executive of the Labour Research Council. In 1922 this information was published in a book entitled *English Prisons Today* which was edited by Stephen Hobhouse and A. Fenner Brockway, who had themselves been imprisoned for their conscientious objection to compulsory military service during the First World War. One chapter of this book specifically considered the mental effects of long-term imprisonment suffered by political prisoners, in this case conscientious objectors confined between 1916 and 1919. In their report, Hobhouse and Brockway defined as long-term prisoners all those who had been subject to imprisonment for a period of twelve months or more.[37] This chapter adopts a similar definition and therefore refers predominantly, but not only, to inmates of convict prisons rather than the local prisons.

The particular psychological effects of long-term imprisonment were identified in *English Prisons Today* not only as individual symptoms but as stages in a process of adaptation to prison conditions. Many of these psychological effects have already been mentioned but they are interesting in this context precisely because they have been placed within a constructed, gradual process of adaptation to long-term imprisonment. One point highlighted by this structured approach is that prisoners began to experience some of the described effects from a very early stage in their imprisonment. This is not to say, however, that such effects would have been experienced in the same way by prisoners undergoing short terms of imprisonment. It seems likely that the knowledge of a long sentence ahead of them would have had a significant impact on the way in which imprisonment was viewed. In addition, no doubt reflecting their own educated background, Hobhouse and Brockway suggested that the process of adaptation, although essentially the same for all prisoners, was more protracted for political prisoners than for juveniles or prisoners who had 'undeveloped mental powers'.[38]

Four stages of mental effects experienced as a consequence of long-term imprisonment were described in *English Prisons Today*. These were, excitation, 'making the best of it', deterioration and finally apathy. The first stage was distinguished by 'an acceleration of mental activity and of emotional response' which ranged in intensity from hysteria to 'intense curiosity'. The next phase consisted of determined and systematic efforts on the part of prisoners to occupy their time in a profitable way. This might include educational and religious study or physical exercise in their cells, but, whatever the activity, it tended to be 'self-centred and introspective'.[39]

---

[37] Hobhouse and Brockway, *English Prisons Today*, p. 488.
[38] Ibid.
[39] Ibid., pp. 488–9.

The third stage was marked by a decline in the activities pursued in the second stage, partly due to 'the exhaustion of the prisoner's internal and external resources'. This was the stage in which mental deterioration began to result in a state of repetitive thought processes. As one conscientious objector remarked, 'Day after day the same thoughts come, and one knows they will come again tomorrow.'[40] The mind often lingered in daydreams, particularly on subjects such as liberty and food. According to the report, prisoners in this stage deteriorated faster if they were apathetic, but were more prone to nervous breakdown if they fought against it. In the latter case, political prisoners recorded feelings of depression or irritability, which led to violent impulses.[41] It was suggested that,

> Perhaps the greater part of the malingering, petitioning and frivolous complaints with which the prisoner annoys the authorities are primarily an expression of this irritability and of the prisoner's desire to assert himself or to relieve the monotony of his life.[42]

But a disturbance of a much more serious nature was described in a personal account by Brockway, who commented that the strain of months of imprisonment was disastrous to self-control.

> One poor fellow who had not been able to stand the strain smashed everything on which he could lay his hands. Within a few minutes from cell to cell the nervous storm spread; every prisoner appeared to be thundering at his door in a fury of pent-up emotions which swept reason away. I had the greatest of difficulty in not joining in. I stood at my door, my fists clenched within an inch of it, my whole body tense, my arms vibrating, my teeth clenched, a bursting pressure in my head. The warders came running along the corridors and dragged off prisoners to the padded cells.[43]

The final stage of the mental decline of long-term prisoners described by Hobhouse and Brockway was one of settled apathy and torpor. The routine of the prison continued mechanically and 'the passage of time [was] no longer noticed'. This was the stage in which prisoners feared that they were becoming institutionalised or had observed what they perceived to be institutionalisation in the behaviour of other prisoners. In this stage, prisoners became accustomed to the lack of individual demands made upon

---

[40] Mason, *Made Free in Prison*, p. 128. Mason goes on to comment that 'Often at the end of a week I have tried to recall events that happened upon such and such a day, but have been unable to remember distinctly even one.'

[41] Hobhouse and Brockway, *English Prisons Today*, p. 490.

[42] Ibid. Also see *The Evening News*, 17 December 1897, 'Story of a Gaol Bird'.

[43] A. Fenner Brockway, *Inside the Left: Thirty Years of Platform* (London: George Allen & Unwin, 1947), pp. 103–4.

them. The dangers of this loss of self-direction or control upon release were clear to Hobhouse and Brockway when they stated that 'the freedom from responsibility or necessity for effort may come in time to be positively preferred to any more active mode of life'.[44]

An important point that is suggested both by Brockway's personal description of a prison outbreak and by consideration of the effects of prison discipline is the interlinking of perceptions of time and space. As Glennie and Thrift have affirmed, 'time is bound up with spatial organisation of society'.[45] The architecture that defined the space within a prison to an extent regulated the direction of movement and also of thought in particular ways. Prison architecture was intrinsic to the prison discipline and routine, and in this way also affected the internal social relations and the time perceptions of individual prisoners. In this respect, Foucault maintained that architecture 'is only taken as an element of support, to ensure a certain allocation of people in space, a *canalization* of their circulation, as well as the coding of their reciprocal relations'.[46]

According to Foucault, four principles directed the spatial separation of individuals. The first of these was 'enclosure'; this defined the boundary of the specific institution, 'the protected space of disciplinary monotony'. The second principle was 'partitioning', which enabled the breaking up of groups and the specifying of space for each individual. The distribution of space was, however, concerned not only with breaking up potentially dangerous communications but also with the creation of useful space, and this can be seen in the prisons by the specification, for instance, of work, exercise and sleeping areas. This composed the third principle of 'functional sites'. Foucault's fourth and final principle regarding the art of distribution is 'rank', and this indicates the importance of the hierarchy that is created by discipline within institutions.[47]

The way in which prisoners described their prison is therefore important; their descriptions reflect not only their physical confinement but their confinement within a disciplined hierarchy. The comparison of a prison cell to a 'human dog-kennel', or prison perceived as a 'kind of living grave', become important indicators of the nature of prison as revealed to those undergoing a sentence within it.[48] The act of a prison warder locking a

---

[44] Hobhouse and Brockway, *English Prisons Today*, p. 491.

[45] P.Glennie and N. Thrift, 'Reworking E.P. Thompson's "Time, Work-discipline and Industrial Capitalism"', *Time and Society* 5, No. 3 (1996), p. 280.

[46] M. Foucault, *The Foucault Reader: An Introduction to Foucault's Thought*, ed. P. Rabinow (Harmondsworth: Penguin, 1991), p. 253.

[47] M. Foucault, *Discipline and Punish: The Birth of the Prison* (Harmondsworth: Penguin, 1979), pp. 141–7.

[48] Cited from a letter received from an imprisoned friend in Hobhouse, 'English Prison from Within', 24; 'No. 7', *Twenty-Five Years in Seventeen Prisons: The Life-Story of an Ex-Convict* (London: F.E. Robinson, 1903), p. 7.

prisoner into a cell both reflects and determines the basic hierarchy and oppositional relations within the prison. Interestingly, for at least one prisoner it was only in his cell that he was able to enjoy a measure of freedom from the constant pace of the prison routine and labour.[49] This was, however, a freedom which could be undermined and interrupted at any point by an eye at the spy-hole in the cell door.

The simplification of life

The grinding routine in which each day was like the last deprived prison time of meaning and merged all the days into an extended present. Within institutions on the scale of many of the convict prisons, there were strong pressures to routinise and standardise so as to produce a simplification of life and experience. For example, the *Report of the Commissioners of Prisons and the Directors of Convict Prisons* for the year ending 31 March 1900 showed that the daily average number of prisoners held in Dartmoor Prison was 960, in Parkhurst Prison it was 700 and in Portland Prison 677. The size of local prisons varied considerably but in the largest the daily average of prisoners could exceed the numbers in the convict prisons. For instance, in the same report for the year ending 31 March 1900, Manchester Prison had a daily average of 698 prisoners, Liverpool Prison had 632, and Pentonville and Wandsworth, both of which were previously convict prisons, had daily average figures of 1,078 and 1,067 respectively.[50]

Discipline established an artificially simplified and ordered existence. Claims that prison dehumanised its inmates were a consequence not only of physical deprivation but of the deprivation of meaningful time. The deprivations of this environment for an extended period of time firmly entrenched the prisoner in the institution, or, in the words of one prisoner, wrapped him in an 'impenetrable cloak'.[51] Mary Gordon, the first female prison inspector, expressed a common feeling when she described the prison as 'a place of suspended animation' in which 'you don't do penance, you do "time"'.[52] In the early twentieth century, she was critical of the prison

---

[49] An example of this opinion is cited in Hobhouse, 'English Prison from Within', p. 28. Even such limited freedom could be reduced either by overcrowding or by being placed in corrugated iron cells in which all the noises made by neighbouring prisoners could be heard. Most of these cells had been replaced by the early twentieth century. See Balfour, *My Prison Life*, p. 74.

[50] BPP, 1900(Cd.380), XLI.65. These figures do not suggest any problem of overcrowding since the number of cells available was 1,158 in Dartmoor Prison, 770 in Parkhurst Prison and 802 in Portland Prison. The lower number of women convicts is shown by the daily average of prisoners held in Aylesbury Prison, numbering only 128 in this year.

[51] Mason, *Made Free in Prison*, p. 131.

[52] M. Gordon, *Penal Discipline* (London: Routledge, 1922), p. 145.

system, especially for women, and remarked that it failed to make any good impressions upon prisoners. She believed in a more 'scientific' individualised treatment of prisoners which would bring about a cure rather than merely impose a punishment.[53]

One important factor in the appropriation and determination of prisoners' time was the peculiarly structured and fragmented nature of social interaction in the prison. Even the architecture of the prison was designed in part to regulate internal 'human sociability'.[54] Anything more than cold and institutional relations between warders and prisoners was generally discouraged, and communications with other prisoners were either forbidden or, at least, severely restricted under the separate or silent systems of discipline. A large proportion of offences against the prison rules and regulations were attempts by prisoners to communicate with one another, which illustrates the value of small independent actions and human interaction to the prisoners.

Fundamentally the silent system entailed the confinement of prisoners in separate cells at night but allowing association at work during the day. The separate system involved the complete seclusion of a prisoner in his cell night and day, although it was intended that he should be visited by prison staff, particularly the chaplain. The adoption of the separate system in English prisons had received an important boost by the advocacy of William Crawford after his investigative visit to North America in 1834; in the following year he had been appointed as one of the new inspectors of prisons.[55] The fact that the operation of the silent system did not necessitate the large-scale improvement or reconstruction of prison buildings and also allowed the prisoners to labour in association was decisive. This meant that a mixture of both systems was adopted in many local prisons and a stage system, beginning with separation and then progressing to silent work in association on the public works, was adopted in the convict prisons.[56]

Realisation of the extent of control that the expropriation of the time of prisoners within these systems of discipline allowed came particularly hard to those who believed that they had been imprisoned for political offences. Jeremiah O'Donovan Rossa, an Irish nationalist who was imprisoned from

[53] Ibid., pp. 222–3.
[54] R. McGowen, 'The Well-Ordered Prison: England, 1780–1865', in *The Oxford History of the Prison: The Practice of Punishment in Western Society* (Oxford: Oxford University Press, 1995), p. 91.
[55] See the evidence of Crawford in *First Report of the Select Committee of the House of Lords appointed to enquire into the present state of the several Gaols and Houses of Correction in England and Wales*, BPP, 1835(438), XI.7–15. Also see Crawford's description of the separate and silent systems of discipline, *Second Report of the Surveyor-General*, BPP, 1847(867), XXIX.17. Also see S. McConville, *A History of English Prison Administration, Vol. 1 1750–1877* (London: Routledge & Kegan Paul, 1981), pp. 170–1.
[56] See Chapter 5 of this publication.

1865 to 1871, expressed how overwhelmed he felt by the power that the British government had over him in Portland Prison. He despaired that the broad arrow signifying government property was stamped on everything, and complained that,

> It was not enough to have it branded on your cap, your shirt and vest, your stockings, jacket-and-trousers, but the nails in your boot or shoe souls were hammered in so that whatever ground you trod left traces that, 'government property' had travelled over it.

He went on to say that if the broad arrow did not 'enter your soul . . . it does find its way into your mouth branded on the bowl of your wooden spoon'.[57]

The lack of personal control or social interaction, the discipline and the silence were all prominent elements of convict prison life in Victorian and Edwardian England. These elements served to affect prisoners' perceptions of time. The present became an undifferentiated and extended arena, the past remote and the future a fantasy or something to avoid thinking about. Hence imprisonment has rarely meant merely the deprivation of liberty; the consequences of this expropriation of time constituted a punishment within the punishment.

Prisoners serving long sentences came to experience time less in terms of the clock than in terms of social time, the relationship of events, such as meals and lock-up times, to one another, or in purely personal terms as each individual worked out their own strategies to cope with prison life. Social relations were determined largely by the discipline and by the tightly routinised prison way of life in which small units of time became significant and useful. Indeed, these schedules composed an institutional time with an internal momentum. Much of this was summed up by one prisoner's description of his imprisonment when he stated, 'Seclusion, silence, shame, separation from one's fellows, a minute and pedantic control exercised by others over all one's actions, a steady, persistent course of official snubbing from morn till eve, these are its [imprisonment's] normal conditions.'[58]

A worker outside the prison could conceivably obtain a greater degree of freedom from being able to sell his time in smaller units. The control over smaller parcels of time could result in an increased independence while also making the worker more flexible in the labour market. In a market culture an individual's time is his property.[59] The time and labour of the prisoner,

---

[57] J. O'Donovan Rossa, *Irish Rebels in English Prisons* (New York: D.J. Sadleir, 1882), p. 114.

[58] Balfour, *My Prison Life*, p. 290.

[59] C. Maier, 'The Politics of Time: Changing Paradigms of Collective Time and Private Time in the Modern Era', in *Changing Boundaries of the Political: Essays on the Evolving*

however, belonged to the state and therefore the division of time into smaller units produced not an increase in independence but rather a more meticulous control over his actions. Time may have been perceived in a different way by prisoners, but the state extended its control through an increased division of time according to the clock.

The manipulation of time through systems of prison discipline was used to impose control and order upon the crime and idleness which had become so closely identified with each other in nineteenth-century liberal social ideology, and not as a means to ensure efficient labour practices. While changes in the organisation of work outside the prison were associated with social progress,[60] the criminal and his idleness were often perceived as representative of an older, more primitive society.

The usefulness of dividing time into defined units in prison cannot be seen in the same terms as the way in which work time was increasingly valued per hour outside of the prison. Gratuity upon discharge or the cost per head to the government of maintaining a prisoner, or even the sentence given as a punishment for non-payment of fines, could be said to associate prison time with money. But the actual proportions of time were not commensurate with proportions of money with the consistency and rigidity that would be required to argue a similarity between outside labour and the position of the long-sentence prisoner. Furthermore, an article by Edmund Du Cane, chairman of the Directors of Convict Prisons for much of the second half of the nineteenth century and of the Commissioners of Prisons from 1878 to 1895, pointed out the manifold problems relating to prison labour that affected its material value. Among these were the lack of skills of most of the prisoners and the fact that the law required a certain period to be served undergoing unproductive and purely penal labour.[61]

In addition, Du Cane claimed that separation, classification and good discipline could not be implemented in the context of large-scale production within the prisons.[62] Efficient time in terms of the productive capacity of labour was not much in evidence in prison.[63] The priorities of prison regimes lay more with control and discipline than with efficient use of labour. The importance of prison labour did not lie in the potential to train an offender to

---

Balance Between the State and Society, Public and Private in Europe, ed. C. Maier (Cambridge: Cambridge University Press, 1987), p. 158. Maier goes on to state that nineteenth-century civilization brought the greatest self-subjection to time and refers to 'serving time' as a prison sentence. He adds to this, however, that 'all of bourgeois culture was involved in serving time'.

[60] D.A. Reid, 'The Decline of Saint Monday, 1766–1876', in *Essays in Social History*, Vol. 2, ed. P. Thane and A. Sutcliffe (Oxford: Oxford University Press, 1986), p. 114.

[61] E.F .Du Cane, 'The Unavoidable Uselessness of Prison Labour', *The Nineteenth Century* 40 (October 1896), pp. 632–42.

[62] Ibid., pp. 640–1.

[63] Cross, *Quest for Time*, p. 17.

enable him to get work after his discharge, but in impressing upon him the ethics of work. As Foucault has suggested, 'penal labour was an apprenticeship not so much in this or that trade as in the virtues of labour itself'.[64] One example of the extent to which labour efficiency was compromised by disciplinary and resource requirements was given by Hobhouse in an article he wrote about his prison experiences. With regard to a 'gardening gang' he observed,

> Whenever one man has the smallest job in another part of the garden, e.g. emptying out some weeds or fetching some vegetables for replanting, and the whole party has to down tools and accompany him; otherwise the warder in charge would be temporarily out of sight or hearing of one portion or other of his gang.[65]

Claims made by prisoners that they were worked like slaves only served to highlight the lack of autonomy and the nature of time to be 'served'; 'there is no heart in a slave's or a prisoner's labour', it was asserted.[66] Prison work was characteristically simple, repetitive and monotonous and did little to alleviate the heavy burden of time or to give a value to time passing. These aspects of prison labour continued into the late twentieth century, and Cohen and Taylor have pointed out that many of the characteristic incentives to work for those outside of the prison, such as 'learning a trade, making something for one's family, financial incentive', are still not evident.[67] Unlike Thompson's industrially employed time, time in prison is not spent but passed.[68]

A report on prison regimes in England and Wales published in 1993, entitled *Doing Time or Using Time*, reiterated the importance of time being usefully employed and expressed concern at the limited amount of work available in modern prisons. This report began with the assumption that 'if prisons are essentially inactive places, those contained in them are locked in a time capsule until release. In conditions of this kind we suggest that those sentenced to imprisonment "serve" time, or are said to be "doing time".' On the other hand, 'if time in custody could be made constructive then it would

---

[64] Foucault, 'Prison Talk', p. 42.

[65] Hobhouse, 'English Prison from Within', p. 28.

[66] Bentley, *Five Years' Penal Servitude*, p. 348.

[67] Cohen and Taylor, *Psychological Survival*, p. 101.

[68] Thompson, 'Time, Work Discipline and Industrial Capitalism', p. 61. According to Thompson, once labour is employed by others the employer must use the time of this labour and see that it is not wasted, 'not the task but the value of time when reduced to money is dominant. Time is now currency: it is not passed but spent.' Also see E. Goffman, 'On the Characteristics of Total Institutions: The Inmate World', in *The Prison: Studies in Institutional Organization and Change* (New York: Holt, Rinehart and Winston, 1966), pp. 62–3.

not be time served, but time used'.[69] The fact that a prison sentence has become so representative of meaningless time and is often referred to as 'doing time' is an indication that efforts to establish constructive work regimes have largely failed in the face of priority being given to security and deterrence.

Several of the accounts of prisoners' experiences show the difficulties of coping with the prison environment and the seemingly endless time. Time itself was one element against which the inmate had to fight, as one stated, 'in a struggle of silence and slow time'.[70] In such a struggle the choices of action available to the prisoner were restricted to obeying or not obeying the rules and regulations. Inherent in this choice was the power to do wrong in the face of authority which had the power to punish.

The committal of even a small offence was a sign of independence. One prisoner explained this in detail. The prisoner

> saves his ego from entire defeat by the secret possession of a nail or a pin or a pencil, anything so long as it is forbidden. The mania for doing wrong things simply because they are prohibited and involve punishment if discovered arises from this craving of the convict to delude himself as to his own powers and freedom.[71]

For a limited time some prison offences offered the prisoners a degree of autonomy as well as an alleviation from routine and from the burden of their time. In this way the short-term rewards gained through participation in or by instigating a disturbance outweighed the fear of the punishment prisoners might receive for it. This provides one explanation as to why some prisoners committed serious offences which seemed to be against their own interests and in circumstances in which punishment was inevitable. Basil Thomson, a retired prison governor, certainly felt that some prison offences were committed as a revolt against the monotony and discipline.[72]

The monotony of prison time might also help to explain why small-scale disturbances in the convict prisons sometimes escalated. For instance, a large-scale disturbance at Chatham Convict Prison in 1861, in which over

---

[69] S. Tumin, *Doing Time or Using Time – Report of a Review by Her Majesty's Chief Inspector of Prisons for England and Wales of Regimes in Prison Service Establishments in England and Wales*, Cm.2128 (London: HMSO, 1993), p. 2.

[70] Mason, *Made Free in Prison*, p. 127. Mason also comments that it was the 'sub-conscious struggle between discipline and mind that embitters the first few months of a first offender's imprisonment', p. 135.

[71] Ibid., p. 141. Mason also comments that the 'convict who possesses an object forbidden flatters his vanity by the reflection that, despite the cleverness and vigilance of the warders, he must be cleverer than they because he can circumvent them'.

[72] B. Thomson, *The Story of Dartmoor Prison* (London: William Heinemann, 1907), p. 265.

800 men were implicated, began with a protest by less than twenty men.[73] Certainly, disturbances in a variety of forms largely shaped by the system of discipline were a common feature of life in Victorian and Edwardian prisons. An awareness of concepts such as time and space in relation to the prison is important, not only because they affect the perceptions of those subject to imprisonment but because they also influence their reactions to their incarceration.

Conclusion

The meaninglessness of passing time and an extended sense of the present were subjective, individual experiences that were nevertheless common in the recorded memories of discharged long-term prisoners. As Forsythe has commented, these writings have value as a historical record and deserve to be inspected for consistent themes.[74] These personal histories combine to give valuable insight into what a long-term prison sentence actually meant for those subject to it, and the way in which prisoners tried to interpret and understand their environment. The recording and publishing of these experiences also indicate an attempt by discharged prisoners to gain some meaning or purpose from their imprisonment. This was certainly the case for political offenders whose accounts attracted a lot of publicity for their causes. Some political offenders were not, however, only concerned with their cause. The conscientious objector Stephen Hobhouse hoped that the prison experiences of himself and others would bring about pressure for reform. As he stated,

> If the evidence of some of those, who are passing through prisons now, may serve to establish true principles by which these institutions may become schools of reformation instead of places of demoralisation and torture, their imprisonment, whatever its other results, will not have been in vain.[75]

In fact the experiences of political prisoners did prove to be a powerful factor in bringing about prison reform.

The prison environment and the extended sense of the present which hung so heavily on long-term prisoners were an intrinsic part of their punishment. This was confirmed by the intentional provision of a monotonous diet and by the regulation and uniformity demanded by security concerns. Prisoners' perceptions of time became dominated less by the clock than

---

[73] See Chapter 3 of this publication.
[74] W.J. Forsythe, *The Reform of Prisoners 1830–1900* (London: Croom Helm, 1987), p. 206.
[75] Hobhouse, 'English Prison from Within', p. 37.

by a self-contained institutional momentum ruled by the times for food, work and sleep. In another sense, time became a more personal experience. Restrictions upon communications drove inmates back upon their own internal resources during the long hours in their cells. The architecture and the discipline of the prison constructed an environment which took away the autonomy, independence and work incentives that gave meaning to passing time for those outside the prison. To use the imagery of a prisoner, prison was felt to be a factory for 'potting human souls'.[76] Socially, prison was a distant and often silent experience which encouraged a dislocation from familiar perceptions regarding not only time but personal identity and social relations. Aspects of life which gave purpose to time outside of the prison, particularly the financial incentives, independence and training obtained through work, held significantly less meaning within the prison.

The systematic manipulation of the conjunction of time and space within the convict prison established a routine, mechanised and physically struc-tured way of life that was relatively static. With these processes, concepts of time and space became predominantly personal and subjective. This resulted in a perception of the present which was considerably extended and which increased the burden of imprisonment. One repercussion of this was to increase the strain and frustration inherent in a long sentence and to increase the likelihood of prison disorder.

[76] Lytton, *Prisons and Prisoners*, p. 188.

3

The Chatham Convict Prison outbreak, 1861: a question of legitimacy?

> The mutiny of the convicts at Chatham had been carefully investigated; but it was very difficult to ascertain precisely the causes and origins of outbreaks of this sort. . . . Some corporal punishment was necessarily inflicted on the ringleaders; but, all things considered, the outbreak was suppressed with as little difficulty as could be expected under the circumstances.[1]

The above quotation is taken from the *Hansard's Parliamentary Debates* of 1861 and indicates that, in the face of difficulties in determining the causes of disturbances, prison officials in the past have tended to emphasise the methods used to deal with such problems and to affirm the successful restoration of order. Prison officials have therefore tended to concentrate upon refining the means of controlling inmates, reflecting an underlying faith in the effectiveness of the prison institution itself. In addition, where there has been investigation into the causes of prison disturbances, concentration has been upon material rather than structural aspects of the prison.

Garland has observed the institutional faith evident in official prison documentation of the nineteenth century. He suggests that so long as fundamental organisational and administrative issues, such as uniformity and the rationalisation of the prison system, remained unresolved, belief in the efficacy of the well-ordered prison continued and was largely unchallenged. His use of the term rationalisation refers to the closing of many small, underused local prisons particularly following the nationalisation of the local prisons in 1877. Until this was achieved, 'any failures or problems of incarceration were laid at the door of inefficient buildings, staff or administration' and the 'model of the prison itself went virtually unchallenged'.[2] According to Garland, this situation applied until the 1890s when it was becoming

---

[1] *Hansard's Parliamentary Debates*, 3rd ser., vol. 164 (1861), col. 649, statement by Sir George Lewis.

[2] D. Garland, *Punishment and Welfare: A History of Penal Strategies* (Aldershot: Gower, 1985), p. 60. Fitzgerald and Sim agree with the dating of this change, although they perceive conditions as constituting only a part of the penal crisis. They assert that due to such changes and uncertainty regarding penal philosophy British prisons have been in a perpetual state of crisis since 1895, M. Fitzgerald and J. Sim, *British Prisons* (Oxford: Basil Blackwell, 1982), p. 3. Also see M. Cavadino and J. Dignan, *The Penal System: An Introduction*, 3rd edn (London: Sage Publications, 2002).

increasingly clear that the failure of the prisons to deter or reform was not merely the consequence of a flawed administration.[3]

Garland's contention does not, however, explain why these administrative issues have retained their prominence in modern official discussion regarding the causes of prison disturbances. Sparks insists that the tendency to define prison problems as being open to technical or repressive 'fixes' remains.[4] Indeed, the term 'crisis' has, he believes, become so associated with this perception that it restricts the range of debate, as he explains:

> It is a term that in its ordinary usage now refers us to the visible symptoms of a problem (in this case overcrowding, insanitary conditions, brutality, riots) rather than the structural problems of the system that generates them. When the word is used in this way a government can announce certain measures (end slopping out, improve visiting arrangements, install some telephones, build some more prisons) and claim, for all relevant purposes, to have averted the crisis, at least for the time being.[5]

The implementation of a multitude of varying fixes within English prisons since the mid-nineteenth century has not yet been able to prevent violent or large-scale prison disturbances. Therefore, an examination of the underlying structural problems that have generated such prison disturbances is necessary. This is not to say that factors such as overcrowding or insanitary conditions are unimportant, but that other more fundamental problems may lie beneath them. In his search for an alternative to a perspective which emphasises the material aspects of the prison, Cavadino has proposed a 'radical pluralist' approach to explanatory problems regarding the concept of a penal crisis. This implies that a complex interaction between material conditions within the prison and ideological influences produced a crisis of legitimacy. The ideological influences Cavadino is directly referring to are the modern collapse of the rehabilitative ideal and the rise of law and order ideology during the 1970s and 1980s.[6] It is this example of a stance which utilises both a materialist and an ideological approach which is followed here.

Chapter 2 of this publication established the point that imprisonment is not merely imposed and submitted to but lived each day in terms of individual experience. This chapter intends to broaden out from this to include a consideration of the moral framework that delineates the structure and maintenance of the prison institution. This is done in the light of

---

[3] Garland, *Punishment and Welfare*, p. 60.

[4] R. Sparks, 'Can Prisons be Legitimate? Penal Politics, Privatization, and the Timeliness of an Old Idea', *British Journal of Criminology* 34 (Special Issue 1994), p. 17.

[5] Ibid., p. 18.

[6] See M. Cavadino, 'Explaining the Penal Crisis', *Prison Service Journal* 87 (1992), pp. 2–12. Also discussed in Sparks, 'Can Prison be Legitimate?', p. 18.

a recent criminological revival of the concept of legitimacy and the assertion by Sparks and Bottoms that the 'combination of an inherent legitimacy deficit with an unusually great disparity of power places a particular onus on prison authorities to attend to the legitimacy of their actions'.[7]

More specifically, this chapter examines the historical legitimacy of the new system of penal servitude established following the running down of transportation during the 1840s and 1850s. This is conducted through an analysis of the causes and effects of one particular large-scale riot that occurred in Chatham Convict Prison in 1861.[8] One reason for considering the concept of legitimacy with regard to a specific major prison disturbance is that such episodes can expose not only the extent to which the day-to-day running of the prison adhered to its rules and regulations and how this was perceived by the inmates, but also the underlying accommodations or understandings which facilitated or obstructed the operation of prison systems. It might then be possible to consider whether these aspects of the prison promoted or hindered the development of a legitimate system. It is by now a truism to state that the prison institution cannot be run by coercion alone.

In addition, this chapter proposes to add another factor to the historical debate which has attempted to explain the shift towards a more deterrent penal policy during the 1860s. It is proposed that the major convict prison disturbances during the late 1850s and early 1860s contributed to the negative public opinion which the system of penal servitude attracted. This negative image of the convict prisons exacerbated existing public and parliamentary concern about crime rates that had been evident since the mid-1850s.[9] Other factors that received publicity and affected social attitudes towards convicts were the ticket-of-leave (a kind of parole on licence system) scares and the sensationalism surrounding the crime of garrotting in London. Furthermore, a general disillusionment with reformative practices in English prisons was highlighted by unfavourable, and largely unfair, comparisons with the Irish prison system during the early 1860s.[10] In addition, Joshua

---

[7] J.R. Sparks and A.E. Bottoms, 'Legitimacy and Order in Prisons', *British Journal of Sociology* 46 (March 1995), pp. 45–62.

[8] Also see A. Brown, 'Legitimacy in the Evolution of the Prison: The Chatham Convict Prison Outbreak 1861', *Criminal Justice History* 18 (2003).

[9] W.J. Forsythe, *The Reform of Prisoners 1830–1900* (London: Croom Helm, 1987), pp. 144–5.

[10] See P.W.J. Bartrip, 'Public Opinion and Law Enforcement: The Ticket-of-Leave Scares in Mid-Victorian Britain', in *Policing and Punishment in Nineteenth Century Britain*, ed. V. Bailey (London: Croom Helm, 1981); J. Davis, 'The London Garotting Panic of 1862: A Moral Panic and the Creation of a Criminal Class in Mid-Victorian England', in *Crime and the Law: The Social History of Crime in Western Europe since 1500*, ed. V.A.C. Gatrell, B. Lenman and G. Parker (London: Europa Publications, 1980); Forsythe, *Reform of Prisoners*, pp. 147–8; S. McConville, *A History of English Prison Administration, Vol. 1*

Jebb, as head of the convict prison directorate, was personally subjected to a hostile press campaign accusing him of being misguided and too lenient on convicts.[11]

The concept of legitimacy

Possibly the most useful consideration of the concept of legitimacy has been offered by David Beetham.[12] His publication, *The Legitimation of Power* (1991), has inspired recent investigation by a few prominent criminologists into the problem of legitimacy with regard to the prison.[13] Beetham contends that all systems of power relations seek legitimation and that legitimacy has a discernible basic structure. This structure of legitimacy takes the form of three criteria. The first criterion is conformity to rules, the second is justifiability of rules in terms of shared beliefs, and the third criterion is legitimation through expressed consent. Each of these criteria has an opposing form of non-legitimate power. A lack of conformity to rules is illegitimate, a lack of justification in terms of shared beliefs is a legitimacy deficit, and a lack of legitimacy through expressed consent is delegitimation. The precise content of these, he contends, is highly variable between different historical societies.[14] Legitimacy is not the only factor necessary to ensure stability and order but it is, according to Beetham, a crucial one. Other important factors in the maintenance of order are organisational capacity, resources and coercion.[15]

An historical view of the concept of legitimacy with regard to the prison offers a more comprehensive and longer-term perspective concerning the problems of disorder that this institution has faced. This approach might also pose the question whether, if such concerns had been given more prominence during the early development of the prison in the nineteenth century, the legitimacy problems experienced by prison systems in later years would have been less pronounced.

Sparks, Bottoms and Hay believe that the concept of legitimacy has been an important undercurrent in most modern investigations into the prison.

1750–1877 (London: Routledge & Kegan Paul, 1981), pp. 441–3. Also see Jebb Papers box 2 and 3.

[11] J. Manton, *Mary Carpenter and the Children of the Streets* (London: Heinemann, 1976), pp. 182–5. For the background to Jebb's career see E. Stockdale, 'The Rise of Joshua Jebb, 1837–1850', *British Journal of Criminology* 16, No. 2 (April 1976), pp. 164–70.

[12] D. Beetham, *The Legitimation of Power* (London: Macmillan, 1991).

[13] J.R. Sparks, A.E. Bottoms and W. Hay, *Prisons and the Problem of Order* (Oxford: Clarendon Press, 1996); J.R.Sparks, 'Can Prisons be Legitimate?', pp. 14–28; Sparks and Bottoms, 'Legitimacy and Order', p. 60.

[14] Beetham, *Legitimation of Power*, p. 20.

[15] Ibid., p. 473.

As they state, 'The problem of legitimation may be one which at least implicitly underpins the concerns of prison sociology from Sykes onwards, though it is largely absent from Foucault's analysis.'[16] According to Connolly, Foucault refused to adopt a theory of legitimation because he saw it as an arbitrary construction. For Foucault, it is power and not legitimacy which is the basis of order, and morality cannot be imposed upon considerations of power and arbitrary disciplines.[17] However, the fact that prisoners had the choice, albeit a restricted one, whether to resist or to submit to the prison rules and regulations and that some prisons were disrupted more than others suggests that individual or combined decisions and judgements were continually being made.[18] Furthermore, these choices were often made with regard to the fairness or morality of a regime or an individual action even if these judgements were ill-informed or prejudiced or if the action taken achieved nothing.[19] At the point of the individual or the group, justice or injustice was subjectively perceived.[20] Foucault himself emphasised the necessity of resistance, which implies that at some point such choices may be made.[21] For Foucault, however, it was the opposition between struggle and submission and not between legitimacy and illegitimacy which provided a better scheme for the analysis of power, although he did indicate his dissatisfaction with his own scheme as well.[22] It is suggested here that the attainment of a level of legitimacy can perpetuate existing systems of power. Nevertheless, this does not detract from evidence which may

---

[16] Sparks *et al.*, *Prisons and Order*, p. 68.

[17] W. Connolly, *Legitimacy and the State* (Oxford: Basil Blackwell, 1984), p. 16.

[18] This statement assumes that the individual is capable of making a reasonably balanced choice, although it is recognised that the specific environment has a strong influence upon such decisions. For instance, in Chapter 2 of this publication it was suggested that the mental effects of long-term imprisonment might inhibit the ability to make rational choices in particular circumstances.

[19] Rawls cites fairness as the fundamental principle in the concept of justice. See J. Rawls, 'Justice as Fairness', *Philosophical Review* 67 (1958), p. 165. Rawls defines justice as 'the elimination of arbitrary distinctions and the establishment, within the structure of a practice, of a proper balance of competing aims'.

[20] E. Carrabine, 'The State of Power: Taking the "New-Old Penology" Seriously in Understanding Prison Riots', paper presented to the British Criminology Conference, July 1995. Carrabine suggests that it is relative as opposed to absolute deprivation that explains the pattern of riots in modern British prisons.

[21] M. Foucault, *Discipline and Punish: The Birth of the Prison* (Harmondsworth: Penguin, 1977), p. 308.

[22] M. Foucault, 'Two Lectures', in *Michel Foucault: Power/Knowledge, Selected Interviews and Other Writings*, ed. C. Gordon (Brighton: Harvester Press, 1980), p. 92. He states his dissatisfaction in the following terms, 'I believe that these two notions of repression and war [legitimacy and his own struggle and submission scheme] must themselves be considerably modified if not ultimately abandoned. In any case, I believe that they must be submitted to closer scrutiny.'

suggest that certain forms or distributions of power are more legitimate than others.

Despite its usefulness in encouraging analysis of the way in which an institution like the prison defines and justifies itself, the concept of legitimacy also poses some problems, particularly with regard to the coercive nature of the prison. In his discussion of the legitimation of power, Beetham begins with the contention that 'Where power is acquired and exercised according to justifiable rules, and with evidence of consent, we call it rightful or legitimate.'[23] Historically, it is difficult to determine intangibles such as consent, particularly in the more marginal sections of the population which rarely left the kind of evidence which would allow a more in-depth understanding of motivations to be made.[24] To an extent, Chapter 2 of this publication, which examines the perceptions of long-term prisoners, is an attempt to counteract this, although much of the evidence upon which this was based was not produced by ordinary prisoners.

Nevertheless, the persistence in Victorian and Edwardian literature and official documentation of the principle of less eligibility would suggest that the material deprivations and discipline imposed in prison were, to a large extent, justifiable in terms of general social beliefs and produced a degree of consent.[25] Of course, this was not a constant and at times the harshness of particular aspects of prison regimes was successfully challenged – for instance, the campaign in the early twentieth century that brought about a progressive reduction in the time convicts spent in separate confinement.[26]

Unlike Weber, whose definition of legitimacy is subjective in that it concerns the beliefs people hold about power, Beetham offers a definition of legitimacy which attempts to lend an objective and moral dimension to the debate. He asserts that a 'given power relation is not legitimate because people believe in its legitimacy, but because it can be *justified in terms of their beliefs*'.[27] Particularly problematic for the use of the concept of legitimacy with regard to the prison is the identification of what constitutes the expression of consent on the part of prisoners. In part, this can be addressed

---

[23] Beetham, *Legitimation of Power*, p. 3.

[24] The problem of 'identifying the relevant beliefs and actions and obtaining evidence for them' has also been highlighted with regard to modern analysis of legitimacy. See R.H.O'Kane, 'Against Legitimacy', *Political Studies* 41 (1993), p. 476.

[25] Prison dietary was one subject that was frequently related to the principle of less eligibility. See, for instance, M. Heather Tomlinson, '"Not an Instrument of Punishment": Prison Diet in the Mid-Nineteenth Century', *Journal of Consumer Studies and Home Economics* 2 (1978), p. 15. Also see A.S. Thompson, 'A Review of Prison Diet in England and Wales', *Prison Service Journal* 68 (October 1987), pp. 19–22.

[26] M. Nellis, 'John Galsworthy's Justice', *British Journal of Criminology* 36 (Winter 1996), pp. 61–84. Also see Chapter 6.

[27] Beetham, *Legitimation of Power*, pp. 9–11. Also see Sparks and Bottoms, 'Legitimacy and Order', p. 48.

by reference to Beetham's contention that a power relation must be justified in terms of beliefs. It has been asserted, for example, that people from the lower sections of society, generally the same classes from which prisoners were often derived, themselves made use of the criminal justice system for redress against the crimes committed against them. For example, Tomes cites cases of men whose assaults upon women outside of their family resulted in them being dragged to the police station by groups from the local community.[28] This suggests that the punishment of at least some offenders was justifiable in terms of the beliefs of at least a proportion of this section of society and also attracted their active consent.

Phillips states that the majority of prosecutions brought by victims of crime in the period 1836 to 1851 were by retail traders and industrialists, but that between 28 and 50 per cent of prosecutions were brought by unskilled and semi-skilled working-class people. As the most common victims of crime, working people were prepared to prosecute those who offended against them.[29] This action implies a degree of acceptance of the values and standards under which the police, the courts and the prisons were run, which constituted 'an acceptance of its [the law's] basic legitimacy as applied to themselves and their affairs'.[30] As Reid has observed, because institutions are unlikely ever to get complete positive consent it is reasonable to see it in voluntary willingness to participate in social institutions.[31] The degree of importance that can be attached to this depends upon the extent to which criminals are seen as constituting a separate class. Certainly, many historians have suggested that, during the nineteenth century at least, any distinction between the working classes and the criminal classes was extremely blurred. Indeed, Jones has commented that most crime in the nineteenth century was committed by people in casual or part-time employment and that the concept of a criminal class was largely a construct used to deflect enquiries into the more fundamental causes of crime.[32]

A further clue as to the form in which evidence of consent may be found is given by Beetham who asserts that, 'what is important for legitimacy is

---

[28] N. Tomes, 'A "Torrent of Abuse": Crimes of Violence Between Working-Class Men and Women in London, 1840–1875', *Journal of Social History* 11 (1978), p. 337.

[29] D. Phillips, *Crime and Authority in Victorian England: The Black Country 1835–60* (London: Croom Helm, 1977), pp. 123–9 and pp. 285–9. Phillips goes on to suggest that there was some distrust of the law and that those cases prosecuted by the working classes constituted only a minority of actual offences committed. Furthermore, some offences were less likely to be prosecuted than others – for instance, the Game Laws seem to have attracted some community sanction.

[30] Ibid., p. 128.

[31] A.J. Reid, *Social Classes and Social Relations in Britain, 1850–1914* (London: Macmillan, 1992), p. 52.

[32] D. Jones, *Crime, Protest, Community and Police in Nineteenth-Century Britain* (London: Routledge & Kegan Paul, 1982), p. 6. Also see Phillips, *Crime and Authority*, p. 287.

evidence of consent experienced through *actions* which are understood as demonstrating consent within the conventions of the particular society'.[33] Thus evidence of consent derived from the actions of prisoners may not be judged in the same terms as that from non-prisoners. To an extent, prisoners existed within a separate society, and actions understood by other prisoners or by prison staff as indicating a degree of consent may have been particular to the environment. This is important since it is not adequate to accept the passivity of many prisoners as evidence of consent, as Scott has asserted in his study of peasant resistance, 'resignation to what seems inevitable is not the same as according it legitimacy'.[34] However, this does make the deciphering of consensual behaviour on the part of prisoners problematic and even precarious, particularly in an historical context.

The institution of the prison has historically experienced legitimacy problems as a result of its coercive and disciplinary approach and the competing demands of differing sections of society. Thus, the considerable evidence of disturbances within English prisons over the previous 150 years provides ample confirmation of a lack of inmate consent. Such problems have also been exacerbated by the great differences that have existed in prison regimes not only over time but between prisons in the same period. Therefore, identifying the existence of consent on the part of prisoners poses three fundamental problems. The first of these is that the prison as a coercive institution was unlikely to elicit consent on the part of prisoners. This is particularly the case in the light of evidence which suggests that abuse of the prison rules and regulations by prison staff has not been uncommon in the past and that prison authorities have tended to place priority upon organisational and coercive resolutions to problems of disorder. The second problem is that the disciplined and routinised prison environment left little opportunity to express consent should it exist. The third and final problem with identifying consent on the part of prisoners is that, should consent have been expressed, it may have been in forms which were particular to prison society.

An alternative to the problem of identifying consent on the part of prisoners has been proposed by Sparks and Bottoms who suggest that, assuming that it existed, then it may at least be possible to 'specify circumstances under which prisoners are more or less likely to confer or withhold degrees of recognition of legitimate authority of prison staff and regimes'.[35] This is a more promising avenue for analysis since it also encourages assessment of the prison in terms of the conditions and treatment that might

---

[33] Beetham, *Legitimation of Power*, p. 12, although Beetham has been criticised for his lack of consideration of non-behavioural factors – see O'Kane, 'Against Legitimacy', p. 477.
[34] J.C. Scott, *Weapons of the Weak: Everyday Forms of Peasant Resistance* (New Haven: Yale University Press, 1985), p. 323.
[35] Sparks and Bottoms, 'Legitimacy and Order', p. 45.

produce consent. This is the approach that is taken in the following examination of the outbreak which occurred in Chatham Convict Prison in 1861.

The context of the Chatham Convict Prison outbreak

The significance of the 1850s and 1860s for penal history in England is that this period witnessed the winding down of transportation. A complete system of convict imprisonment had, therefore, to be established. Public works convict prisons were established by the government at Portland (1849), Dartmoor (modernised 1850), Portsmouth (1852) and Chatham (1856), in order to facilitate the transition of England's convict system from reliance upon transportation to the retention of its convicts wholly within the country. The accommodation provided by the public works prisons also enabled the gradual abolition of the notorious prison hulks. Public work in these convict prisons consisted of labour in naval dockyards, quarrying and agriculture. Because the ending of transportation was largely due to growing opposition from Australia, Bartrip has referred to the establishment of a system of penal servitude in Britain as a 'classic case of the functional imperative – of reform through pressure of events rather than principle'.[36]

Public works prisons were to provide the second stage of a penal servitude system in which the first stage was spent in separation in Millbank or Pentonville prisons and the third stage was release on conditional licence, or ticket-of-leave. The Directors of the convict prisons hoped that the progressive stage system and the gratuities that prisoners could earn would stimulate industry and encourage reform through the inculcation of the habit of work. Indeed, the governor of Portland Convict Prison stated in his report of 1852–3 that,

> When it is considered that scarcely any of the convicts were ever employed on such work before, and that they have neither the aptitude, the physical strength, nor the diet of the quarrymen or labourers engaged in such operations, the result is remarkable, and can only be attributed to willing and persevering industry, induced by the encouragement held out under the present system.[37]

Bartrip points out that the problem of having to accommodate offenders within the country should not be exaggerated, since many transportees were already being dealt with in British prisons and hulks, and also transportees

---

[36] Bartrip, 'Public Opinion', p. 153.
[37] *Report on the Discipline and Management of the Convict Prisons*, BPP, 1852–3(1572), LI.30.

constituted a minority of all convicted offenders.[38] Nevertheless, the fact that all offenders were now to be retained within the country caused public alarm, and the threat posed by ticket-of-leave men was exaggerated and sensationalised.

Public alarm was exacerbated by newspaper accounts of disturbances in these new prisons. This, therefore, brings into the discussion the effects of public and political opinion on penal policy. Of course, the nature of public opinion in this period is problematic, but Bartrip provides a useful definition. He states that 'the term "public opinion" signified a rationalisation and propagation of views or prejudices held in high places. It might be, in other words, a clarion call for action which was difficult to resist.'[39] The multidimensional nature of this is one reason for the usefulness of the concept of legitimacy in an examination of this subject. As Sparks has observed, the conceptual power of legitimacy

> lies in the connections which it illuminates between the interior life of penal systems, and the social relations that characterize them, and the centrally important 'external' issue of the conditions under which it is judged appropriate to impose prison sentences in the first place.[40]

The prison was certainly exposed to wider public and political opinion in this evolutionary period, which proved decisive in determining the direction of penal policy during and after the 1860s.

What made some of the prison disturbances of this period distinctive was their scale. The strike at Portland Prison in 1858 involved as many as 350 inmates, and some 850 inmates were initially implicated in the riot at Chatham in 1861. Dartmoor Convict Prison also experienced serious disciplinary problems. A prison official was later to maintain that assaults committed in Dartmoor Convict Prison in this period had 'become so common that the records ceased to give names or particulars, and the temper of the men was so dangerous that arrangements were quietly made for drawing upon the Plymouth garrison if necessary'.[41] These problems seemed to confirm the worst fears about retaining convicts within the country

---

[38] See Bartrip, 'Public Opinion', p. 173.

[39] Ibid.

[40] Sparks, 'Can Prison be Legitimate?', p. 16.

[41] B. Thomson, *The Story of Dartmoor Prison* (London: William Heinemann, 1907), p. 244. According to the *Report of the Commissioners of Prisons and the Directors of Convict Prisons*, BPP, 1914(Cd.7601), XLV.389–90, Basil Thomson joined the prison service in 1896, and became, successively, governor of Northampton, Cardiff, Dartmoor and Wormwood Scrubs prisons. In 1908 he was made Secretary to the Prison Commission and in 1913 left the prison service to take up a post as Assistant Commissioner of Police.

and prompted alarmist comments like that in *The Times* which stated that such outbreaks constituted a 'strategy of war on our own island'.[42] The disturbances were contained but the consequent publicity was damaging. The system of penal servitude in the convict prisons seemed to ensure neither the safe custody of its inmates nor their reformation.

The realisation that all convicts now had to be retained within the country served to concentrate government and public attention on the gap between the rhetoric and the actual performance of the system of penal servitude. Expectations of the system pulled in several directions. Deterrence and less eligibility required a strict and sparse discipline, but at the same time any damaging physical or psychological effects on inmates as a result of a strict regime had potential for public scandal. These lessons had been learnt during the previous three decades in the administration of Millbank and Pentonville convict prisons and also in the scandals produced by regimes in the local prisons at Birmingham and Leicester.[43] Importantly, there was also recognition that to maintain order and encourage reformation through the inculcation of habits of industry, penal servitude had to establish justifiable standards upon which to base its discipline.

In the event, the effects of convict disturbances upon political and public opinion helped to create a climate which favoured the shift towards a more deterrent penal philosophy. An article which appeared in *The Edinburgh Review* in 1865 was critical of the 'supposed reformatory system' which, it was claimed, actually meant 'lightness of punishment, laxity of discipline, deference to the will of the convict, and the prospect of liberty under great advantages'.[44] Under such conditions, the article continued, 'we can hardly wonder much at the mutinies in our prisons', and it asserted that, 'We have heard so much of reformatory schemes in our convict prisons, and we have seen so much of their failure, that we have lost faith in all attempts to reform, at any age, and under any circumstances.'[45] Thus, at this early point, short-

---

[42] 23 August 1858, p. 11, col. a. This comment refers directly to the outbreak at Portland Convict Prison in 1858.

[43] See U.R.Q. Henriques, 'The Rise and Decline of the Separate System of Prison Discipline', *Past and Present* 54 (1972), p. 84. Henriques points out that the 'public suspicion, alternating between general demands for greater severity and outcries against individual cases of cruelty, was one factor in the decline of the separate system'. Also see D. Roberts, 'The Scandal at Birmingham Borough Gaol 1853: A Case for Penal Reform', *Journal of Legal History* 7 (1986), pp. 315–40; McConville, *English Prison Administration*, ch. 6; *Report of the Commissioners appointed to inquire into the Condition and Treatment of the Prisoners confined in Birmingham Borough Prison*, BPP (1854), XXXI, pp. 1–38; *Report of the Commissioners appointed to inquire into the Condition and Treatment of the Prisoners confined in Leicester County Gaol and House of Correction*, BPP (1854), XXXIV, pp. 467–79.

[44] Anon. [H.Martineau], 'Life in the Criminal Class', *The Edinburgh Review* 122 (July–October 1865), pp. 361 and 358.

[45] Ibid., pp. 360 and 358.

term pressures heavily influenced penal policy and, given the instability of the convict prisons, the necessary priority assigned to security. The minority who asserted that increased deterrence would degrade criminals further were, according to Heather Tomlinson, 'shouted down by the majority who feared for themselves'.[46] These circumstances overwhelmed any nascent attempts by Joshua Jebb, the Director of the Convict Prisons, to establish a disciplinary system which might achieve a more equal balance between deterrence, custody and reform.

The Chatham Convict Prison outbreak and its causes

One particular disturbance in Chatham Convict Prison on 11 February 1861 played a large part in exposing the inadequacies of the existing system of penal servitude. The disturbance at Chatham was large-scale – initially up to 850 convicts were implicated in the riot by the prison authorities – and received a lot of public attention. As late as 1904, Arthur Griffiths referred to this disturbance as 'the famous Chatham mutiny of 1861'.[47] Radzinowicz and Hood have more recently commented that it is Chatham which stands out in the history of prison disobedience.[48]

A disturbance on 11 February, as the prisoners were paraded for labour at the public works, resulted in thirty-five of the ringleaders being secured in the punishment cells. Later the same day a large number of inmates became unruly and demanded the release of the prisoners under punishment. The situation quickly escalated and in the time it took for troops to arrive the convicts became 'masters of the interior of the prison'. They got possession of the keys and released all the convicts locked in their cells and created 'terrible havoc' and destruction. A total of 850 men were later implicated in the disturbance. In the face of the combined power of the prisoners, the ability of the prison staff to enforce their primary task, the secure custody of the inmates, had been seriously challenged, and when it came to re-imposing control the prison warders were ruthless. Before the arrival of reinforcements from the nearby garrison and the Metropolitan Police, the prison warders drove the mutineers into their cells using their staves freely against any opposition.[49]

---

[46] M. Heather Tomlinson, '"Prison Palaces": A Re-appraisal of Early Victorian Prisons, 1835–77', *Bulletin of the Institute of Historical Research* 51 (1978), p. 71.

[47] A. Griffiths, *Fifty Years of Public Service* (London: Cassell, 1904), p. 178.

[48] L. Radzinowicz and R. Hood, *A History of English Criminal Law, Vol. 5 The Emergence of Penal Policy* (London: Stevens, 1986), p. 522.

[49] The above is a summarised account collated from various sources of evidence. *Report of the Directors of Convict Prisons*, BPP, 1862(3011), XXV.577–611; *The Times*, 13 February 1861, p. 12, cols c–d, 'Revolt of the Convicts at Chatham'; *Report of the Commissioners appointed to Inquire into the Operation of Acts relating to Transportation and Penal Servitude* (hereafter the Penal Servitude Acts Commission), BPP, 1863(3190), XXI.335–8,

News of the disturbance rapidly spread through the town. According to a report in a local paper, *The Chatham News*, on 16 February 1861, 'the horrible hubbub created by a thousand felons in mutiny, and the arrival of bodies of troops, attracted much attention, and many persons congregated'.

Radzinowicz and Hood have described the Chatham disturbance in detail, yet they conclude that to

> disentangle the basic causes of the precipitating factors of a major disturbance in a major institution over 100 years ago is a hopeless task. A variety of explanations were provided but to weigh them up would be an exercise in sheer speculation. It may be that there was some truth in all of them.[50]

It may be the case that all of the available explanations contain some truth, but that is largely because the evidence has a consistency which is convincing and which builds up to an argument which, if not concrete, is much more than 'sheer speculation'. Moreover, one source that offers exceptional insights into the period prior to the disturbance, the journal of the governor of Chatham Convict Prison, Folliot Powell, was not used by Radzinowicz and Hood.[51] In the light of this assertion and the availability of a variety of sources of evidence, the 'interaction history' of one particular, even sensational, episode in the history of the prison system can be constructed. In sociological terms the 'interaction history' of an event has been described in the following way:

> The scene or setting, the quality of relationships, the structure of opportunities, the meaning of events, prospective costs and benefits, change constantly. Every violent episode, whether it is an altercation between two friends, a mugging, or a riot, is the product of such an interaction history.[52]

qu.571–98 and 387–91, qu.1201–33, the evidence of Sir Joshua Jebb, and the evidence of Captain Folliot Powell, Governor of Chatham Convict Prison. Also see *Returns relating to the recent Convict Disturbances at Chatham*, BPP, 1861(125), LII.3; *Hansard's Parliamentary Debates*, 3rd ser., vol. 161 (1861), cols 472–4 and vol. 164 (1861), cols 649–59. In agreement with Radzinowicz and Hood, Arthur Griffiths' claim that the Director, Captain Gambier, 'went into the thick of the menacing throng and knocked the ring-leader down with his own hands' seems like prison service mythology. See Griffiths, *Fifty Years of Public Service*, p. 178. Also see, *The Chatham News*, 16 February 1861, 'Convict Mutinies at Chatham'.

[50] Radzinowicz and Hood, *History of English Criminal Law*, p. 524.
[51] PRO PCom2/427, journal of the governor of Chatham Convict Prison, 1 June 1859 to 8 March 1861.
[52] A.K. Cohen, 'Prison Violence: A Sociological Perspective', in *Prison Violence*, ed. A.K. Cohen, G.F. Cole and R.F. Bailey (Lexington, Mass.: D.C. Heath, 1976), p. 8.

It is clear from the Reports of the Directors of the Convict Prisons that all of the convict prisons were at this time experiencing quite violent resistance by prisoners. The public works convict prisons, including Chatham, were particularly prone to disturbances. As McConville has pointed out, there were control problems inherent in large numbers of prisoners labouring together under relatively light supervision.[53] This makes it more difficult to identify the particular combination of factors which determined the scale and form of the disturbances within a particular prison. The general organisational characteristics referred to by McConville were undoubtedly decisive, and, since the pattern and level of disturbances within the convict prisons during this period varied, it implies that the nature of specific prison regimes and of the relationships between the prisoners and the prison staff was also important.

The journal of the governor of Chatham Convict Prison indicates that there was a build-up of tension and evidence of a lack of discipline on the part of both staff and prisoners prior to the disturbance of 11 February. One incident described in the governor's journal is particularly revealing about the condition of the internal relations of the prison at this time. On 30 January 1861 a violent incident occurred in which

> A brutal assault was committed upon . . . John Anderson by some convicts . . . the outrage was not seen by either the Officer or Guard but Anderson states that it was committed by two convicts of the names of Clerk and Gallagher. It was reported to the Princl [sic] Warder Webb on Monday that this assault was intended, and that certain prisoners had an iron instrument for this purpose and was again brought to this officers notice in writing on Tuesday but he took no steps in the matter, nor made any report of the circumstances.[54]

According to the governor's journal, there were no repercussions as a result of the failure of this senior officer to act to prevent the assault. There was no investigation as to whether the two named prisoners were responsible, nor was any punishment recorded against them. The lack of action by the governor in the face of such a dereliction of duty by the principal warder seems inexplicable and yet the governor makes no attempt to cover this up or to offer any mitigating circumstances.

Convict prison records of the period, including those regarding Chatham, show that the conduct and disciplining of staff were a priority, as evident, for example, in the punishment of warders who had been on guard when a prisoner had attempted to escape.[55] On both Thursday 8 November 1860 and

---

[53] McConville, *English Prison Administration*, p. 440.
[54] PRO PCom2/427, journal of the governor of Chatham Convict Prison, 30 January 1861.
[55] Ibid.

Sunday 9 December 1860 warders at Chatham were automatically suspended from pay and duty pending investigation by the Visiting Director, Captain Gambier, for allowing convicts to escape while they were on duty. These and other events prior to the major disturbance of 11 February, including two violent assaults on warders and a search on 14 January for skeleton keys believed to be in the possession of prisoners, combine to establish a first impression of a lack of control as well as possible collusion by officers with the prisoners.

An article published in *The Cornhill Magazine* attributed the disturbances at Chatham Convict Prison primarily to corrupt prison warders, and suggested that the prisoners' own perceptions of the fairness of prison procedures was important, even if such prison conventions did not actually adhere to the rules and regulations. The article maintained that some 'right screws', that is prison warders who were corrupt, were trafficking for the prisoners at extortionate rates or keeping the money received from friends and relatives of prisoners' which made the convicts 'desperate'.[56]

Soon after the disturbances an official letter was enclosed with convicts' letters to family and friends outside and also circulated within the convict prisons. This letter warned correspondents against sending money to prisoners 'in any way except by letter addressed to them directly through the post-office'. The letter also explained that 'Some persons employed about the prison have obtained money from friends of prisoners, and have used it for their own purposes, or have given a part of it to the prisoners contrary to the regulations and to law.'[57] In the months prior to the riot, Folliot Powell, the governor of Chatham, had disciplined officers for such offences. On Friday 19 October 1860, Assistant Warder Loughlin was allowed to resign after being found guilty of writing part of a letter to a prisoner's friend for the purpose of obtaining £2.10s. On Saturday 7 December 1860 the governor suspended the schoolmaster from pay and duty for corresponding with the friends of a prisoner, Samuel Smith, and trying to obtain money from them.[58]

In his evidence to The Penal Servitude Acts Commission, Jebb laid much of the blame for the disturbances upon the presence in Chatham of certain prisoners and warders – 'the dregs' – from the old prison hulks which had been notorious for their lack of discipline and violence.[59] It was later commented about these prison ships that,

> Every evil that can be supposed to arise from the unchecked association of men
> of foul lives and unrestrained passions, with no more restraint than was enforced

---

[56] Anon. [H.W. Holland and F. Greenwood], 'Revelations of Prison Life', *The Cornhill Magazine* 7 (January–June 1863), p. 644.

[57] Ibid.

[58] PRO PCom2/427, Journal of the Governor of Chatham Convict Prison.

[59] BPP, 1863(3190), XXI.336, qu.573.

by gaolers of a very inferior class, and with extremely imperfect ideas of discipline, prevailed on board.[60]

Folliot Powell had reported that some of the senior officers transferred from the hulks, on whom he ought to have been able to depend, were secretly acting against him and the officers from the other convict prisons and colluding with the prisoners. This, according to Powell, brought about a situation in which 'those officers who did their duty were looked upon by the prisoners as tyrants, and those who did not were regarded as comparatively good fellows'.[61] It appears that measures had been taken to discharge, with pensions, these senior officers prior to the disturbances of February 1861. The officers in question were aware of this, but the discharges had not yet been carried out. What seems clear is that, in the face of such corruption and internal division, the possibilities of establishing and maintaining a stable and consistent system of adherence to the rules and regulations of the prison would be severely limited. Following the Chatham 'mutiny', ten warders were suspended from duty on full pay; six of these were then transferred to other prisons. The remaining four, all senior warders, were discharged. These four senior warders were almost certainly those previously identified by the governor as unsatisfactory.[62]

Embroiled in the internal divisions within Chatham Convict Prison were convicts who had been returned from penal servitude in Bermuda and who had another grievance.[63] Some of these men had been sentenced under the Penal Servitude Act of 1853, the first to establish by law that penal servitude could be carried out in England rather than overseas. This Act substituted for sentences of transportation shorter sentences of penal servitude but with no remission.[64] Convicts sentenced later, under the 1857 Penal Servitude Act, although subject to longer sentences were able to obtain remission for industry. The 1857 Act did not extend remission to those previously sentenced under the Act of 1853. According to Tomlinson, the main reason for the hard line taken by the Home Office on the issue of

---

[60] E.F. Du Cane, 'Experiments in Punishment', *The Nineteenth Century* 6 (November 1879), p. 873.

[61] *The Penal Servitude Acts Commission*, BPP, 1863(3190), XXI.336, qu.576 and 387, qu.1206.

[62] Ibid., evidence of Captain Folliot Powell, governor of Chatham Convict Prison, 387–91, qu.1201–33.

[63] It should also be noted that in some cases particularly unruly prisoners had been consigned to Bermuda in the past and some of these may have been included with this group. See McConville, *English Prison Administration*, p. 411.

[64] McConville has asserted that this was largely a bringing together of existing practice; as he states, 'This was no leap in the dark, but rather a regularisation and combination of existing measures, renamed and presented in a manner calculated to allay and soothe public anxieties', ibid., pp. 386–7.

remission was to try to build public confidence in penal servitude served wholly in England.[65]

Naturally the issue of remission created resentment and friction between prisoners sentenced under different legislation when they came to work side by side in the convict prisons.[66] This was exacerbated by those sentenced under the 1857 Act baiting and jeering at those sentenced under the 1853 Act. With reference to Portland Convict Prison the Directors reported that 'the 1857 Act men taunted them [those sentenced under the 1853 Act] . . . and jeered at them for working so hard for nothing. This feeling at last showed itself by large bodies of men striking work and refusing to labour any more.'[67] The serious disturbance at Portland Convict Prison in 1858, in which over 300 men had refused to work, was largely a result of these defects in the legislation. According to the governor, the prisoners had themselves stated 'that they considered themselves ill used in having no remission of sentence for good conduct such as the men under the Act of July 1857 had'.[68] By 1862, Jebb had implemented a certificate system, which effectively gave remission to those sentenced under the 1853 Act.[69] Indeed, Chatham Convict Prison was the last prison to experience a major disturbance in which this grievance played a part.

The practice in the convict prisons of transferring troublesome prisoners was common; similar tactics were no doubt used in this case on the staff. The majority of the prisoners involved in the disturbances were retained at Chatham, although at least seven of those who were perceived to be the ringleaders of the Chatham mutiny were sent to imprisonment in Gibraltar.[70] The Directors of the Convict Prisons, and Joshua Jebb personally, wanted to prove they were able to suppress disobedience and re-establish control. This was particularly important in the light of the disturbances that had occurred at other convict prisons and the critical press they had received. The fact that other convict prisons were experiencing disciplinary problems also limited the usefulness of transferring large numbers of prisoners between the small number of convict prisons.

---

[65] M. Heather Tomlinson, 'Penal Servitude 1846–1865: A System in Evolution', in *Policing and Punishment in Nineteenth Century Britain*, ed. V. Bailey (London: Europa Publications, 1981), p. 134.

[66] Ibid., pp. 132–3.

[67] *RDCP* (Report of the Directors of Convict Prisons), PP, 1859 s.2 (2556), XIII, Pt.1.191 and 338.

[68] PRO PCom2/359, journal of the governor of Portland Convict Prison, Mr Clay, 21 April 1858 to 5 March 1861, entry dated Monday 30 August 1858.

[69] Indeed Jebb was later to comment that 'until every man sentenced between 1853 and 1857 (altogether about 10,000) were disposed of, the state of the convict prisons was much less satisfactory than previously, or than it is at present', *The Penal Servitude Acts Commission*, BPP, 1863(3190), XXI.28.

[70] McConville, *English Prison Administration*, p. 394.

The stance taken by the local newspaper, *The Chatham News*, was unsympathetic to the prisoners and labelled the convict prison system lax in discipline and over-generous with the diet, especially in the provision of meat. It was asserted that prison conditions compared favourably with workhouses, the military and with the standard of living of ordinary labourers. The 'paper's view' stated, 'Certainly, the people in this locality feel indignant that such unworthy objects should be so well treated, and they think that the too good treatment has rendered the convicts rebellious.'[71] Mismanagement was also cited; one of the problems was felt to be that the governor and deputy governor did not have sufficient power and authority in the prison, which was in part due to the bad influence of convicts and staff transferred from the hulks. However, more fundamental weaknesses were implied. It was suggested that there was a 'reign of terror' over prison officers to prevent the truth about the mutinies becoming public.[72] There is little doubt from Jebb's papers that the position of the head of the prison service was undermined and weakened by such publicity. Indeed, a pamphlet was quoted in *The Chatham News* which referred to the official explanation for the Chatham Mutiny as 'lame'.[73]

Jebb recognised that it was not enough only to suppress disobedience. Following the 'mutiny' he sent a letter to Folliot Powell stating that he did 'entirely approve of the prompt and vigorous manner in which the warders acted in regaining possession of the prison and restoring order'. Nevertheless, he went on to call the governor's 'serious attention' to the prison rule which prescribed that,

> prisoners shall be treated with kindness and humanity, &c. It is by firmness and decision, united with consideration for the feelings of the men, who will, of course, long continue to remember and feel the humiliation of such a defeat as they experienced, that a right and proper feeling between warders and prisoners will be re-established.[74]

There is a clear appreciation here that the operation of prison discipline needed the co-operation of the prisoners, not their complete humiliation. Effective working relations between warders and prisoners in English convict prisons could not be re-established, or indeed established in the first place, simply by brutality or coercion.

The report of the Penal Servitude Acts Commission of 1863 was to be instrumental in bringing into being the more deterrent penal system which existed from the middle of the 1860s, but it also emphasised the need

---

[71] *The Chatham News*, 16 February 1861.
[72] Ibid., 23 February 1861.
[73] Ibid., 23 March 1861.
[74] *Returns relating to the recent Convict Disturbances at Chatham*, BPP, 1861(125), LII.3.

for consistency. Indeed, consistency and deterrence were not opposing concepts but associated ones. They represented the linking of a classical penal philosophy, which espoused certainty, proportionality and predictability in punishment, and a utilitarianism, which emphasised deterrence as the primary purpose of punishment. The report concluded that,

> it is necessary that the most scrupulous good faith should be observed towards convicts, in fulfilling expectations they have been authorized to entertain, with respect to indulgences to be granted to them for good conduct, and as to the regulations to which they are to be subject.[75]

Consistency was essential to facilitate the socialisation of prisoners to their prison environment and to the routinisation of their time. However, the reference made in the report to faith does imply a concern with fairness.

Wider considerations

There are several issues highlighted by the disturbance in Chatham Convict Prison that were reflective of a system of penal servitude still in its infancy. Clearly the attempts to construct a more disciplined and regulated environment clashed with the previous experience of the staff and prisoners from the hulks. In addition, prisoners were aware of the lack of confidence in the new system shown in the press and in Parliament, which added to their perceived justification to rebel. Powell had stated that before the outbreak prisoners had obtained copies of 'penny newspapers' critical of the prison authorities.[76] Some may also have felt robbed of a new start in the colonies through transportation, although assertions of this tended to come from those unlikely to ever be subject to transportation. The governor of Portland Convict Prison, commenting upon the serious disturbance there in 1858, had stated that 'the long sentenced men who are very numerous and many of them very bad characters were disappointed in not being embarked for public works abroad'.[77] Ultimately, the lack of consistency experienced by a domestic system of penal servitude in its infancy, exacerbated by the inadequacies of the Acts of 1853 and 1857, undermined efforts that had been made to construct a fair or legitimate system of penal servitude.

Reference to the concept of legitimacy itself was not generally made by contemporaries, but the language of legitimacy was used. Terms such as fairness, faith and justice were occasionally invoked, usually with regard to

---

[75] *The Penal Servitude Acts Commission*, BPP, 1863(3190), XXI.71.

[76] Ibid., 387, qu.387.

[77] PRO PCom2/359, Journal of the Governor of Portland Convict Prison, 9 June 1860. Also see McConville, *English Prison Administration*, p. 439.

the prison system, but also, if less frequently, with regard to values held by prisoners. That prisoners themselves should adhere to some standards of justice seemed to be a novel idea as far as *The Times* was concerned. It was a curiosity that the strike at Portland Convict Prison in 1858 had occurred in defence of 'a species of civil rights', namely the grievances over remission. It was admitted that, even though misguided, there did 'seem to be notions of justice as well as honour among thieves'.[78]

One important point to make here is that standards and ideas about fairness were not restricted to being defined only within a system of rules and regulations. Ideas about fairness were also evident in non-legal but often conventional areas of social interaction within the prison. For instance, in the convict prisons of the 1850s and 1860s it was accepted that warders would profit from trafficking, but, as demonstrated at Chatham, it seems that there existed an informally recognised limit to the amount of profit that was justifiable. Stealing money from the relatives and friends of prisoners undermined respect for warders, who were representatives of the prison system, and created considerable bitterness. Yet, if the evidence of Jebb and Powell is to be believed, it was the warders who were doing their duty who were the most hated. This was possibly because the other warders, in not following the rules and regulations, allowed more latitude to the prisoners, at least to the strongest prisoners or those with the most influence with their fellow convicts.

In order to prevent victimisation, convicts needed to be protected from each other as well as from the power wielded by the warders. Prison discipline was intended to secure the protection as well as the custody and good behaviour of prisoners. This is not to say that discipline is by definition fair. Discipline is a mechanism, a means to regularise and control behaviour; of itself it has no morality. Morality must be provided by wider philosophies and the extent to which the prison authorities have the will to address the interests of those subject to their rules. The first aim of prison discipline and of prison staff was to secure the custody of the prisoners. Historically, compliance and obedience have been the primary expectations made of prisoners; active consent has not been a major requirement, nor have the routinised and often large-scale prison regimes given much opportunity for the demonstration of such consent even if it was present. On the other hand, the existence of a lack of consent, to the extent that prisoners disrupted the prison routine, was much more demonstrative and visible.

Control in prisons has tended to rely to a large extent upon the power of the prison authorities over rewards and punishments. One aspect of this was to nurture an atmosphere of reciprocal obligation. Joshua Jebb referred to this obligation in his evidence to *The Penal Servitude Acts Commission* in 1863, when he stated that the 'convicts received great advantages, and

[78] 23 August 1858, p. 8, col. e.

therefore we had the right to expect ready obedience and cheerful industry'.[79] With regard to this type of reasoning, however, Beetham has asserted the difference between 'the use of incentives to encourage cooperation, within a predominantly coercive regime, and the claim that a power structure is justified because it serves the interests of the subordinate'.[80]

Conclusion

Individually, or in combination, prisoners could resist authority, but this was not only an expression of force. In an examination of riots in modern prisons in the United States, Wilsnack has suggested that riots were more likely when prisoners perceived themselves to be otherwise powerless. He further contends that rioting is more indicative of protest, as opposed to non-riot resistance which is more indicative of direct confrontation. Non-riot resistance involves bargaining or negotiation to some extent, whereas rioting is a last resort and may possibly intend to enlist support from outside the prison as a result of the publicity consequent upon the riot.[81]

Large-scale disturbances in particular could have important repercussions beyond the prison, but they could also make the prisoners liable to severe punishment. Of those involved in the Chatham outbreak, forty-eight were punished with three dozen lashes of the military cat-o'-nine-tails each. The most basic power of the prisoners, the force of their numbers, was weak compared to that of the forces that could be mustered by the prison authorities. In retaliation against serious challenges to authority made by the prisoners, the Directors of the Convict Prisons could publicly justify the use of severe and exemplary punishment. They could also call in the troops, as they did at Chatham Convict Prison in 1861. But the reality of the position of the prisoners was not just emphasised on the few occasions on which troops were called into the convict prisons; prisoners were every day faced with the coercive nature of the prison regime and their own low status within it.

---

[79] BPP, 1863(3190), XXI.336, qu.578.

[80] Beetham, *Legitimation of Power*, p. 87.

[81] R.W. Wilsnack, 'Explaining Collective Violence in Prisons: Problems and Possibilities', in *Prison Violence*, ed. A.K. Cohen, G.F. Cole and R.G. Bailey (Lexington, Mass.: D.C. Heath, 1976), p. 73. Some British criminologists have also affirmed the meaningfulness of rioting behaviour, for instance, Cavadino and Dignan, *Penal System*, pp. 18–19. In his historical analysis of protest by convicts in Australia in the first half of the nineteenth century, Atkinson states that physical or verbal attack represented a fundamental rejection of authority, as opposed to other forms of protest which imply some kind of appeal to or wish to bargain with authority. See A. Atkinson, 'Four Patterns of Convict Protest', *Labour History* 37 (November 1979), p. 29.

In the aftermath of the Chatham 'mutiny' a letter was sent from H. Waddington, on behalf of the Secretary of State, Sir George Lewis, to the governors of the convict prisons, detailing the permitted use of force in the event of resistance by convicts. This letter was circulated specifically in relation to an assault upon a prison warder by a convict at Portsmouth Convict Prison. It stated that the governor, in the absence of a magistrate or director,

> may order the warders, or the military called in to assist them, or both, to fire upon or charge with the bayonet the prisoners, or any of them, if such a course is, in their deliberate judgement, absolutely necessary to prevent the mutineers from getting the upper hand and over-powering the officers who have charge of them.[82]

Some of the elements which had culminated in the outbreak in Chatham Convict Prison on 11 February 1861 were left behind as the system of penal servitude evolved and as those convicts who had experienced the weaknesses and inconsistencies of this period in penal history were discharged. However, many of the problems that had brought about such disturbances were not resolved.

Neither the public, Parliament nor convicts were convinced that the system of penal servitude established during this period was legitimate. This is evident in the considerable criticism of convict prisons in Parliament, and also in the media, which Jebb records with anguish in his personal papers. In the face of such criticism the prison authorities fell back upon the organisational capacity and coercive strengths of the prison.

The shifts in penal philosophy and politics were reflective of a recognition of the failure to establish a legitimate penal system and a search for solutions to this failure. In the years under the leadership of Du Cane in the latter half of the nineteenth century, both convict and local prison systems did become more uniform and, in this respect at least, more fair. However, prisons retained their individual autonomy because of the large degree of discretion within which they continued to operate, and also because of the particular mix of personalities to be found in each institution. Unofficial accommodations and compromises continued and have become part of the mechanisms that maintain order or otherwise in prisons, although they do not necessarily contribute to the fairness of individual prison regimes. The priorities of penal policy over the next thirty years were established in this evolutionary period in the history of the prison. The prison authorities, politicians and the public demanded that primacy be given to security and

---

[82] *Copy of all reports made by any of the Warders to the Governor of the Convict Prison at Portsmouth, relative to the Attack made upon Mr George Deane, a Warder of that Establishment, by a Convict of the name of Lewis Francis*, BPP, 1863(114), XLVIII.343.

deterrence. In the 1860s, it was the advocates of deterrence that were in the ascendancy.[83]

Investigations into the causes of the serious disturbances that have occurred in British prisons since the 1970s emphasise that the problem of how to establish legitimate social relations within an essentially coercive institution has yet to be resolved. The tension between the prison's need for legitimacy and the public's demand for deterrence is a persistent problem in penal policy. The onus upon prison authorities to build upon best practice remains. As Sparks has suggested,

> All prison systems confront severe legitimacy deficits, especially from the vantage point of the confined. But such deficits are not always total. Nor are they everywhere equally severe. This being so, for as long as we must have prisons, it is indeed possible to distinguish clearly between better and worse, preferable and less preferable, stronger and less strong justifications both in the conditions which externally govern their use and in their internal practices.[84]

---

[83] Henriques, 'Rise and Decline of Separate System', p. 88.
[84] Sparks, 'Can Prisons be Legitimate?', p. 26.

4

A local prison before nationalisation: reform and inmate society

Informal accommodations and compromises were an important part of the internal relationships of the prison and influenced the nature of inmate society. Access by individual prisoners to resources obtained, for instance, through trafficking could be a source of power in any internal hierarchy among prisoners.[1] Generally, the nature and quality of prison relationships at all levels could operate as an obstacle or aid to the implementation of prison reform. With regard to prison society there has been disagreement between writers on the subject of the survival of inmate subcultures. Subcultures emerge where a social group adopts its own sense of identity and practices in relation to wider power, often in response to restricted or blocked aspirations and/or an ambiguous or low status. Ignatieff, for example, has asserted that by the 1850s 'the inmate collectivity' had been 'broken up and silenced' by the imposition of new disciplinary techniques which left the prisoners more open to abuse within the prison than previously.[2]

Even within a restricted environment certain modes of behaviour and social habits persist through shared needs and a shared culture.[3] Subcultures are expressions of particular cultural and material experiences that are in some sense distinct from the wider culture.[4] Hence they have been described as being 'socially transmitted and collectively maintained life-styles

---

[1] For a detailed consideration of the value to inmates of such resources see E. Goffman, 'On the Characteristics of Total Institutions: The Inmate World', in *The Prison: Studies in Institutional Organization and Change*, ed. D.R. Cressey (New York: Holt, Rinehart and Winston, 1966), pp. 53–4.

[2] M. Ignatieff, *A Just Measure of Pain: The Penitentiary in the Industrial Revolution 1750–1850* (London: Macmillan, 1978), p. 208.

[3] This does not, however, follow for environments that were not only restricted but which had little or no accepted or predictable standards, such as the Jewish experience in Nazi concentration camps during the Second World War. Cohen maintains that life within these camps bore no relation to that outside, therefore, 'Theft, egotism, lack of consideration for others, pitilessness, disregard of the laws, all of this was prohibited in pre-concentration camp days: inside the concentration camp, however, it was normal.' E.A. Cohen, *Human Behaviour in the Concentration Camp* (London: Jonathan Cape, 1954), p. 137.

[4] J. Clarke, S. Hall, T. Jefferson and B. Roberts, 'Subcultures, Cultures and Class: A Theoretical Overview', in *Resistance through Ritual: Youth Subcultures in Post-War Britain*, ed. S. Hall and T. Jefferson (London: Hutchinson, 1976), pp. 10–13.

informed by distinctive beliefs, values, and focal concerns'.[5] There has been disagreement among sociologists and criminologists about the specific form that inmate subcultures have taken, which has been described as the divide between prisonisation and importation perspectives. The first perspective, prisonisation, depicts inmate subculture as a specific reaction to the prison environment. The second perspective asserts that inmate subcultures reveal aspects not only of the reaction to imprisonment but also of the culture from which prisoners are derived, their parent culture.[6]

Inmate subcultures during the nineteenth century no doubt varied between prisons and particularly between local and convict prisons. The nature of inmate society was affected by the extent of discipline and by the general culture of the individual prison regimes. Although direct evidence is scarce, it is likely that in local prisons during this period the high turnover of inmates and the presence of offenders who served repeated short sentences would have resulted in inmate subcultures of these prisons being an expression of commonly held values and modes of behaviour derived from their lives in the community outside, as well as a representation of the adaptation of prisoners to their common institutional environment. Zedner has suggested with regard to Tothill Fields, which was a local prison for women in London, that the pattern of short but repeated sentences led to a blurring of 'the divide between life inside and their own communities outside'.[7]

Prison inmate subculture was, therefore, in part an expression of the experience of an enforced and restricted confinement which itself placed quite strict limitations upon the nature of that expression. This, of course, results in problems for the historian with regard to finding and interpreting evidence of the existence of such forms of social behaviour. Similar problems were described in relation to identifying the existence of consent in Chapter 3. Precisely because of the informal and illegitimate nature of subcultural forms of behaviour the historical evidence regarding it is fragmented, diverse and often implicit rather than explicit. Conclusions made from such evidence must therefore be tentative, and the strength and continuity of inmate subcultures during the period covered by this chapter should not be over-drawn.

This chapter examines the condition of local prisons during the forty years prior to nationalisation and the extent to which this represented the diffusion of reformative practices.[8] Concentration will be upon the administration of

---

[5] A.K. Cohen, 'Prison Violence', in *Prison Violence*, ed. A.K. Cohen, G.F. Cole and R.G. Bailey (Lexington, Mass.: D.C. Heath, 1976), p. 11.

[6] R. Adams, *Prison Riots in Britain and the USA* (London: Macmillan, 1994), p. 209.

[7] L. Zedner, *Women, Crime, and Custody in Victorian England* (Oxford: Clarendon Press, 1991), p. 5.

[8] Also see A. Brown 'Hull Prison and its Inmates', in *Aspects of Hull* (Bradford: Warncliffe Publications, 1999); A. Brown 'A Disciplined Environment: Penal Reform in the East

one particular local prison, the United Gaol and House of Correction in Kingston-upon-Hull (hereafter Hull Prison), which was at that time in East Yorkshire.[9] In this way an assessment can be made of the practical implementation of discipline on a local level and of the inter-connections between prison discipline, inmate subcultures and the level of prison offences and punishments. This is important because, as Forsythe has pointed out, 'practice at local level often differs substantially from the intentions of theorists, legislators and propagators of new approaches'.[10]

Revisionists and counter-revisionists

One of the most basic criticisms of revisionist historians has been that they have tended to assume that by the mid-nineteenth century prison discipline had achieved a maturity and refinement that the records of both local and convict prisons do not substantiate.[11] These historians have been defined as revisionist because they have endeavoured to revise the pre-eminent Liberal or Whig view which depicted the development of the modern prison as a process of progressive reform. Thus, this older liberal view of the development of the modern prison in England maintains that there has been, inspired by increasing social concern and humanitarianism, steady progress in the improvement of conditions and in the treatment of prisoners. Revisionists have asserted that a disciplined, highly regulated and increasingly uniform order was established in prisons by the mid-nineteenth century. Foucault dated the completion of the 'carceral system' more precisely as being achieved by 22 January 1844, the official opening of Mettray Reformatory. The reason he gives for this precision is that Mettray 'is the disciplinary form at its most extreme, the model in which are concentrated all the coercive technologies of behaviour'. Foucault goes on to comment,

Riding House of Correction', *Family and Community History* 4, No. 2 (November 2001), pp. 99–110.

[9] By the mid-nineteenth century, the distinction between houses of correction and prisons had largely disappeared. To be consistent, therefore, the word prison will be used throughout this study. The Prison Act of 1865 formally abolished any distinction.

[10] W.J. Forsythe, *The Reform of Prisoners 1830–1900* (London: Croom Helm, 1987), p. 92.

[11] The most prominent revisionist historians in this field are M. Foucault, *Discipline and Punish: The Birth of the Prison* (Harmondsworth: Penguin, 1977); Ignatieff, *Just Measure of Pain*, although Ignatieff later criticises his previous position, see M. Ignatieff, 'State, Civil Society and Total Institutions: A Critique of Recent Social Histories of Punishment', in *Social Control and the State*, ed. S. Cohen and A. Scull (Oxford: Robertson, 1983); D.J. Rothman, *The Discovery of the Asylum* (Boston: Little, Brown, 1971).

'This disciplinary effect upon the body had a double effect: a "soul" to be known and a subjection to be maintained.'[12]

There is evidence to suggest that many local prisons did become more disciplined over the first half of the nineteenth century, but they by no means attained the machine-like efficiency that has been claimed for Pentonville Prison, opened in 1842, for example.[13] Ignatieff accepts that the reformative faith placed in the Pentonville regime barely survived the 1840s, but suggests that the separate system retained its appeal for deterrent rather than reformative purpose's partly as a means of social control through the creation of a division between respectable and deviant among the lower social classes. In fact, uncertainty and controversy regarding prison discipline persisted in the convict and local prisons throughout the first half of the nineteenth century and beyond.[14] In 1850, *The Times* still maintained that, as regards prison discipline, 'We are confessedly in the dark, groping our way to daylight.'[15] In 1866 another contemporary writer maintained that one reason why the reformatory prison system was not better understood by society and the magistracy was because it included 'a mischievous confusion of ideas'.[16]

Uncertainties and inconsistencies in the adoption of reforms led Zedner to accuse Foucault of losing sight of the actual extent of disorganisation and variation existing in the 'reformed' prisons.[17] Wiener has also asserted that Foucault and Ignatieff exaggerated the 'thoroughness of the transformation' in prison discipline, although he believes them to have been correct in directing attention to an important shift in penal practice in the first half of the nineteenth century.[18] Furthermore, Wiener suggests that this shift did compose a restructuring of the environment of the criminal and an attempt to 'reorient' his mind. The changes in the treatment of the criminal, Wiener maintains, represented a distinctive mode 'of constructing human reality, of envisaging human nature and social priorities'.[19]

Forsythe observes that reformatory techniques, typified by 'active chaplains, prison schools, ranges of separate cells, rigorous prevention of communication, purpose-built chapels and cubicled treadmills', were evident in most of the larger city and county prisons in England by the 1860s,

---

[12] Foucault, *Discipline and Punish*, pp. 292–4.

[13] Ignatieff, *Just Measure of Pain*, p. 5; he maintains that the 'prison was run like a machine'.

[14] See Chapter 3 with regard to convict prisons.

[15] 14 August 1850, p. 5, col. a.

[16] Anon. (Harriet Martineau), 'Life in the Criminal Class', *The Edinburgh Review* 122 (July–October 1865), pp. 337–71.

[17] Zedner, *Women, Crime, and Custody*, p. 95.

[18] M.J. Wiener, *Reconstructing the Criminal: Culture, Law and Policy in England, 1830–1914* (Cambridge: Cambridge University Press, 1990), p. 101.

[19] Ibid., p. 102.

although he allows for some uneven implementation.[20] What this constituted was the gradual construction of institutions in which the discipline and the daily routine were increasingly uniform. As Wiener has commented, 'Variety and uncertainty in penal conditions were perceived as impractical or unjust in an altered ideological climate that was coming to equate legitimacy with equity and morality with predictability.'[21]

The debate with regard to the practical implementation of policy in local prisons centres upon the speed of the transformation from the unreformed, insanitary, and badly organised institution in which inmate subcultures flourished or were even encouraged, to the reformed, more disciplined, and sanitised prison. In accepting that 'local custom and idiosyncrasy ameliorated the panoptic visions of the central state and penal ideological dogma until 1865', Forsythe is advocating a position between the ideological totalities of Foucault and the detailed but fragmented nature of counter-revisionist writers, such as De Lacy and Zedner.[22] Forsythe acknowledges that there was in some cases a considerable gap between rhetoric and reality, but emphasises the extent of the change in English prisons between the late eighteenth century and the mid-nineteenth century. He states that,

> Foucault was entirely correct to define a new panopticon carceral grounded on techniques of education, proselytisation, behavioural conditioning and so forth, the prison of the mid-19th century as a new and very formidable institution for measuring and defining the criminal 'other' and subjecting the prisoner to methods of education and training which were entirely unknown to the prisons of the 1760s or 1770s.[23]

De Lacy and Zedner assert that in many cases the regimes in the local prisons were so far from being disciplinary machines that they contradict the revisionist thesis.[24] Neither De Lacy nor Zedner examines local prisons after nationalisation and they therefore offer no conclusions about the effects of nationalisation upon local discipline. Forsythe, however, asserts that, following nationalisation, local prison discipline became closer to the image

---

[20] W.J.Forsythe, *Reform of Prisoners*, pp. 95–6. Also the convict prisons, built and managed under direct state control, had established more uniform and efficient systems of discipline by the mid-1860s. See M. Heather Tomlinson, 'Penal Servitude 1846–1865: A System in Evolution', in *Policing and Punishment in Nineteenth Century Britain*, ed. V. Bailey (London: Croom Helm, 1981).

[21] Wiener, *Reconstructing the Criminal*, p. 103.

[22] W.J. Forsythe, 'Women Prisoners and Women Penal Officials 1840–1921', *British Journal of Criminology* 33, No. 4 (Autumn 1993), p. 528.

[23] W.J. Forsythe, 'The Garland Thesis and the Origins of Modern English Prison Discipline: 1835 to 1895', *Howard Journal* 34, No. 3 (August 1995), p. 266.

[24] M. De Lacy, *Prison Reform in Lancashire 1700–1850: A Study in Local Administration* (Manchester: Manchester University Press, 1986); Zedner, *Women, Crime, and Custody*.

of the prison presented by Foucault in that it was 'uniform, unwinking, unmoved, its systems surveying all and – panopticon like – brooding over all'.[25]

Forsythe emphasises the extent of the spread of reformatory practices in local prisons by the 1860s, and criticises De Lacy for selecting her evidence from the very early years of the Victorian period to support her conclusion that the diffusion of reformatory practices was uneven and very gradual.[26] Yet if the original point for debate is the arguments of revisionists, then it should be re-emphasised that Foucault specified the achievement of the disciplinary form as being in 1844 and Ignatieff by 1850. Judgements regarding the degree of implementation of reformatory practice and the associated disciplinary systems are clearly affected by quite small differences in the period of time and the size and type of prison examined. Pentonville Prison, that 'monument to faith in an ideal',[27] with its rigid regime, separate exercise yards, separate chapel stalls, and peaked caps, was, by the 1840s, clearly much closer to the revisionists' conception of the prison than many of the smaller local prisons by 1860 or even the late 1870s.[28]

An important factor which has affected the debate over the rate of the expansion of reformatory practices is that until the late 1980s the bulk of research in this field related to convict prisons. This was due partly to the better quality and larger quantity of evidence on convict prisons. As institutions owned and administered by central government, convict prisons were more of a new departure than local prisons, although this is not to underestimate the large investment in local prisons during the first half of the nineteenth century. The survival of local prison records has been uneven and fragmented, although some good sources, such as those relating to Hull Prison, have been found in local archives. In the light of these considerations, this chapter will concentrate upon one of the medium-sized, provincial local prisons, Hull Prison, about which there is a good body of evidence. This chapter will cover the period from about 1840 until the opening, in 1869, of its replacement institution, the Hull Prison which remains a part of England's prisons estate in the twenty-first century.

---

[25] W.J. Forsythe, 'Centralisation and Local Autonomy: The Experience of English Prisons 1820–1877', Journal of Historical Sociology 4, No. 3 (September 1991), p. 340.

[26] See Forsythe, Reform of Prisoners, ch. 4.

[27] R. McGowen, 'The Well-Ordered Prison, England 1780–1865', in The Oxford History of the Prison: The Practice of Punishment in Western Society, ed. N. Morris and D.J. Rothman (Oxford: Oxford University Press, 1995), p. 101.

[28] M. Heather Tomlinson, '"Prison Palaces": A Re-appraisal of Early Victorian Prisons, 1835–77', Bulletin of the Institute of Historical Research 51 (1978), pp. 62–3.

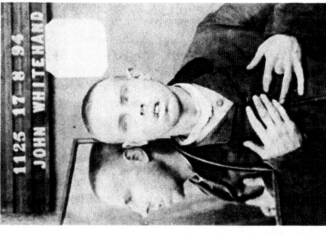

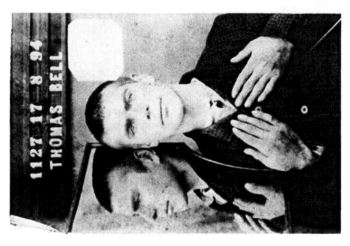

Figure 1 These indicate the kinds of photographs that were commonly taken of offenders in prisons across Britain. Importantly, they remind us of the subjective experience of imprisonment and give us glimpses of, for example, how individuals responded to having their photograph taken, their dress, disability, etc. Unfortunately, no photographs of prisoners from the United Gaol and House of Correction have survived. These photographs are of convicted offenders in the East Riding of Yorkshire and would have been imprisoned in the East Riding House of Correction at Beverley, the closest prison to Hull.

Local government and the prison inspectorate

During the nineteenth century the introduction of general social and industrial reform increasingly entailed the establishment of government inspectorates to enforce legislation. The Prison Act of 1835, for example, enabled the appointment of five government inspectors who entered into every local prison and opened them up to regular and detailed central government and public scrutiny. However, as Bartrip has pointed out, the appointment of inspectors did not guarantee the observation of legislation.[29] The new prison inspectors were given no legal or financial means to enforce their recommendations, and responsibility for prison conditions remained in the hands of local authorities until nationalisation in 1877.[30]

In the early nineteenth century the local financing, administration and control of prisons was largely unquestioned. The basic principle for the local control of such institutions was '*local provision, for local wants, locally identified*'.[31] The limited powers allowed to the prison inspectors were an indication of the sensitivity of central government to local authority. As the century progressed, however, central government began to increase its influence in local affairs. One of the purposes in creating a prison inspectorate was as a means to reduce the difference between the more uniform central government prisons and the variety existing in local prisons.[32]

Hennock identifies another, related purpose of the inspection systems. He maintains that 'inspectors, travelling the country on behalf of central government departments, were able to assemble standardized information about different localities'.[33] This information represented the centralisation of knowledge, which enabled comparisons to be made between localities, and national norms to be established. The centralisation of knowledge was, therefore, an important step in changing the balance of knowledge and power between central and local authorities, and this, in many cases, led to the gradual increase in central control.[34] The possession of greater knowledge by central government officials in the movement towards nationalisation of the prisons has also been stressed by Forsythe. He states that the onslaught

---

[29] P.W.J. Bartrip, 'State Intervention in Mid-Nineteenth Century Britain: Fact or Fiction?', *Journal of British Studies* 23, No. 1 (Fall 1983), p. 67. Bartrip is largely referring to the factory and mines inspectorate in this article but he makes some important general comments. He goes on to state, for instance, that 'Inspection was subject to a range of constraints not the least important of which was limitation of the resources allocated for the achievement of legislative ends.'

[30] Ibid., p. 154.

[31] E.P. Hennock, 'Central/Local Government Relations in England: An Outline 1800–1950', *Urban History Yearbook* (1982), p. 39.

[32] Wiener, *Reconstructing the Criminal*, p. 105.

[33] Hennock, 'Central/Local Government Relations', p. 40.

[34] Ibid., pp. 40–1.

against locality was based upon the confidence of central government officials in their 'greater knowledge or science of prison government' over locally based officials depicted as 'archaic' and parochial.[35]

Government inspectors, appointed to monitor and inform on the workings of the local institutions, were an important instrument in gradually undermining the credibility of local authorities to administer their prisons, and the publicity their reports attracted became a subtle weapon. This was a weapon that was effectively directed against the 'pre-separation modes of prison discipline'.[36] Regarding the work of the inspector for southwest England, it has been commented that, 'From 1842 onwards . . . new methods of inspection, carried out with the clear intention of disseminating hostile publicity rather than producing an atmosphere of discussion and slow change, were used unremittingly against the borough prisons.'[37] The public questioning of local competence and credibility in relation to the prisons paved the way for incremental centralisation and the nationalisation of the prisons under an Act of 1877 which came into force on 1 April 1878.[38]

In addition to the inspectors' use of publicity, their accumulated specialised experience began to be recognised by some regional authorities and they became involved in local discussions on penal policy.[39] This enabled 'the establishment of a communications – information – administrative link between central government and local authorities'.[40] The prison inspectorate of the 1840s, especially, was part of the gradual professionalisation of the administration of the prison, which enabled the implementation of reforms. Ignatieff sees this professionalisation as a shift in influence from organisations outside of the prison and other social institutions to those internal to it.

[35] Forsythe, 'Centralisation and Local Autonomy', p. 21.

[36] W.J. Forsythe, 'Prisons and Panopticons', Social Policy and Administration 18, No. 1 (Spring 1984), p. 75. Also see Forsythe, 'Centralisation and Local Autonomy', pp. 326–7.

[37] W.J. Forsythe, A System of Discipline: Exeter Borough Prison 1819–1863 (Exeter: Exeter University Press, 1983), p. 81.

[38] L.J. Blom-Cooper, 'The Centralization of Governmental Control of National Prison Services, with Special Reference to the Prison Act 1877', in Prisons, Past and Future, ed. J.C. Freeman (London: Heinemann, 1978), pp. 68 and 74–5. Blom-Cooper maintains that local participation in the prisons was lost through nationalisation, 'Local power created local interest and a sense of local responsibility.' He is also critical of the lack of a modern local prison inspectorate, particularly in the light of the increasing use of local services, such as hospitals and after-care hostels, by the prisons. A modern prison inspectorate was instituted in 1980 when a Chief Inspector was appointed. See G.S. Frouxides, 'The English Prison Inspectorate 1835–1877: Its Role and Effectiveness', Ph.D. thesis, University of London, 1983, p. 452.

[39] Forsythe, Reform of Prisoners, p. 103.

[40] Frouxides, 'English Prison Inspectorate', p. 150.

As he states, 'The professionalization of reform was accompanied by the professionalization of prison and police staff.'[41]

The reports of the prison inspectors, particularly before the late 1850s when inspections became increasingly lax, remain one of the most comprehensive and revealing historical sources for analysis of nineteenth-century local prisons. Excepting a small number of omissions, the prison inspectors reported centrally on an annual basis, although individual prisons were not necessarily inspected on an annual basis. These reports offer extensive statistical data and descriptive information, even references to individual staff members and prisoners, and have been called 'the single most valuable source of data on prison discipline in England during the period 1835–1877'.[42] Unfortunately, as central government control and responsibility expanded, the prison inspection system was allowed to run down. Although five inspectors had been appointed in 1835 there were only two by 1863.[43] Reports became less descriptive and more statistical, and once the local prisons were nationalised the prison authorities became increasingly circumspect about giving information.

McConville has suggested that, as well as trying to curb criticism of a government sector which had great potential for scandal due to the sheer volume of prisoners dealt with, Du Cane, the head of the Prison Commission between 1877 and 1895, sought to severely restrict the flow of information from the prisons because of his own 'soldier-civil servant's distrust of outsiders'. This restriction of information enabled Du Cane to consolidate his own position of power.[44] In addition to the reduction of information in the inspectors' reports, other local historical sources regarding these prisons begin to deteriorate or come to an end during the 1870s, in the years before nationalisation. This deterioration in the quality of evidence has a negative effect upon the depth of analysis of local prisons, including this examination of Hull Prison.

The rate of reform in Hull Prison

Hull Prison was opened in 1829 and was closed by the end of 1869 when a new prison was opened on Hedon Road on the outskirts of the town. Built on the radial design it was part of a wave of nation-wide prison construction which by 1830 left few of the pre-1779 prison buildings remaining

---

[41] Ignatieff, *Just Measure of Pain*, p. 189.

[42] Frouxides, 'English Prison Inspectorate', p. 150.

[43] E. Stockdale, 'A Short History of Prison Inspection in England', *British Journal of Criminology* 23 (1983), p. 220.

[44] S. McConville, *English Local Prisons 1860–1900: Next Only to Death* (London: Routledge & Kegan Paul, 1995), p. 236.

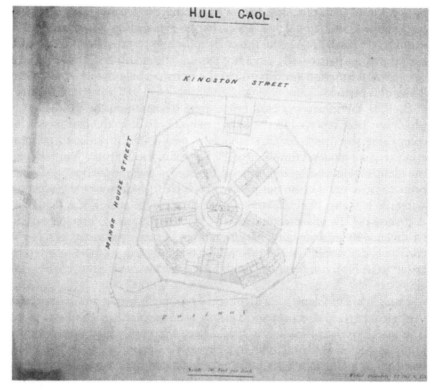

Figure 2 Plan of the United Gaol and House of Correction for the town of Kingston-upon-Hull. Original plan held with architectural drawings at Hull City Record Office.

(see plan of prison, Figure 2). *The Hull Advertiser* had commented upon its appearance that, 'Without any pretence at architectural splendour it may be pronounced neat, if not tasteful.'[45] In accordance with the directions of the Prison Act of 1823, Hull Prison was to be regularly inspected by local magistrates, no commercial trading within the prison was to be allowed, and the prison governor was to receive a salary. Little has been written about Hull Prison; no scandal within it attracted nation-wide publicity, nor did the prison seem to have any reputation outside of Hull for being particularly progressive.[46] The foreword to the *Judicial Statistics* did, on a few occasions

[45] 8 May 1829.
[46] The incident within the prison which seems to have attracted the widest attention during the period covered by this study was not until 1918, when a conscientious objector died as a result of the inhalation of liquid food while being force fed, *The Hull Daily Mail*, on 22 March 1918, announced, 'CO'S DEATH IN PRISON, HULL VERDICT: NO NEGLECT'. Also see PRO HO144/1490/356124.

in the 1860s, pick out Hull Prison as having the lowest average annual costs per head in England and Wales, but no explanation was given for this thriftiness.[47] Furthermore, the size of the prison in terms of its inmate population, neither particularly large nor particularly small, and Hull's relative geographical isolation contributed to the unremarkable nature of its prison during this period.

By 1831 the inmates of Hull Prison were labouring on the treadwheel,[48] which was later reported in the local paper as providing 'the best means for compelling the most refractory, indolent, or sluggish prisoner to perform a fair, regular and profitable task'.[49] By 1836, Hull Prison had adopted the silent system, and by 1849 a 'model prison' of some twenty-two cells had been constructed within the prison in which to implement the separate system.[50] It seems likely, however, that this 'model prison' was deficient. A governor of the prison commented in 1852 that 'many . . . obstacles would be obviated by separate confinement, but not in such apartments as those in our newly converted "model prison". I have had charge of the new model prison in Dublin, completed in 1848, I am, therefore, well aware of the great difference.'[51]

Disciplinary problems were highlighted repeatedly by the prison inspectors in their reports and on some occasions were reported in the local press. The management of Hull Prison had been vigorously denounced by the prison inspector, Frederick Hill, in a large-scale inquiry as late as 1848. The dismissal of a female warder for drunkenness and opium smoking on duty and the resignation of the chaplain for neglect of duty followed directly from this, although the inspector's recommendation that the governor also be dismissed was not taken up by the magistrates.[52] The prison was in a 'bad

---

[47] BPP, 1863(3181), LXV.468, average annual cost per head £24.3s.4d, average annual cost per head in Hull Prison £17.5s.3d. BPP, 1866(3726), LXVIII.519, average annual cost per head £24.3s.3d, average annual cost per head in Hull Prison £14.15s.10d. BPP, 1867–8(4062), LXVII.55, average annual cost per head £26.13s.0d, average annual cost per head in Hull Prison £16.17s.0d.

[48] The Hull Advertiser, 1 April 1831. This article states that, 'Several persons have recently been committed to the treadmill for vagrancy.'

[49] Ibid., 16 April 1852. The treadwheels in Hull Prison were used initially to grind corn.

[50] 3rd Report of the Inspectors of Prisons (NE) (hereafter RIP), BPP, 1837–8(141), XXXI.99–100. Also see miscellaneous records relating to the Hull Gaol Committee Minutes, TCGL 15. It seems likely that the 'model prison' in Hull was built, with some delay, partly on the recommendation of Joshua Jebb, the Surveyor-General of Prisons, who visited Hull Prison in early 1842 with regard to planned alterations to the building. During this visit he 'suggested the probability of an Act of Parliament being passed in a few years for the purpose of requiring all prisons to be made upon the principles of the Model Prison'. The 'Model Prison ' referred to by Jebb is presumably Pentonville. See the Annual Report of the Justices of the Peace in Gaol Sessions, BPP, 1843, XLIII.242.

[51] The Hull Advertiser, 29 November 1852.

[52] Ibid., 10 November 1848. This may have been an example of the way in which local

state', prisoners were dirty, ragged and neglected by both the chaplain and the surgeon. The diet did not distinguish between gender or the type of work the prisoners were doing, and large numbers of punishments were given for prison offences. In the year 1847–8, over 800 punishments were recorded when total commitments were 1233.[53]

Discipline and organisation within Hull Prison were evidently at a relatively immature stage by the mid-nineteenth century. Some of the recommendations for change in the prison made by the inspector in 1848 reinforce this impression. As part of his inquiry the inspector suggested that officers should wear uniforms 'in order to distinguish them at once from prisoners', and that every convicted prisoner should be supplied with a complete set of prison dress and have a bath a least once a month.[54] Previously prison clothes had been given only when 'absolutely necessary'.[55] How literally this had been taken prior to 1848 was shown by observations made by an ex-prisoner in 1833 who had seen the 'Naked thighs before and behind, naked backs, naked legs, and naked feet' of his fellow inmates in Hull Prison.[56]

Reform in Hull Prison since the mid-1830s had been very gradual. In his report of 1837–8 the prison inspector had observed that the prisoners received no medical examination upon entry and were generally very dirty, that there was no paid schoolmaster, and that the debtors in the prison were smoking, gambling and drinking alcohol in the prison. Upon further investigation, the inspector found that the educational instruction that was given in the prison was in a room 'uncontrolled by the presence of any officer' and by an inmate who, according to the inspector, 'was most certainly one of the last persons who ought to have been selected'.[57] Although the Gaol Committee for Hull Prison resolved in 1838 that a schoolmaster should be appointed, as far as can be determined this was not done until the early 1850s.[58] Furthermore, the dietary guidelines produced by central government in 1843, in an effort to increase uniformity of dietary in the local prisons, were not adopted in Hull Prison until 1851.[59] One important early improvement, however, was that after 1841 the custom of allowing each member of staff to keep a pig on the premises was curtailed.[60]

---

magistrates protected their own appointees against the inspectors. Also see Forsythe, 'Prisons and Panopticons', p. 75.

[53] 14th RIP (NE), BPP, 1849(1055), XXVI.230.

[54] Ibid.

[55] 3rd RIP (NE), BPP, 1837–8(141), XXXI.99.

[56] J. Jackson, A Peep into the Prison House (Hull, 1833), p. 14.

[57] 3rd RIP (NE), BPP, 1837–8(141), XXXI.99–101.

[58] The Hull Advertiser, 15 April 1853, report of the governor.

[59] 17th RIP (NE), BPP, 1852–3(1600), LII.91. The nearest other prison to Hull geographically, the East Riding Penitentiary at Beverley, had adopted the official dietaries in 1844, 9th RIP (NE), BPP, 1844(595), XXIX.341.

[60] 6th RIP (NE), BPP (1841), s.2, I, p. 38.

Hull Prison soon became overcrowded both in terms of the number of offenders confined within it and in terms of the buildings constructed around it. For instance, total committals to Hull Prison rose from 416 in 1835 to 891 in 1840.[61] Despite extensions to the prison buildings in the early 1840s and in 1864, Hull Prison was dogged by problems associated with persistent over-crowding throughout its lifetime.[62] In his third report (1837–8), the prison inspector had observed that the prison stood 'in a fine open space close to this populous and important town'.[63] By 1849, the inspector was recom-mending that as the site of Hull Prison had become confined and overlooked it should be sold and the East Riding Penitentiary, at Beverley, enlarged to house the prisoners from Hull.[64] In a period of rapid population growth as well as urban and industrial expansion this was not an uncommon problem for urban prisons.[65] In 1850, for instance, Manchester's new borough prison was situated two miles from the town but the inspector anticipated that it would be surrounded by buildings before long due to the 'rapid extension of the town in all directions'.[66] With regard to the New Bailey Prison in Salford, the inspector stated in his report of 1837 that,

> The crowded numbers and the impurity of the air make it almost intolerable. The security of the prison will be much impaired by the Bolton Railway, now in progress, passing within a few feet of the exterior wall, and commanding, by its elevation, a view of the interior.[67]

Not all local authorities, however, chose either to build new prisons or to situate them outside of the town. Lincoln, Lancaster and York, for example, continued to use as prisons their historic castle buildings located in the heart of these towns.[68]

---

[61] *The Hull Advertiser*, 29 October 1841.

[62] The extension completed in the early 1840s was in part a consequence of the increased committals as a result of the enlargement of the borough since municipal reform in 1835.

[63] *RIP (NE)*, BPP, 1837–8(141), XXXI.98.

[64] *14th RIP (NE)*, BPP, 1849(1055), XXVI.169. For primary information relating to the East Riding Penitentiary see miscellaneous material QAG/2(1819)–QAG/27(1859) held at the East Riding County Record Office, at Beverley.

[65] De Lacy points out that one of the main problems experienced by administrators in Lancashire's prisons was overcrowding. M. De Lacy, 'Grinding Men Good? Lancashire's Prisons at Mid-Century', in *Policing and Punishment in Nineteenth Century Britain*, ed. V. Bailey (London: Croom Helm, 1981), p. 226.

[66] *16th RIP (NE)*, BPP, 1851(1355), XXVII.513.

[67] *2nd RIP (NE)*, BPP, 1837(89), XXXII.595. The site of Hull Prison was later sold to the North Eastern Railway Company, Gaol Committee Minutes, TCM 110, 16 July 1870.

[68] The Gladstone Report of 1895 later expressed its dissatisfaction that most prisons were located in large towns and 'populous places' and suggested that some of them should be closed and the prisoners transferred to 'country districts'. *Report from the*

Overcrowding within Hull Prison placed stress upon existing systems of categorisation and discipline at the same time as pressures from central government to improve standards were mounting. In the years from 1852–3 to 1857–8 (years ending 30 September), for instance, Hull Prison had the capacity to confine 105 prisoners in separate cells, but during the same period the daily average number of inmates never fell below 141, and this disguised considerable seasonal fluctuations.[69] The Prison Act of 1835 had urged the need for increased uniformity within local prisons and this was restated in the 1850 *Report from the Select Committee on Prison Discipline*.[70] From 1835 money was given by central government to help cover the local costs of assize and quarter sessions prosecutions and also the costs of transferring prisoners from local to convict prisons. This funding was extended in 1846 to include the maintenance of prisoners, and the 1865 Prison Act gave the Home Secretary power to withhold this grant-in-aid from prisons which did not comply with the provisions of that Act.[71] Central government legislation also tried to get local authorities to deal with problems of overcrowding which were inhibiting the take-up and operation of the separate system. The 1865 Prison Act stated, for example, that,

> In every Prison separate Cells shall be provided equal in Number to the Average of the greatest Number of Prisoners, not being Convicts under Sentence of Penal Servitude, who have been confined in such Prison at any Time during each of the preceding Five Years.[72]

In addition, all cells used for the separate confinement of prisoners had to be certified by the prison inspectors as adequate.[73] Saunders has identified a further means by which central government pressurised local authorities into building new prisons. With regard to Warwickshire she states that in order to force the local magistrates into building a new prison the Home Office refused to approve any alterations to the existing county prisons.[74]

Departmental Committee on Prisons (Gladstone Committee), BPP, 1895(C.7702), LVI.37, para. 90.

[69] *18th–24th RIP (NE)*, 1856–9.

[70] BPP, 1850(632), XVII.3. The committee stated that 'Parliament has long been anxious to see established such an uniform system of Prison Discipline as would ensure the sentences of Prison Discipline being strictly carried into effect'.

[71] S. McConville, *A History of English Prison Administration, Vol. 1 1750–1877* (London: Routledge & Kegan Paul, 1981), pp. 256–9. Also see Forsythe, 'Centralisation and Local Autonomy', pp. 332–3.

[72] Prison Act: 28 & 29 Vict., c.126, para. 17.

[73] Ibid., para. 18.

[74] J. Saunders, 'Institutionalised Offenders: A Study of the Victorian Institution and its Inmates with Special Reference to Late Nineteenth Century Warwickshire', Ph.D. thesis, Warwick University, 1983, p. 108.

Persistent overcrowding seriously affected the ability of the staff within Hull Prison to implement any system of discipline effectively. The governor himself admitted in 1852 that 'the present construction of the building does not afford sufficient accommodation for the average number of prisoners, and is ill adapted for enforcing essential discipline'.[75] The overcrowding in Hull Prison was also the subject of repeated reports by the visiting justices and of conflict between the visiting justices and the town council over the need to build a new prison.[76] In 1864 the prison inspector reported that the 'magistrates are very desirous to build a new gaol, but the town council are not favourable to the proposal'. He recommended 'that the council be required to co-operate with the magistrates, and to proceed immediately with the preparation of plans for building a new gaol'.[77] Tensions mounted as punishments rose; in 1861–2, for example, the total number of prisoners committed to the prison was 1237 while the total number of punishments for prison offences in the same year was 1470.[78]

The citing of high punishment figures does not mean that an increase in punishments necessarily correlated with an increase in overcrowding. The levels of punishment within a prison are a function of a complex mix of factors which might include overcrowding, prison design, the disciplinary system, the nature of the internal administration or changes in that administration. Nevertheless, as De Lacy has pointed out, when used with care such statistics can be useful and can indicate increased tension within individual prisons.[79] It is also important to point out that the level of prison offences and the level of prison punishments are not necessarily numerically directly related. Individual prisons had differing policies on which offences should be punished and which merely admonished. In addition, the number of recorded offences reflects not only the number of offences but the willingness to detect them and the efficiency of the prison staff in doing so. Unfortunately, the statistical information for Hull Prison regarding committals and punishments is fragmentary until the mid-1850s. Nevertheless, in the context of other evidence, it is clear that the strain of overcrowding exposed the weaknesses in the management and organisation of the prison and inhibited the extent to which the reformatory practices contained in central government legislation were taken up. One indication of such strain is that the number of

---

[75] *The Hull Advertiser*, 16 April 1852. The governor of Hull Prison also stated that the untried prisoners had 'every opportunity of communicating to each other'.

[76] Conflict over prison reform between these two local bodies has been identified in other localities. Evidence of such conflict has been found with regard to Exeter Borough Prison in the mid-1830s. See Forsythe, *A System of Discipline*, pp. 57–8. In Warwickshire the local magistrates were divided over the cost and necessity of building a new prison. See Saunders, 'Institutionalised Offenders', pp. 89–108.

[77] *Correspondence relating to a Report on Prison Discipline*, PP, 1864(313), XLIX.580.

[78] *28th RIP (NE)*, BPP, 1863(3234), XXIII.200.

[79] De Lacy, 'Grinding Men Good', pp. 195 and 197.

punishments given for prison offences continued to rise from the mid-1850s until at least 1862.[80]

In the opinion of the prison inspector, the high rate of prison punishments in Hull Prison was largely a product of overcrowding. McConville has pointed out that due to population increase and mobility, borough prisons tended to suffer more from overcrowding than other provincial prisons, and this seems to have been the case in Hull.[81] By 1854, the visiting justices were complaining that the untried prisoners were not separated, except by sex, and that, 'in the part of the Gaol devoted to females, the case is even worse, for the untried and the tried, old and young, felons and misdemeanants, at present amounting to 42 in number, are all in one day-room'.[82] In 1858 the prison inspector commented that, in 'the crowded day-rooms of Hull Gaol it seems indeed almost a mockery to attempt to enforce the silent system'.[83] By the time of the inspector's report of 1864 the number of prisoners was 'at all times greatly in excess of the accommodation provided'.[84] In the following year, many men were sleeping three to a cell, given no means of employment and were not supervised.[85] In such circumstances it appears that the overcrowding and disorganisation in Hull Prison in the 1850s and 1860s prevented the maintenance of strict discipline or adequate supervision and led to a higher level of prison offences.

Table 1 below shows that the level of punishments for prison offences relative to total commitments and the daily average of prisoners was consistently high in Hull Prison. Unfortunately, the prison statistics do not record how many prisoners committed these offences.

It is clear that, although total committals and the daily average number of offenders in the prison remained fairly high, the number of punishments began to decline, especially in the last three years covered by the table. It is difficult to account for the decline in punishments during the early 1860s but the most likely explanations are multiple and interlinking.

In his report of 1863 the prison inspector observed that the inmates in Hull Prison were 'insolent and insubordinate' and that 'the ordinary punishments by the governor are found insufficient to control them'.[86] The decline in the level of punishments may, therefore, have been a reflection of disillusionment with the effectiveness of disciplining prisoners in this way.

[80] See Table 1 below.

[81] McConville, *English Prison Administration*, p. 365.

[82] Minute Books of the Gaol Committee, Kingston-upon-Hull, Report of the Visiting Justices of the Gaol to the Justices in Gaol Sessions Quarter ending December 1854, TCM 109.

[83] Report of the Visiting Justices in Gaol Sessions (Hull Prison), Michaelmas 1858, TCM 109.

[84] *Correspondence Relating to a Report on Prison Discipline*, BPP, 1864(313), XLIX.580.

[85] *31st RIP (NE)*, BPP, 1866(3715), XXXVII.341.

[86] *28th RIP (NE)*, BPP, 1863 (3234), XXIII.201.

Table 1 The number of prisoners confined in Hull Prison and total punishments

| Year | Commitments | | Total | Daily | Total |
	Male	Female	average	punishments	
1854–5	723	250	973	142	1530
1855–6	663	296	959	162	1745
1856–7				168	1636
1857–8	928	440	1368	167	1506
1858–9					
1859–60					
1860–1					
1861–2	859	378	1237	141	1470
1862–3	960	458	1418	160	956
1863–4	915	366	1281	149	899
1864–5	700	363	1063	170	624

Sources: 16th–31st RIP (NE), BPP (1851–66). The Hull Gaol Committee Minute Books, TCM 108–13, 1836–78, and miscellaneous material relating to the Hull Gaol Committee Minute Books, TCGL 1–39.

Related to this, there would also have been a lower detection rate within a system of discipline under stress. Some telling comments by the prison inspector lend credence to a further aspect of the problems within Hull Prison. These suggest that the decline in prison punishments was a consequence of punishments not being recorded, no doubt because of the criticism that the high levels of punishments had attracted. In the early 1860s it was apparent that handcuffs and leg irons were being used as methods of control and punishment without any written authority or even an entry being made in the governor's journal. The inspector had to warn the governor that 'handcuffs should not be used as a means of punishment, but only to restrain prisoners from doing violence to themselves or others, or from wilfully destroying prison property'.[87]

The available historical evidence regarding Hull Prison suggests, therefore, that persistent overcrowding affected the establishment of an effective disciplinary system. One consequence of this was disillusionment with the efficacy of lesser forms of punishment, particularly when disorganisation affected the ability to detect prison offences. Furthermore, criticism attracted by high punishment rates and the use of illegal punishments may well have led to punishments not being recorded.

---

[87] Ibid., 201 and *29th RIP (NE)*, BPP (1864), XXVI.145.

An assault and a strike in Hull Prison

Evidence regarding the dynamics of inter-relationships within the local prisons is scarce. However, one incident which occurred in Hull Prison, an assault upon a prison officer by an inmate, and which was reported in the local newspaper when it came to court, is interesting because of the statement made by the defendant, Charles Thompson. He pleaded that,

> I am a poor prisoner, and when I went to gaol I felt that I was a prisoner . . . I felt that I was justly punished. But if that man [the warder] had not acted as a tyrant I should not have struck him . . . I have been treated by him more like a wild beast in a den than like a prisoner.[88]

This may partly be a case of post-event justification, but the statement made by the prisoner does indicate that certain standards of behaviour and fair treatment were expected precisely because inmates were identified predominantly as prisoners whose treatment was stipulated by the rules and regulations of the prison. As Ignatieff has commented, prison rules were not only 'an enumeration of the inmate's deprivations, but also a charter of their rights'.[89] That the prison rules and regulations were seen to be applied, and that there were procedures for redress if they were not, was fundamental to the establishment of a legitimate system.

The magistrate presiding over the trial considered it necessary to warn Thompson against any further retaliation. Thompson was punished with an addition of two months to his existing prison sentence and was warned that, 'if you, or any of your friends and companions in the gaol, try to do anything of this kind, the same leniency which I have just extended to you will not be shown to yourself or them'.[90] It is implicit in this exchange that Thompson's actions were felt to reflect the views of other inmates in Hull Prison towards this particular prison officer and that the judge certainly feared some joint retaliation might result from Thompson's conviction for assault.[91]

Another area of prison life which revealed aspects of the internal dynamics of the prison was the official complaints made by prisoners. The fact that such complaints were not uncommon implies a degree of acceptance of the systems

---

[88] *The Hull Advertiser*, 5 December 1863.
[89] M. Ignatieff, 'The Ideological Origins of the Penitentiary', in *Crime and Theory: Readings in History and Theory*, ed. M. Fitzgerald, G. McLennon and J. Pawson (London: Routledge, 1981), p. 54.
[90] *The Hull Advertiser*, 5 December 1863.
[91] This agrees with the comment that 'Individual or non-group behaviour can be subcultural so long as it reflects values of an existing subculture.' M.E. Wolfgang and F. Ferracuti, *The Subculture of Violence: Towards an Integrated Theory in Criminology* (London: Tavistock, 1967), p. 102.

established by the prison rules and regulations. They also suggest that there must have been some hope that grievances would be addressed. A serious problem in this respect could be difficulty in gaining access to authority above the level of prison warder. Thus, Charles Thompson, the prisoner who had assaulted a prison warder in Hull Prison, complained that 'I have made repeated applications to be allowed to see the governor, but I do not believe that he ever heard them.'[92]

That convicted criminals who, in most cases, had been imprisoned for depriving others of property should claim fair treatment for themselves seemed hypocritical to some contemporaries. Michael Davitt, an Irish nationalist convict, referred to this in relation to fellow convicts in Dartmoor Prison, observing that,

> An individual who would never be troubled by such a thing as conscience in robbing another of all he might possess in the world will threaten to bring the director and Secretary of State down upon the whole prison staff if he thinks there is an ounce of meat below the stipulated quantity in his shin-of-beef soup, or if his loaf of bread should chance to be a fraction lighter than the weight mentioned in the rules as his due.[93]

Other complaints made by the prisoners in Hull during this period include a petition by a debtor which stated that 'his health had been permanently damaged by the damps in the sleeping cells'[94] and a complaint by one prisoner that when he complained of 'illness and inability to labour on the wheel, he was placed in solitary confinement without being first brought before the surgeon'.[95] Unfortunately, the outcome of these complaints is not recorded.

The most overt threat to prison discipline, other than outright mass riot, was organised collective action by prisoners. Most breaches of prison rules and regulations, violent or otherwise, were committed by individuals and therefore were much easier to repress. Collective action established a prisoners' discipline to rival the prison discipline and displayed the existence of a consensus among prisoners that could give their action credibility. There is only one recorded incidence of a strike by the prisoners in Hull Prison during this period, but this was small-scale and never seriously threatened the order of the prison. The report of the governor, Neill, published in *The Hull Advertiser* on 31 March 1854, stated that twelve prisoners had 'recklessly' refused to work the treadwheel and had,

---

[92] *The Hull Advertiser*, 5 December 1863.
[93] M. Davitt, *Leaves from a Prison Diary, or Lectures to a 'Solitary' Audience* (Shannon: Irish University Press, 1972), p. 141.
[94] Miscellaneous material relating to the Gaol Committee Minutes for Hull Gaol, letter dated 15 July 1851, TCGL 16/5.
[95] *9th RIP (NE)*, BPP, 1844(595), XXIX.347.

by concerted arrangement expected the others to unite with them to stop the wheel, &c., but they soon found that the 'strike' did not improve their position or prospects, and were convinced that, however painful the punishment, or severe the treatment they endure, they are consistent with the spirit of the penal laws and the prison rules, in support of which, the repeated visits and enquiries of the learned Recorder, in addition to those of the District Inspector, the Chief Magistrate, and visiting justices, have had a modifying influence. Moreover those habitual idlers who are unwilling to labour when at liberty, feel a fair day's work more severely when in prison. It therefore appears to me, that coercive industry is the soundest system of prison discipline; its deterring or reformatory tendency may fail in its object, but there is always a moral certainty in the pecuniary result.

In the face of this strike, the governor, Neill, felt it necessary to reassert and justify the 'penal laws and the prison rules' as well as the use of the tread-wheel about which there had been persistent controversy.

The strike was not accepted as a justifiable form of protest but was asserted by the governor to be an indictment of the prisoners who refused to recognise the legitimacy and justice of their punishment. Part of the governor's justification of the prison rules involved a reinforcement of his own administration and management of the prison, even giving a list of local luminaries whose role it was to ensure that a fair system was operated. A further tactic was to attack the character of the strikers by accusing them of that most Victorian of sins, idleness. The main aim of this report by the governor was to undermine any credibility the strikers may have had, and if his arguments did not succeed in convincing the public of the legitimacy of their punishment then the final appeal on financial grounds might.

Local prison policy and inmate subcultures

Much of this chapter has emphasised the ways in which Hull Prison did not live up to the reformatory ideal, and indeed many of the prison inspector's reports did likewise. However, some movement towards the adoption of contemporary reformatory practices was made. By the early 1850s a schoolmaster was employed for the first time, although he was also employed as clerk to the prison; prisoners were better clothed; all the prison staff were uniformed; and the instance of epidemic disease within the prison was low.[96] Thirty-one cells had been certified by the inspectors as suitable for separation, and a hard-labour machine, or crank, was in use as well as the treadwheel. In addition to this, a Discharged Prisoners' Aid Society had been established

---

[96] *The Hull Advertiser*, 15 April 1853, report of the governor; *28th RIP (NE)*, BPP, 1863(3234), XXIII.201.

in 1857 in which the prison chaplain was active.[97] Furthermore, a variety of industrial employments had been taken up, including mat-making, tailoring, shoemaking, and washing and sewing by the female prisoners.[98] Nevertheless, prior to nationalisation Hull Prison, like many other local prisons, remained far from the reformatory ideal. Rather than embark upon a wholesale take-up of reformatory practices the prison authorities in Hull made attempts to build upon existing practice under difficult conditions and with competing local priorities in mind. According to Zedner, this was evident in other local prisons. She asserts that 'Compromise and accommodation to existing structures were more salient features of the efforts to improve local prisons than any coherent programme of radical reform.'[99] Evidence regarding the character of the changes implemented in the local prisons during this period indicates that the separate system was often introduced on a partial and modified basis.[100]

In their analyses of mid-nineteenth-century local prisons, Zedner and De Lacy both found evidence of the survival of inmate subcultures in widespread trafficking, bartering, victimisation, and even sexual intimacy between prisoners and between prisoners and prison warders.[101] In Hull Prison too, the governor feared that the crowded conditions allowed prisoners to 'freely communicate their worst passions' and commented that trafficking and bartering went on, especially with regard to prisoners trying to get notes and messages out of the prison.[102] De Lacy has also suggested that one effect of the survival of inmate subcultures was that prisoners turned on other individual inmates who were perceived to be misfits or who were foreign or of other religious persuasions.[103]

There is no doubt that reformatory practices did not eradicate abuses, even if they were taken on wholesale. On a local level the prison was one obligation among competing interests and priorities. Among the local priorities cited by Zedner were the concept of less eligibility and the 'eagle eye for economy', the kind of priorities that long delayed the building of a new prison in Hull.[104] Local prisons were much closer to the workhouse

---

[97] 30th RIP (NE), BPP, 1865(3520), XXIII.357. By 1862 the society was having problems attracting donations. A report in The Hull Advertiser, 17 May 1862, admitted that the 'subscriptions and donations during the past year, considering the size and population of Hull, are so diminutive that we are almost ashamed to publish the amount'. The donations amount to '£1.4s.6d., and the subscriptions to £2'.

[98] 29th RIP (NE), BPP (1864), XXVI.143.

[99] Zedner, Women, Crime, and Custody, p. 133.

[100] Saunders, 'Institutionalised Offenders', p. 9.

[101] Ibid., pp. 160–5; De Lacy, Prison Reform in Lancashire, pp. 198–201.

[102] The Hull Advertiser, 29 October 1852 and 6 January 1855, reports of the governor.

[103] De Lacy, Prison Reform in Lancashire, p. 199.

[104] Zedner, Women, Crime, and Custody, p. 133. Also see Saunders, 'Institutionalised Offenders', p. 308.

system than the convict prisons, so that the principle of less eligibility was more overt.[105] Certainly the reports of the governor of Hull Prison were very much concerned with finances.

The reformative priorities evident in Pentonville Prison during the 1840s were less clear-cut in local prisons. This was in part due to limited expectations of reform in the light of the short sentences of most offenders held in these prisons. Indeed, Joshua Jebb, the chairman of the Directors of the Convict Prisons, commented in 1862 that 'During very short periods [of imprisonment] . . . no reasonable expectation can be entertained that a man can be reformed: and if measures be not taken to deter, the opportunity of making an impression is lost.'[106] In the local prisons, deterrence and economy remained the predominant concerns over a reformative philosophy that envisaged the reform or moral reconstruction of the individual. Although some progress was made in the local prisons to reduce neglect prior to nationalisation it is clear that 'local politics, interests, inertia and rates bills', as well as the debate over the purpose of imprisonment and over disciplinary systems, were prominent determinants of local prison policy.[107]

The fact that the rate of reform in local prisons was much more variable than in convict prisons also had a bearing on the nature of subcultures within these institutions. That subcultures existed in the prisons of the period has been argued in opposition to the contention by Foucault that the spread of reformatory practices and disciplinary techniques resulted in correction and submission through normalisation and to that by Ignatieff that the reformed prison 'broke up and silenced' the 'inmate collectivity'.[108] According to Foucault, the construction of disciplinary techniques must

> master all the forces that are formed from the very constitution of an organised multiplicity; it must neutralize the effects of counter-power that spring from them and which form a resistance to the power that wishes to dominate it; agitations, revolts, spontaneous organizations, coalitions – anything that may establish horizontal conjunctions.[109]

By this understanding of the change that occurred in penal practice during the first half of the nineteenth century, reformatory practices and the associated disciplinary mechanisms resulted in a neutralising of resistance.

One of the main rationales for the introduction of reformatory practice and discipline within prisons was to circumvent inmate subcultures

---

[105] Ibid.

[106] J. Jebb, 'Prison Discipline', *Transactions of the National Association for the Promotion of Social Science* (1862), p. 435.

[107] Forsythe, *Reform of Prisoners*, p. 105.

[108] Foucault, *Discipline and Punish*; Ignatieff, *Just Measure of Pain*, p. 208.

[109] Foucault, *Discipline and Punish*, p. 219.

and expose prisoners to reform.[110] These subcultures had sometimes been quite powerful. In eighteenth-century Newgate Prison, individuals elected from among the prisoners played a major role in enforcing order within the gaol, although they also at times encouraged abuse and intimidation. They established codes of conduct and sat as a tribunal to punish offenders. These prisoners, known as 'partners' or 'swabbers', also supervised the cleaning of the prison and collected 'garnish money' from the prisoners to pay for necessities, such as soap, coal and candles.[111]

By the mid-nineteenth century, the kind of internal society that had once existed in Newgate Prison, and which had in some cases been relied upon by the prison authorities to maintain order, had been eradicated. However, some of the older customs survived, especially in the debtors wards of the local prisons. In his report of 1842, the prison inspector covering the north and eastern district of England noted that in the debtors ward in Hull Prison garnish was still collected.

> Two shillings is required from every person upon entrance, one of the number being appointed garnish master. There being no coals allowed for the debtors wards, this money is described as being applied for that purpose, and the surplus, when unfortunately any, distributed among the prisoners.[112]

Despite being constricted by the spread of reformatory and disciplinary techniques, inmate subcultures formed, and continue to form, part of the social life of the prison. The continued existence of an inmate society was observed in nineteenth-century prisons and was even defined by one ex-prison official as the positive expression of a form of 'social conscience' amongst prisoners, a social life which 'pulses steadily below the surface'.[113] The conventions of such an inmate society have been described in modern terminology as the 'rules of the social life' or 'rules of relationship' as opposed to 'rules of task', which largely made up the working of the discipline.[114] Using the influence and power that inmate subcultures afforded, 'prisoners appropriated, distorted, and recast the values of disciplinary society'.[115] Thus,

---

[110] Ignatieff, 'State, Civil Society and Total Institutions', p. 81. Also see W.J. Forsythe, 'The Aims and Methods of the Separate System', *Social Policy and Administration* 14, No. 3 (1980), p. 251.

[111] W.J. Sheehan, 'Finding Solace in Eighteenth-Century Newgate', *Crime in England 1550–1800*, ed. J.S. Cockburn (London: Methuen, 1977), pp. 229–45.

[112] *6th RIP (NE)*, BPP, 1841 S.2 (339), V.37.

[113] B. Thomas, *The Story of Dartmoor Prison* (London: William Heinemann, 1907), pp. 279 and 274. Thomas associated the existence of inmate society with the existence of 'decency' in prisoners.

[114] E. Finkelstein, *Prison Culture: An Inside View* (Aldershot: Avebury, 1993), p. 3.

[115] P. O'Brien, 'The Prison on the Continent: Europe, 1865–1965', in *Oxford History of the Prison*, p. 206.

the shaping and defining of prison discipline was not only the result of policy determined by local and central government officials, the prisoners themselves had a role in this and also in shaping the behaviour of one another. An inmate subculture within a stable prison discipline could be a positive factor in the maintenance of order since significant disorder could also disrupt the existence and hierarchy of the inmate subculture. In addition, an inmate society, no matter how fragmented, was one way of attempting to manage the monotonous and alien way of life enforced by the prison.

Henriques maintains that inmate subcultures were the product of a general criminal class subculture. She suggests that 'the criminal subculture which flourished in gaols was not created by them' but that the roots of this were to be found in the social experience preceding arrival in prison.[116] Nield has referred to such social experience with regard to prostitution. He describes nineteenth-century prostitutes as being born into 'the sub-culture of chronic urban poverty and petty criminality, in the alienation of a culture to which the moral and economic aspirations of surrounding society were visible but utterly unattainable, a world of overcrowded housing and blighted expectations of work and wages'.[117] Whether this constituted what could be termed as a criminal class is debatable, but inmate subcultures in the local prisons were partly a product of the life experiences of the poorest classes whose earnings from work were often precarious and whose only other means of survival was criminality. For many this experience was reinforced by their prison treatment and the affirmation of their inferior status.

The 'revolving doors of short term imprisonment'[118] in the local prisons, which brought in time and again those recidivists who often lived together in the poorer areas, reflected the culture of the lower social classes. The inmate culture of the local prisons in this period was linked to the local community, bringing in both its negative and positive elements and contributing to the diversity of the local prisons. In the mid-nineteenth century the families of the prison warders themselves were also liable to be included in this culture. As McConville has maintained, 'there were apt to be ties of familiarity and sentiment between local officials and their prisoners. Family names, backgrounds, and places allowing officials and offenders to meet on a human plane'.[119]

[116] U.R.Q. Henriques, 'The Rise and Decline of the Separate System of Prison Discipline', *Past and Present* 54 (1972), p. 92.
[117] K. Nield, *Prostitution in the Victorian Age* (Farnborough: Gregg, 1973), p. 2.
[118] L. Radzinowicz and R. Hood, *A History of English Criminal Law, Vol. 5 The Emergence of Penal Policy* (London: Stevens, 1986), p. 776.
[119] S. McConville, 'The Victorian Prison: England, 1865–1965', in *Oxford History of the Prison*, p. 145.

Community ties that were transferred into local prisons were affected by nationalisation. For instance, after nationalisation, senior officials were required to serve in several prisons during their career to produce more homogeneous administrations. A consequence of this, and of central pressure to adhere to penal legislation, was the decline in strictly local practices. A much more regulated system had been constructed by 1880, which was characterised by 'a central command structure in London, a philosophy of economy, uniformity, distance between officials and prisoner, and pessimism about the reformation of prisoners'.[120] Wiener broadly agrees with this timing, stating that the 'Victorian transformation of the prison experience' was not completed until the 1880s as a result of the effects of successive legislation which established the principles of uniformity and predictability.[121]

Conclusion

The hustle and bustle of many urban local prisons with relatively large numbers of offenders being received and discharged daily must have taxed prison discipline and management.[122] But if some local authorities gave priority to resourcing their prison, many prisons like that in Hull seem to have been the subject of disagreement regarding local jurisdiction between the town council and the gaol committee, and resistance to committing the large sums of money required to modernise prison buildings.[123] The town council in Hull was reluctant to spend money on a new prison to resolve the obvious problems of overcrowding and an over-burdened system of discipline. Finally, the Secretary of State threatened to withdraw central government finance, which had become quite significant after 1846,[124] unless the council agreed to build a new prison. A report of 1864 referred to this, stating that the 'magistrates are very desirous to build a new gaol, but the town council are not favourable to the proposal. We recommend that the council be

---

[120] Forsythe, 'Women Prisoners', p. 532, although I disagree with Forsythe that this system could be termed 'wholly efficient'. Also see Forsythe, 'Centralisation and Local Autonomy', pp. 338–9.

[121] Wiener, *Reconstructing the Criminal*, p. 108.

[122] For example, according to Zedner, at Tothill Fields prison for women, in London, 10 per cent of the prison population entered or were set free every day. See Zedner, *Women, Crime, and Custody*, pp. 152–3.

[123] *The Hull Advertiser*, 5 September 1851. Councillor Jalland referred to the dispute between the gaol committee and the town council stating that 'though the council possessed a veto on the justices' actions under some circumstances, yet they could not interfere with the internal management of the gaol'.

[124] McConville, *English Prison Administration*, p. 258.

required to co-operate with the magistrates, and to proceed immediately with preparations of plans for building a new gaol.'[125] Prisoners were being transferred to the new prison on Hedon Road in Hull by 1869.

The persistence of inmate subcultures was one blemish upon the image of the 'reformed' local prison. An increase in disciplinary regimes or even a decline in disorder in individual prisons did not necessarily signal an end to inmate subcultures as they were able to adapt to these changes. Inmate subcultures provided a means of resisting in the same manner in which the group of prisoners in Hull Prison refused to labour on the treadwheel, but they also had an interest in maintaining the order which allowed them to exist and which determined the framework of their operation.

Inmate society could itself be seen as a means of cultivating a degree of order although not necessarily consent. Within an organised and stable prison regime, inmate subcultures can be seen as a means of cultivating a collective passivity or of managing low-level conflict, but within a disorganised regime inmate subcultures could provide an unpredictable element leading to increased individual or combined disturbances.

Prison offences and punishments tended to represent the conflicts rather than the accommodations made, or as Zedner has suggested, punishments appear 'less as failures than the outer delimiting boundaries of accepted behaviour'.[126] In some respects, prison offences and punishments were the forcing edge of inmate subcultures, a means of determining the limits of operation. Prison offences, like prison subcultures, were an everyday part of the prison.[127] Certainly the persistence and even necessity of inmate subcultures and unwritten conventions in prisons have been accepted in modern discussion of the phenomenon.[128]

A significant degree of autonomy remains in modern prisons and is influenced by the behavioural conventions of the inmate subcultures existing in individual prisons. These conventions represent power at a low level concealed by both prisoners and staff. According to Philip Wheatly, inmate subcultures can be a positive element of the modern prison and he emphasises that it can be 'an excellent form of time filling, the battle to beat the system and come out ahead can fill the prisoner's day with excitement and

---

[125] *Correspondence Relating to a Report on Prison Discipline*, BPP, 1864(313), XLIX.350.

[126] Zedner, *Women, Crime, and Custody*, p. 160.

[127] Adams, *Prison Riots*, p. 36. As Adams has asserted with regard to prison riots, 'The fragmented narrative opens the way for the prison riot to be viewed, like the rest of the continuum of actions by prisoners, as part of the day-to-day practices of the prison institution.'

[128] For instance, P. Wheatly, Governor 4, HMP Leeds in 1981, 'Riots and Serious Mass Disorder', *Prison Service Journal* 44 (1981), p. 3; V. Stern, Director of the National Association for the Care and Rehabilitation of Offenders, 'An Open Letter to Lord Justice Wolf', *Prison Service Journal* 77 (1990), p. 11.

interest. It is obviously much more enjoyable than the boredom of the official routine.'[129]

Inmate collectivity in culture and action is a source of power and credibility. A prison inspector's report on Hull Prison published in 1992 commented on interviews with eight inmates, 'Their degree of unity added to their credibility.'[130] The threat that such power could convey was also made clear when these inmates asserted that 'inmates would have to take matters into their own hands if management would not or could not improve conditions in Hull'.[131] One of the most difficult tasks for the prison authorities has been to recognise and assess inmate subcultures as an inherent part of prison life and develop strategies to integrate them.

---

[129] Wheatly, 'Riots and Serious Disorder', p. 3
[130] *Report of a Short Inspection by HM Inspectorate of Prisons*, 1992, p. 11.
[131] Ibid., p. 12.

5

The principle of deterrence in the public works convict prisons

By the middle of the nineteenth century it had become clear that the separate system of prison discipline was not the panacea for criminality and that the 'model prisons' were not going to bring about wholesale reform. Indeed, concern about the psychological effects of the long-term separate confinement of convicts brought about the amelioration of the separate system in use at Pentonville Prison.[1] In 1848, the initial period of separation undergone by convicts was reduced from 18 months to 12 months, and in 1853 this was further reduced to 9 months.[2] In the public works convict prisons, incidents of violence and large-scale disturbances in the late 1850s and early 1860s had been blamed on defective and lax supervision of the large numbers of convicts associating together at labour, and upon a lenient and ineffective system of penal servitude.[3] Reformative penal philosophy was increasingly overshadowed by demands for a more deterrent penal system as a solution to problems regarding legitimacy and discipline.

This chapter examines the most deterrent period in the history of the modern prison, during the years from the mid-1860s to the mid-1890s, and will concentrate on the experience of inmates in the public works convict prisons. The aim of this chapter is to highlight the extent to which the severity and deterrence of the penal system during this period were a cause of disorder. The severity of the system imposed at this time can be seen, for example, in the monotonous and sparse dietary and in the exacting nature of penal labour. The potential for excess which existed under this overtly deterrent system resulted in individual cases of callous treatment of convicts and some of the most extreme cases of violence and self-injury by convict prison inmates. The most extreme cases of self-injury occurred within Chatham Convict Prison during the early 1870s. Chatham Convict Prison became notorious for convicts injuring their limbs under the wheels of moving trucks or engines. In 1871 this had resulted in the medical officer performing thirty-three amputations. To an extent such behaviour was the

---

[1] S. McConville, *A History of English Prison Administration, Vol. 1 1750–1877* (London: Routledge & Kegan Paul, 1981), pp. 405–6.
[2] P. Priestly, *Victorian Prison Lives: English Prison Biography 1820–1914* (London: Methuen, 1985), p. 39. Also see U.R.Q. Henriques, 'The Rise and Decline of the Separate System of Prison Discipline', *Past and Present* 54 (1972), p. 90.
[3] See Chapter 3 of this publication.

product of severe conditions and the harsh system of punishments used by the prison authorities to deal with disobedience, although the particularly strict system of penal servitude at this time was itself a reflection of prevailing social attitudes.

This chapter will also examine whether there were sufficient administrative checks upon the excesses which could potentially be allowed under such an overtly deterrent prison system. The autonomy and independence of the Prison Commission as well as the lack of any formal notion of prisoners' rights meant that individual cases of brutality on the part of prison staff went largely uninvestigated. However, the problems faced by the prison authorities in dealing with violent and self-destructive behaviour by convicts led to the development and refinement of organisational and administrative methods, some of which are still in use in the early twenty-first century. This has entailed the marginalisation of prisoners who have been persistently violent or troublesome.

The concept of deterrence will not be considered primarily in terms of the effectiveness of a sentence of penal servitude to discourage criminality, in either the individual or society as a whole, but as a means to assess the severity of the public works convict prisons. This is because the operation of deterrence depends not only on the likelihood of being punished but on the nature of the punishment itself.[4] This is not to suggest that the most severe punishment necessarily provides maximum deterrence. As Zimring and Hawkins have suggested, there are several variables to be considered in determining the effectiveness of a punishment. They state, for instance, that there 'is a reciprocal relationship between punishment policy and the system that administers it. Judges and juries may affect punishments, but punishments may also affect judges and juries.'[5]

Evidence that punishments can be mitigated or used selectively as part of wider, less formal control strategies can be seen in the reluctance of juries in the eighteenth century to convict for an offence for which the death penalty might be given, as well as in the frequency of pardons given for those who were sentenced to death.[6] Such strategies could influence another important determinant of the effectiveness of deterrence by reducing the level of the real or perceived risk of being caught and punished for criminal

---

[4] J. Andenaes, *Punishment and Deterrence* (Michigan: University of Michigan Press, 1974), p. 24.

[5] F.E. Zimring and G.J. Hawkins, *Deterrence: The Legal Threat in Crime Control* (Chicago: University of Chicago Press, 1973), p. 62.

[6] Ibid., pp. 62–3. Also see D. Hay, 'Property, Authority and the Law', in *Albion's Fatal Tree: Crime and Society in Eighteenth Century England*, ed. P. Linbaugh, J. Rule and E.P. Thompson (New York: Pantheon, 1975), pp. 17–63, and J. Brewer and J. Styles, 'Popular Attitudes to the Law in the Eighteenth Century', in *Crime and Society: Readings in History and Theory*, compiled by M. Fitzgerald, G. McLennon and J. Pawson (London: Open University Press, 1981), pp. 29–36.

behaviour.[7] Consideration of risk would bring into the discussion issues such as the rise and efficiency of the new police and factors that influenced individual tendencies to be optimistic or pessimistic in assessments of risk. The inclusion of such factors in assessing individual and general deterrence would necessitate much broader examination of the social context of the punishment of imprisonment than can be undertaken here and would take this chapter outside the terms of reference of this publication. Therefore, this chapter concentrates upon the severity of the punishment itself and specifically upon the nature and intensity of deterrence in the system of penal servitude that was operated between the mid-1860s and the mid-1890s.

The practical implications of a deterrent penal philosophy

The 1863 report of the Commission appointed to inquire into transportation and penal servitude did not eschew reformatory policies but was directed more to the primacy of deterrence. Where the issue of reform did arise it was largely seen in terms of the assertive encouragement of positive habits, such as hard labour, rather than the reform of individual character.[8] The Commission presented its report in the context of a public alarmed by the convict prison disturbances of the late 1850s and early 1860s and by the necessity to retain convicts in the country as a result of the curtailing of transportation. The report, and the Penal Servitude Act which followed in 1864, instigated a more organised, uniform, and deterrent convict prison system.[9] This system represented both a shift in penal philosophy and a continuation of the methods established under Joshua Jebb, Chairman of the Directors of the Convict Prisons from 1850 to 1863. In 1865, the Directors of the Convict Prisons asserted that it 'may reasonably now be hoped that penal servitude will become, as it ought to do, the last and most dreaded result of heinous offences against life and property short of capital punishment'.[10]

Edmund Du Cane, the Chairman of the Directors of the Convict Prisons from 1869 to 1895, has been criticised for his role in constructing a severe system of penal servitude, and there is little doubt that Du Cane's name 'will always be written large in the history of English prison administration'.[11] Certainly, Du Cane enjoyed a commanding and even autocratic position

---

[7] Zimring and Hawkins, *Deterrence*, pp. 160–7.
[8] *Report of the Commissioners to Inquire into the Operation of the Acts (16 & 17 Vict., c.99 and 20 & 21 Vict., c.3) relating to Transportation and Penal Servitude*, BPP, 1863(3190), XXI.
[9] Penal Servitude Act, 1864: 27 & 28 Vict., c.47.
[10] RDCP, BPP, 1865(3573), XXV.5.
[11] RCPDCP, BPP, 1904(Cd.1800), XXXV.32.

within the prison directorate, although his achievements were largely in the areas of increased administrative efficiency and uniformity.[12] McConville has asserted that Du Cane perceived imprisonment 'as little more than a series of administrative and technical problems' and that he showed little interest in 'the human experience and consequences of this'.[13] Harding offers a rather more sympathetic assessment of Du Cane. He emphasises Du Cane's single-minded approach to the prison service and depicts him as 'a very hard-working and committed administrator' who introduced some ameliorative as well as deterrent measures into the prison system. Among the ameliorations Harding cites are an end to flogging parades and the use of shot drill, Du Cane's support of Prisoners' Aid Societies and his campaign against insanitary conditions.[14]

In the context of a contemporary view, particularly among medical men, which increasingly referred to criminals as being an inferior type of humanity, Forsythe has suggested that Du Cane was

> less the initiator of a new policy than the administrator of a system whose priorities had been established in the 1860s and validated by the greater pessimism about the nature of criminal man which characterised almost all writing on the subject in the late-1860s and 1870s.[15]

The view of criminality as being perpetrated by a section of the population who had lower or more primitive mental development reinforced pessimism regarding the potential to reform criminals.[16] Overall, Du Cane's administration of the convict system must be seen in the context of legislative measures which favoured deterrence and also public pressure for a shift in

---

[12] Several historians and contemporaries have asserted the predominance of Du Cane in the determination and practical application of penal policy in this period. For example, S. McConville, *English Local Prisons 1860–1900: Next Only to Death* (London: Routledge & Kegan Paul, 1995), pp. 166–71; L. Radzinowicz and R. Hood, *A History of English Criminal Law and its Administration from 1750*, vol. 5 (London: Stevens, 1986), p. 527. Radzinowicz and Hood comment that 'He [Du Cane], more than anyone else during this period, determined the way penal sanctions were administered and the nature of prison regimes.' Also see A. Griffiths, *Fifty Years of Public Service* (London: Cassell, 1904), pp. 258–9. Griffiths comments regarding Du Cane that 'he had no advisors, no coadjutors; he would brook no interference'.

[13] McConville, *English Local Prisons 1860–1900*, p. 173; for McConville's detailed examination of the social and penal ideas of Du Cane see ch. 4.

[14] C. Harding, 'The Inevitable End of a Discredited System? The Origins of the Gladstone Committee Report on Prisons', *Historical Journal* 31 (1988), p. 606.

[15] W.J. Forsythe, *The Reform of Prisoners 1830–1900* (London: Croom Helm, 1987), p. 199. Also see W.J. Forsythe, 'The Garland Thesis and the Origins of Modern English Prison Discipline: 1835 to 1939', *Howard Journal* 34, No. 3 (August 1995), pp. 264–5.

[16] Ibid., pp. 197–202.

the same direction. For example, Du Cane cannot be held responsible for the increase in the minimum sentence of penal servitude from three to five years for first offenders and to seven years for any subsequent offence under the 1864 Act.[17] Du Cane's priorities and philosophy were entrenched in the prevailing pessimistic social attitudes towards criminality and the public and parliamentary pressure for more deterrent prison regimes. His views on punishment were predominantly classical and were combined with a bureaucratic concern with economy. Du Cane espoused a rational, uniform and deterrent system which related the severity of the sentence to the seriousness of the crime. By the particular methods Du Cane used when translating a deterrent penal philosophy into deterrent practice he left his mark on the history of the prison in England.

Under Du Cane's supervision the previous lax administration of the length and completeness of the initial period of separation was tightened up.[18] In addition, educational provision was reduced and pushed into the evening so as not to interfere with work, and writing materials were restricted. Furthermore, following the report in 1864 of a parliamentary committee headed by Dr Guy, the medical superintendent at Millbank, the diet in the public works prisons was reduced. This was despite the comments made by the committee about the monotony of the existing diet.[19] A more strict enforcement of the rule of silence while at work was also introduced later in 1878.[20]

The deterrent philosophy which became dominant under Du Cane's administration was also expressed in a more meticulous system of progressive stages with privileges and punishments recorded in a character book.[21] Radzinowicz and Hood have suggested that the privileges available in this period were so limited that this constituted a more 'emaciated progressive stage system' than previously employed.[22] During their first nine months in separation and in their three months' probation on the public works, convicts

---

[17] It has been claimed that Du Cane had an important influence in the construction of a later piece of legislation, the Prison Act of 1877. See P. Tibber, 'Edmund Du Cane and the Prison Act 1877', *Howard Journal* 19 (1980), p. 10. However, by this time Du Cane was a more influential figure in penal politics.

[18] McConville, *English Prison Administration*, pp. 406–7.

[19] McConville, *English Prison Administration*, pp. 418–19. Also see *Report of the Committee to Inquire into the Dietaries of Convict Prisons*, BPP, 1864(467), XLIX. McConville claims that the diet in the public works prisons remained unchanged yet the Directors refer to such a reduction having been implemented in all government prisons. They also comment that a 'mutiny' occurred in Portland Prison 'where the reduction was greatest and most severely felt'. See *RDCP*, BPP, 1865(3573), XXV.11. Radzinowicz and Hood also assert that the diet was reduced, *History of English Criminal Law*, pp. 533–4.

[20] An Act to amend the Penal Servitude Acts, BPP, 1864, XLVII.

[21] A. Cook, *Our Prison System* (London: Drane, 1914), p. 45. Cook describes Du Cane as 'that prince of detail'.

[22] Radzinowicz and Hood, *History of English Criminal Law*, p. 533.

were allowed no gratuities, visits or correspondence and only one exercise period on Sundays. In the third class, convicts in the public works prisons were allowed a gratuity of 12s per year, one visit lasting twenty minutes, and to send and receive one letter every six months. Prisoners in the second class were allowed two exercise periods on Sundays, the choice of tea and two ounces of additional bread instead of gruel. In the first class, prisoners were allowed 30s per year in gratuity, one visit lasting half an hour, to receive and send one letter every three months, three exercise periods on Sundays, and to get baked instead of boiled meat.[23] It was the prospect of a remission of their sentence that was thought to be the main inducement to industry and good behaviour.[24] A male convict could earn remission of up to a quarter of his sentence, excluding the separate stage and time in the penal class or on second probation for bad conduct.[25]

Advance through the (initially) three stages of the public works prisons was determined by a more exact accounting system of units, or marks, than previously used.[26] Good conduct alone was no longer considered a sufficient requirement for the awarding of marks and remission, because good conduct, according to Du Cane, could mean 'little more than passive [sic], or abstaining from acts of indiscipline or irregularity'.[27] After 1864, eight marks a day could be earned.[28] Industry accompanied by good conduct would be rewarded by gratuities, privileges and remission through the stage system, although not with additional food as this was felt to be 'an appeal to the baser feelings'.[29]

Disobedience was to be confronted primarily by the forfeiture of marks, and hence remission, and also by relegation in stage and the loss of associated privileges. More physical punishments included a bread and water diet for a set number of days, solitary confinement or flogging. If the prisoner continued to misbehave he could be sent to the penal class or, if he persisted in being disobedient throughout his sentence, he could be ordered to pass the last six months of his sentence in separate confinement, 'so that the

---

[23] Ibid., pp. 532–3.

[24] For instance, John Campbell, a medical officer in the convict service, claimed that the inducement to good behaviour offered by remission was 'very great'. See *Thirty Years Experience of a Medical Officer in the English Convict Service* (London: T. Nelson, 1884), p. 116.

[25] Radzinowicz and Hood, *History of English Criminal Law*, 404.

[26] For a detailed account of the origins and philosophy of the marks system see M.J.Wiener, *Reconstructing the Criminal: Culture, Law and Policy in England, 1830–1914* (Cambridge: Cambridge University Press, 1990) pp. 111–22.

[27] E.F. Du Cane, *The Punishment and Prevention of Crime* (London: Macmillan, 1885), p. 164.

[28] Standing Order no.146: 'Regulations – Marks System', 22 July 1864.

[29] Du Cane, *Punishment and Prevention*, pp. 162–3.

deterrent effect of that discipline may be impressed on his mind when he is set free'.[30]

An impressive array of forms of action or indeed lack of action was subject to punishment under the prison rules and regulations. Indeed, behavioural restrictions were so tight that some prisoners felt unable to avoid committing offences.[31] Davitt pointed out the all-encompassing and intrusive nature of the prison rules and regulations which gave the prison staff immense discretion in the determination of what constituted an offence. He stated that to

> speak, sing, whistle, or walk; to attempt to ornament the cell; to offer to, or take from, a neighbour an ounce of bread; to exchange a book; to possess a needle or a pin; to stitch a button upon a garment without permission; to look out of the cell-window into the prison-yard; to protest against bad or light-weight food; to refuse to strip naked whenever the warder requires this to be done for the purpose of searching the prisoner – all this, with a hundred other nameless, irritating, ceaseless, mind-killing worries and degradations, is what separate cellular life and work means to a prisoner undergoing 'reformation' by the Du Cane plan.[32]

Of course, these were activities that would often have constituted offences prior to the 1860s, but during this period enforcement of the rules and regulations became more rigid and intense.

Labour and diet in the public works convict prisons

In spite of his claim that the system operated in the public works was intended to be reformative as well as deterrent, Du Cane was sceptical about the potential for reform of the kinds of people who experienced penal servitude. He advocated the primacy of general deterrence to deter those outside the prison from crime, and strict and exact discipline, particularly for adult recidivists,[33] that 'class of fools whom even experience fails to teach'.[34]

---

[30] E.F. Du Cane, *An Account of the Manner in which Sentences of Penal Servitude are Carried out in England* (London: HMSO, 1872), p. 26.

[31] J.S. Balfour, *My Prison Life* (London: Chapman and Hall, 1907), p. 63. After tasting this system from the convict point of view, Balfour sarcastically commented that the only way to avoid offence or punishment was not to do anything and that if he succeeded he would be considered a well-conducted prisoner.

[32] M. Davitt, 'Criminal and Prison Reform', *The Nineteenth Century* 36 (December 1894), p. 880.

[33] Du Cane Papers, Bodleian Library, Mss.Eng.hist.c.649/73. Memorandum on punishment by Sir Edmund Du Cane, 16 March 1885.

[34] Du Cane, *Punishment and Prevention*, p. 3.

This was because punishment was primarily 'to prevent crime by the warning held up to those who might, but for such influences, fall into it'.[35]

Hard labour was a fundamental part of the philosophy of deterrence in the public works prisons and this took precedence over considerations of profit or the training of prisoners. Although some important work was completed by convicts, including the building of Wormwood Scrubs Prison and the dockyard construction at Chatham, convict prison labour was primarily an expression of servitude.[36] As Foucault has suggested, penal labour was primarily the 'constitution of a power relation'.[37] Penal labour was a relational issue and overtly demonstrated the divide between the convict and the prison staff as well as the degraded status of the convict.

The reports of the Directors of the Convict Prisons and the detailing of accidental injuries show how dangerous labour was on the public works. For example, it was reported that at Portland Convict Prison during 1865 one death and 282 accidents had occurred on the works. In the same year, there were twelve fractures and 'several serious accidents' on the works at Chatham Convict Prison. Similarly, at Portsmouth Convict Prison one man was crushed, and at Dartmoor Convict Prison one man died and another was severely injured by an accidental blast.[38] The governor of Portland Prison commented that, 'It cannot be a matter of surprise that accidents are numerous, when the nature of the labour the men are employed on is taken into consideration.'[39] Of course, such accidents were common in similar working environments outside the prisons, but the monotony, sparse diet and under-investment may have increased the frequency of accidents. According to McConville, convict labour was used when horse-power would have been safer and more efficient; in effect prisoners were used as beasts of burden.[40] One account of convict life during this period stated that,

> I have myself fainted more than once on returning to my cell after putting in a day's work at the brickfields at Chatham, and the work done in the brickfields was

---

[35] Du Cane, *Account of Penal Servitude*, p. 17.

[36] Radzinowicz and Hood, *History of English Criminal Law*, pp. 538–9. Radzinowicz and Hood maintain that penal labour was deterrent and unlikely to effectively defray costs or enable convicts to learn a trade. Often the prison authorities were merely making work for convicts to do.

[37] M. Foucault, *Discipline and Punish: The Birth of the Prison* (Harmondsworth: Penguin, 1977), p. 243.

[38] RDCP, BPP, 1866(3732), XXXVIII.111, 141, 169 and 190, reports of the prison medical officers.

[39] RDCP, BPP, 1859, XIII, Pt.1.333.

[40] McConville, *English Prison Administration*, pp. 397–8. In 1861, Jebb had been opposed to the use, for example, of 12 or 14 men for hauling a cart which could have been pulled better by one horse, cited in M. Heather.Tomlinson, 'Penal Servitude 1846–1865: A System in Evolution', *Policing and Punishment in Nineteenth Century Britain*, ed. V. Bailey (London: Croom Helm, 1981), p. 137.

light in comparison with that done in 'the basin,' where more human blood was spilt and more human lives lost through excessive labour than in any other prison in the country.[41]

Many convicts were not used to such strenuous labour and were physically weak, particularly after spending nine sedentary months in separation at Millbank or Pentonville. The implementation of penal labour was reinforced by a system of awarding marks that meant that convicts in the infirmary could earn only six marks per day, which was enough to maintain their position but not to earn them remission.[42] This was an attempt to prevent convicts feigning or inducing illness in order to receive the better food and conditions that the infirmary offered. Such 'malingering', where it occurred, was a form of passive resistance undertaken by convicts.

Penal labour and the system of rewards and punishments were designed to induce submission and composed a form of behavioural conditioning. This system, with the addition of an initial period in separate confinement, constituted the basis of penal servitude, or to use McConville's description, penal servitude consisted of 'a system of inducements and threats, and a period of initial purging and breaking'.[43] So restrictive was this system that even minor acts were punished severely. In a manifestly deterrent system, to strip down daily life to its barest essentials served to exacerbate the severity of prison punishments.[44] A punishment of three days on bread and water could undermine the health of a man already on a sparse diet. One medical officer commented that the 'effect of the dietary punishment is far more serious to health than the bodily pain, for it sometimes lays the foundation for maladies of a fatal nature'.[45] This was particularly a problem given the poor health in which many of the prisoners were received into prison. In the *Report of the Directors of the Convict Prisons* for 1868, for example, it was recorded that of 1237 convicts who were allocated to other convict prisons from Millbank only 55 per cent were sent to the public works prisons as fit for hard labour, a further 11 per cent were certified as fit for only light labour, and the remainder had to be sent to invalid prisons.[46]

The convict prison dietary was particularly sparse during this period, although even in the late 1890s and early twentieth century convicts, such

---

[41] 'No. 7', *Twenty-Five Years in Seventeen Prisons: The Life-Story of an Ex-Convict* (London: F.E. Robinson, 1903), p. 104.

[42] McConville, *English Prison Administration*, pp. 397–8.

[43] S. McConville, 'The Victorian Prison', in *The Oxford History of the Prison: The Practice of Punishment in Western Society* (Oxford: Oxford University Press, 1995), p. 136.

[44] M. Davitt, 'The Punishment of Penal Servitude', *The Contemporary Review* 44 (August 1883), p. 181. Davitt refers to penal servitude as imposing an 'animal existence' which produced an 'unceasing conflict between every feeling in the prisoner that is superior'.

[45] Campbell, *Medical Officer in Convict Service*, p. 120.

[46] BPP, 1867–8(4083), XXXIV.519.

as Jebez Spencer Balfour, remained critical of convict prison food. Balfour commented that 'to a great number of prisoners penal servitude is certainly not starvation or semi-starvation, but one long hunger'. He also maintained that prisoners suffered constant indigestion due to the poor quality of the food that was supplied.[47] There was something quite pathetic, he observed, in a man being able to weigh exactly the loaf in his hand.[48] Du Cane had commented in a matter-of-fact way about the spartan convict diet that it 'in fact is fixed at the minimum necessary to enable a man to execute the work required of him, but if he should be idle and not execute the work, then the amount of his food is reduced'.[49]

This period witnessed the most rigid combination of a sparse diet, exhausting and monotonous labour, and a mechanical accounting of the submission or conflict between the prisoners and the staff under the marks system. One indication of the severity of penal servitude in this period is the evidence of persistent conflict over food. Several references were made by convict prison medical officers and discharged convicts to the items that hunger induced convicts to eat; these included dead shellfish found on the works, candles, and worms.[50] Prison medical officers also commented repeatedly on the prevalence of abscesses, boils and carbuncles among the prisoners, which is another indication that the diet was poor. But perhaps the most overt indication that the diets in the public works prisons were inadequate was that in 1867 an increase in the diet at Chatham Convict Prison caused friction and insubordination in Portland Convict Prison where no such increase had been allowed. The small increase in the diet at Chatham was authorised by the Directors, a decision which may have been influenced by disturbances there in 1861.[51] Despite this increase, the diet in Chatham was still felt by the medical officer to be 'scarcely sufficient to make them effective for the hard labour of this place'.[52]

---

[47] Balfour, My Prison Life, p. 262.

[48] Ibid., p. 264.

[49] Du Cane, Account of Penal Servitude, p. 25.

[50] For example, RDCP, BPP, 1870 (C.204), XXXVIII.267, report by the medical officer of Chatham Convict Prison regarding the death of two prisoners caused by eating dead shellfish. Also see Griffiths, Fifty Years of Public Service, p. 176.

[51] RDCP, BPP, 1867(3928), XXXVI.174–5. Also see The Times, 30 August 1866, p. 12, col. c. This article reported 'several open acts of insubordination' at Chatham caused by recent change in diet. Clearly the riot of 1861 remained in the public memory and was evoked in this article which stated that 'it was feared [that these disturbances] would lead to a repetition of the disturbances enacted at the same convict prison a few years since, which then resulted in the assistance of the military being called in'.

[52] RDCP, BPP, 1867(3928), XXXVI.71, reported by the governor of Portland Convict Prison.

Convict violence and self-injury

The actions of some convicts suggested that they were unable or unwilling to cope with their sentence. In the *Report of the Directors of the Convict Prisons* published in 1874, the medical officer of Pentonville Prison described the suicide of one of the convicts:

> All the ordinary precautions to frustrate suicide continued to be taken, and yet on the following night he succeeded in strangling himself by means of a bandage around his neck, tied to a looped sheet, in the bight of which he placed his feet, and by extension tightened the ligature. The act was unexampled for cunning and determination. Covered by his bedclothes, and refraining from any noise, he appeared to the officer on night duty, who passed and repassed all night in full view of him, to be sleeping naturally.[53]

Prior to his suicide this convict had 'commenced a course of malingering' which included destroying books, bedding and the window glass in his cell. He was then hospitalised as a result of his refusal to eat and then 'added muteness to his other eccentricities'. He had finally, on the day before his death, assured the medical officer that he would end his attempts to feign insanity.[54]

It is difficult not to feel sympathy and even horror at the desperation of committing suicide in this way. Such an act cannot be regarded as typical of the experience of convicts in this period, but this incident does offer an example of a downward spiral that was not uncommon and was referred to in this case as a 'usual routine'.[55] This kind of spiral might begin with verbal threats, escalate into physical assaults upon staff and prisoners as well as destruction of prison property, and end with extreme forms of self-injury and suicide. Evidence of such a catastrophic progression as well as of other individual acts of violence and self-injury exposed the potential for excess and inflexibility inherent in a predominantly deterrent penal system. This was also evidence of the intensity and isolation of the convict prison experience.

The frequency of the transferral of individual convicts was, in some cases, a facet of the kind of downward spiral evident in the behaviour and punishment of some convicts. In spite of criticism, some troublesome prisoners were repeatedly transferred, spreading the responsibility for the management of their disobedience. Their record and reputation preceded them. In a letter to *The Times* dated 7 October 1880, William Tallack, Chairman of the Howard League, complained that the efficiency of the

---

[53] BPP, 1874 (C.1089), XXX.115.
[54] Ibid.
[55] Ibid.

schoolmaster and chaplain was impaired by the 'irregular and arbitrary manner in which prisoners are removed from one gaol to another'.[56] Although transfers were not officially a punishment, they could be used as such and represented an additional instrument of control available to the prison authorities. Jabez Balfour, for example, complained about the frustration of the arbitrary manner in which transfers were conducted and felt that the staff took 'an infantile and malicious delight' in keeping such information from the prisoners until the last moment.[57]

For those inmates who made a cry for help, nothing could exceed an attempt at suicide for, what one medical officer cynically referred to as, 'a one-act extravaganza'.[58] Violent or self-destructive behaviour was one means of calling attention to the helplessness and perhaps desperation of an individual's circumstances. In an environment in which choices were restricted, committing such extreme acts must have involved a weighing up of the costs and benefits, a calculation that could be distorted by stress or mental instability. As Cohen has pointed out, violence was one of the few resources that was available to all and was therefore a source of universal uncertainty.[59] This could create an atmosphere of anxiety and even fear in a confined prison environment, and also highlighted the need for co-operation. Although the prison authorities during the second half of the nineteenth century held considerable power over the prisoners, this could not be complete. It has been observed that 'The characteristic feature of power is that some men can more or less entirely determine other men's conduct – but never exhaustively or coercively.'[60]

The degree of conflict between prisoners is an area rarely touched upon in the Directors' reports unless a serious injury resulted from it. It may be that such conflict was considered to be so common, and perhaps inevitable among the class of people undergoing penal servitude, that it did not merit attention. Yet conflict between prisoners was one product of internal tensions in the prison. In 1873, for example, a prisoner at Portland Prison died after receiving a fractured skull 'caused by one prisoner kicking another on the temple during a quarrel'.[61]

During the late 1870s there was a wave of serious assaults among convicts in Portland Convict Prison, although the extent of recorded violence among

[56] 7 October 1880, p. 4, col. f.

[57] Balfour, My Prison Life, pp. 54–5.

[58] D. Nicolson, 'Feigned Attempts at Suicide', Journal of Mental Science 17 (January 1872), p. 485.

[59] A.K. Cohen, 'Prison Violence: A Sociological Perspective', in Prison Violence (Lexington, Mass.: D.C. Heath, 1976), pp. 5–7.

[60] D. Lacombe, 'Reforming Foucault', British Journal of Sociology 2 (June 1996), p. 343.

[61] RDCP, BPP, 1874(C.1089), XXX.239. A statement made by the medical officer of Portland Convict Prison.

convicts had dissipated by 1880. In 1878, there were 87 violent assaults committed by prisoners upon other prisoners, in 1879 this had declined to 79, and by 1880 the recorded number of assaults between prisoners was only 43.[62] The governor of Portland Prison attributed much of this to trafficking, usually in food or tobacco.[63] Basil Thomson, who had been a prison official, maintained that 'convicts suffer far more from the malevolence of their fellows than from the discipline of the place', but he failed to make any link between the two.[64] Fights between convicts were, it seems, even on occasion allowed to continue as a means of defusing tension, resolving conflicts or as entertainment, although again evidence is limited. Balfour commented that when a fight occurred at Dartmoor 'the combatants are almost invariably allowed the privilege of a round or two before they are separated'.[65]

Possibly the most violent and self-destructive behaviour recorded in the prisons of the period was in the public works prisons, Chatham and Portland, and to a lesser extent Portsmouth, and the 'light' labour prison, Dartmoor. These convict prisons combined severe discipline with labour in association on the public works following the initial period in solitary confinement. Extreme acts of self-injury were committed in all convict prisons but it was Chatham that became notorious for one form of self-injury in particular, that of convicts placing their limbs between the wheels of moving trucks or engines and the tracks they ran along. In 1871, the medical officer at Chatham recorded that as a result of these acts it had been necessary to perform thirty-three amputations. He observed that,

> prisoners never denied the fact, but said that they had done it intentionally, pleading a violent fit of passion which they could not restrain at the moment, on being placed to doing some work which they disliked.[66]

Arthur Griffiths, an ex-prison official, referred to this practice as being 'endemic' and stated that the motive 'has been variously attributed to abject despair, the reckless desire to end a life of misery, and to deliberate craft,

---

[62] *RCPDCP*, BPP, 1878–9 (C.2446), XXXV.382. In his report of 1878–9 the governor of Portland Prison commented that 'Of late years I have observed a growing tendency amongst the convicts to commit murderous and violent assaults upon each other.' Interestingly, this wave of violence had been preceded by an increase in serious assaults upon prison warders at Portland Prison, which had occurred in the early 1870s. In 1873 and 1874 there were 27 and 25 assaults upon prison officers respectively. See *RCPDCP*, BPP, 1878 (C.2175), XLIII.383.
[63] *RCPDCP*, BPP, 1881(C.3073), LII.382
[64] B. Thomson, *The Story of Dartmoor Prison* (London: William Heinemann, 1907), p. 278.
[65] Balfour, *My Prison Life*, p. 297.
[66] *RDCP* BPP, 1872(C.649), XXXI.688.

aiming at a long and recuperative detention in the comparative ease of the hospital'.[67] It was common for prison staff to attribute self-injury to attempts by convicts to avoid work. This neatly fitted in with the stereotype that it was idleness that led to crime, and also avoided the need to consider any wider culpability.

In his report for 1872, the medical officer at Chatham Convict Prison stated that of the fractures he had treated during the year, 27 had been produced intentionally, and of these 16 required immediate amputations. He also estimated that of 358 other contusions and injuries 163 had been inflicted wilfully.[68] In the Chatham medical officer's report for the previous year, 1871, he had described some of the other terrible acts of self-injury committed by convicts and gave an account of the practice of intentionally infecting wounds and sores with copper wire, verdigris, lime and glass amongst other things.[69] This practice was not new; comments had been made regarding this practice in 1866. The medical officer at Chatham had detailed one case of self-injury in which the prisoner,

> J.K. bruised the fore-finger of the right hand purposely, and mutilated the fore-finger of the left hand by chopping it with a knife, opening the joint, and producing so much inflammation that the whole finger required to be removed. This prisoner afterwards feigned insanity, and also pretended to attempt suicide while under observation in a separate ward in the infirmary.[70]

In that year it had been assumed prematurely that the practice of punishing malingering, and of light labour and restricted diet when under treatment for it, had put a stop to such self-injury. The Directors later investigated the most extreme forms of self-injury and concluded that 'self infliction of injury is merely a form of malingering, which appears in recent years to have become the vogue among the convicts at Chatham'.[71] They did, however, recommend that as far as possible prisoners be removed from the facilities for such acts, that is trucks or engines, that prisoners should be made to understand that such behaviour would be severely punished, and that the unreasonableness of these acts in the light of the consequences for those who had already committed them should be made clear.[72]

[67] Griffiths, *Fifty Years of Public Service*, p. 177.
[68] RDCP, BPP, 1873(C.850), XXXIV.329.
[69] RCDP, BPP, 1872 (C.649), XXXI.687.
[70] RDCP, BPP, 1866 (3732), XXXVIII.141–2. Report of the medical officer of Chatham Convict Prison.
[71] RDCP, BPP, 1873(C.850), XXXIV.8.
[72] Ibid., p. 331.

Investigation into the diet at Chatham Convict Prison as a possible cause of self-destructive behaviour found that it was not insufficient, although it was admitted that it was an area of difficulty.[73] The medical officer disagreed and stated that on several occasions it had been necessary to remove convicts from the punishment cells to the infirmary. He proposed a small increase in diet as an inducement to labour on the public works. He also asserted that he was 'led to this conclusion from the emaciation which this labour induces and by the admission to the infirmary on this account alone without any specific disease amounting to 245'. According to the medical officer's report, total casualties, including all forms of illness and injury, numbered 19,633 in 1872. This made the daily average of those in ill health 53. The total number of convicts in the prison during 1872 was 2123.[74] Little seems to have been done by way of improving conditions as a possible means of reducing the rate of self-injury, aside from a small change in the diet and the issue of a brown jersey against the cold weather.[75]

According to the accounts of some discharged convicts, those who feigned illness and committed acts of self-injury were generally unpopular, as this meant that the genuinely ill were also suspected of malingering.[76] Furthermore, in prisons holding large numbers of convicts, 'malingerers' would take up the time of already hard-pressed medical staff to the detriment of the genuinely ill. Prison medical officers were the arbiters of decisions regarding the fitness of prisoners' often 'patrolling the narrow straits that separate hunger from starvation and punishment from outright cruelty'.[77] John Campbell, a medical officer in Dartmoor and Woking Convict Prisons during this period, recognised the difficulty of this position and stated that a medical officer in the convict service would be fortunate to 'escape the ungenerous charge of being too strict on the one hand or easily deceived on the other'.[78] The root of this dilemma was in the sometimes contradictory roles of the medical officer to both maintain discipline and preserve the physical and mental health of the convicts in the context of an overtly deterrent penal system. An imbalance in the priority given to the disciplinary over the medical role on the part of a medical officer could have severe implications for the welfare of convicts. It could also result in open conflict between prison medical officers and prisoners. As Sim has suggested, this has been a persistent and continuing problem in the prison medical service, in

---

[73] Ibid., p. 9.

[74] Ibid., pp. 329–31 and 283.

[75] Griffiths, *Fifty Years of Public Service*, p. 177.

[76] M. Davitt, *Leaves from a Prison Diary, or Lectures to a 'Solitary' Audience* (Shannon: Irish University Press, 1885), p. 141. F. Maybrick, *My Fifteen Years Lost* (New York: Funk & Wagnalls, 1905), p. 118.

[77] Priestly, *Victorian Prison Lives*, p. 190.

[78] Campbell, *Medical Officer in Convict Service*, p. 71.

which 'the will to discipline has had a profound impact on the level of medical care that prisoners have received since the end of the eighteenth century'.[79]

One case, which resulted in a court hearing, and involved a Fenian, Daniel Reddin, highlighted the repercussions of a prisoner being accused by a medical officer of 'malingering'.[80] Reddin stated that during his imprisonment in Chatham Convict Prison he complained repeatedly of being ill and unable to work but received no medical aid. As a result of this neglect, Reddin claimed that he became paralysed and was unable to walk without assistance. The medical officer of the prison, Dr John Burns, believed Reddin to be feigning his illness and in consequence Reddin was, on successive occasions, punished for refusal to work. Reddin was kept on a light diet or in a solitary cell in the infirmary, his legs were burned and pierced with needles, and he was also given electric shocks and blistered.[81]

There were several inquests into the deaths of prisoners in public works prisons during this period, which indicate the extent to which the treatment given by the prison medical officers could mean the difference between life and death.[82] These inquests also reinforce the impression that prison discipline, at this time, was very harsh, perhaps especially in Chatham which gained the nickname of 'the slaughterhouse'.[83] Arthur Griffiths, who spent some time as a deputy governor at Chatham during this period, was later to condemn the severity of the regime at the prison, although this has to be seen in the context of the wholesale condemnation of Du Cane's regime during and after the 1890s. Despite Griffiths' recognition that Chatham was 'the largest [convict prison] in the kingdom, probably the finest, the best

[79] J. Sim, *Medical Power in Prisons: The Prison Medical Service in England 1774–1989* (Milton Keynes: Open University Press, 1990), p. v.

[80] Daniel Reddin was convicted for his involvement in the attempt to rescue two prominent Fenians from a police van in Manchester in 1867, Radzinowicz and Hood, *History of English Criminal Law*, pp. 422–3. Also see J. O'Donovan Rossa, *Irish Rebels in English Prisons* (New York: D.J. Sadleir, 1882), p. 276. According to this account, Rossa received a message from Reddin asking for help and stating that 'They have me nearly dead. I am now doing twenty days bread and water, and have no bed at night. My name is Dan Reddin; I am one of the Manchester men.' See Chapter 7 for a further consideration of the circumstances of political prisoners in English prisons.

[81] Copy 'of all Affidavits used in the Court of Queen's Bench, either in obtaining or showing Cause against a Conditional Order for a Criminal Information made in last Hilary Term, on the Application of Daniel Reddin against Dr Burns, the Medical Officer, of Chatham Convict Prison', BPP, 1873 (366), LIV.286–376.

[82] For example, *Inquiry into the Alleged Ill-Treatment of the Convict Charles M'Carthy in Chatham Convict Prison*, BPP, 1878 (C.1978), XIII.769–860, and *Copies of Evidence given before the Jury at the Inquest held recently in Portland Prison on the Death of a Convict*, PP, 1875 (302), LXII.286–383.

[83] J.E. Thomas, 'Killed on Duty', *Prison Service Journal* (July 1972), p. 9.

organised and best run', Griffiths also described it as imposing a 'very vicious system of reports and punishments'.[84]

Evidence given before the Kimberley Commission in 1878 revealed some of the tensions and abuses which existed in the convict prisons of the time.[85] Forsythe has categorised these under six main developments, which provide a useful summary of some of the evidence discussed here. The first was that there was much unjustifiable violence towards convicts; the second that 'institutionalised over-reaction to the slightest suspected disrespect was typical'. The third indictment of the convict system that emerged in the evidence to the Kimberley Commission was that conditions were degrading and cruel; the fourth that staff who protested were ushered out of the service. The fifth indictment was that in response to organisations interested in prison reform and conditions the prison authorities were 'evasive and obstructive'. Forsythe's final category referred directly to medical practice within the convict prisons. It states that prison medical staff were using methods such as the infliction of electric shocks and red hot pokers against suspected malingerers.[86]

The weaknesses of checks on deterrence

By the late-1870s the worst practices of self-injury were less evident. There had been little real will to uncover the causes of this 'epidemic' and the Directors continued to profess their ignorance, at least in their published reports. In their report of 1875, they commented that,

> three years back it became quite the fashion at Chatham for prisoners to attempt to mutilate themselves. No reasonable cause for it could be discovered, but it ceased as soon as the convicts became convinced that besides the pain and injury they inflicted on themselves by their own act, they would also certainly be subjected to severe punishment.[87]

In 1873 Du Cane ordered a convict who had thrown himself under a moving truck, but whose injury was not life-threatening, to be flogged. The Directors then attributed the decline of this form of self-injury to the fact that convicts from then on knew that they would be severely punished for it. Administrators of a deterrent system had sought and used a deterrent answer to the problem of self-destructive behaviour among convicts. This was

---

[84] Griffiths, *Fifty Years of Public Service*, pp. 162–3.
[85] *Report of the Commissioners Appointed to Inquire into the Workings of the Penal Servitude Acts*, BPP, 1878–9 (C.2368), XXXVII.
[86] Forsythe, *Reform of Prisoners*, p. 203.
[87] RDCP, BPP, 1875 (C.1346), XXXIX.7.

an indication of unwillingness to address grievances of convicts or to accept criticism of the convict system in the context of the faith that was placed in deterrence. The choice of this solution was justified partly by these offences of self-injury being seen as wholly the responsibility of the convict; the Directors neither sought nor accepted culpability.

Hart has asserted that 'in relation to any social institution, after stating what general aim or value its maintenance fosters we should enquire whether there are any and if so what principles limiting the unqualified pursuit of that aim or value'.[88] In order to prevent others from committing extreme acts of self-injury in the future, Du Cane's rather utilitarian philosophy legitimated the flogging of an injured man who had placed himself under a moving truck. The problem with a philosophy that emphasised deterrence was that it could potentially legitimate any punishment on the pretext of preventing others from committing similar acts.

Administrative checks are one mechanism used to prevent the worst of such possible excesses, but in this period all communications from prison staff went through the Directors. The 'absolutism' of the administration of the prison was criticised in an article in *The Contemporary Review* in 1884. The article commented, for instance, that 'the Prison Chairman can constitute his own court, in cases of complaint by subordinate officers, against himself or colleagues'.[89] Similar complaints about lack of accountability and 'excessive centralisation' were made in the 1890s by William Morrison, an ex-prison chaplain whose criticisms of the prison system under Du Cane were published frequently.[90] He maintained that centralisation had resulted in 'machine-like methods of dealing with human beings'.[91] No independent inspection system existed in the convict prisons until 1880, and the system of unpaid philanthropic visitors that was established at that time proved to be ineffectual.[92] According to Morrison, these visitors had little power and 'no real knowledge of the facts of prison life'.[93]

The superficiality of the investigations by the Home Office into the petitions of prisoners during this period may be a further indication of the control over the flow of information possessed by the Directors of the

---

[88] H.L.A. Hart, 'Principles of Punishment', in *Philosophical Perspectives on Punishment*, ed. G. Ezorsky (Albany, NY: University of New York Press, 1972), p. 161.

[89] F. Peek, 'Official Optimism', *The Contemporary Review* 46 (July 1884), p. 85. Francis Peek was the Chairman of the Howard Association.

[90] For example, W.D. Morrison, 'Prison Reform', *The Fortnightly Review* 69 (January–June 1898), p. 782. Also see W.D. Morrison, 'Are Our Prisons a Failure?', *The Fortnightly Review* 61 (April 1894), pp. 459–69; W.D. Morrison, 'Prisons and Prisoners', *The Fortnightly Review* 69 (May 1898), pp. 781–9; W.D. Morrison, 'The Increase of Crime', *The Nineteenth Century* 31 (1892), pp. 950–7.

[91] Morrison, 'Prison Reform', p. 782.

[92] Radzinowicz and Hood, *History of English Criminal Law*, pp. 570–1.

[93] Morrison, 'Prison Reform', p. 783.

Convict Prisons.[94] The *Commission Appointed to Inquire into the treatment of Treason-Felony Convicts in English Prisons*, which reported in 1871, was critical of the procedures for petitioning by prisoners to the Home Secretary. They reported not only that the practical limitations on the use of petitioning varied between prisons but that its exercise was 'too dependent upon the discretion of the very authorities whose conduct may be impugned to be of much value as an appeal in the last resort'.[95] The Commission went on to examine the procedures for the trial and punishment of prisoners for prison offences and seriously questioned whether the procedures for this were 'consistent with the attainment of that which is the object of all inquiry, viz., the knowledge of the real facts of the case'. One of the 'doubtful points of the system' emphasised by the Commission was the standard practice of disallowing the evidence of one prisoner in corroboration of the evidence of another.[96]

The long-held conventions operating in individual convict prisons with regard to trial procedures for the judgement of prison offences died slowly. Over thirty years later, in a statement dated 27 August 1902, the governor of Dartmoor Convict Prison asserted that,

> it is, in my opinion, highly undesirable to admit one prisoner to give evidence in favour of another. They would invariably either combine against the officer, or, in isolated cases, pay off an old score by attacking their fellow-prisoners. If prisoners' evidence were admitted in one case it would have to be admitted in all.[97]

According to the Prison Commissioners, the governor and Board of Visitors of Dartmoor Convict Prison were, by this time, exceptional in their adherence to this principle and this was attributed partly to the physical isolation of the prison. Because of the length of the journey to the prison it was claimed that the Board of Visitors had less time to hear cases.[98] As a result of an investigation in 1902 into internal trial procedures at Dartmoor it was decided that one of the Directors, Mitford, was to travel to the prison once a month in order to

> relieve the Board of Visitors of dealing with ordinary cases but leaving to them the trial of prisoners which may result in corporal punishment and also complaints of

---

[94] This suggestion can only be tentative as the existing historical records of the Home Office have in part been determined by the various criteria under which they have been preserved.

[95] BPP, 1871 (C.319), XXXII.9, para. 32.

[96] Ibid., 10, para. 35.

[97] PRO HO144/564/A612219/25, investigation following the petition of prisoner William Simmons for wrongful punishment.

[98] PRO HO144/558/A60074/8, memorandum dated 13 December 1901.

prisoners against officers which were considered to be the special subjects for investigation by these bodies.[99]

The investigators do not make it clear why the Board of Visitors were thought to be more capable of dealing with serious offences committed by convicts. However, the petitions which had instigated the investigation into trial procedures at Dartmoor had referred only to disproportionately severe punishments being given for petty offences.[100]

It is predictable that it is the petitions from convicts that question the partiality of official procedure and documentation most directly. Convicts were not only the people most affected by unfairness in the procedures for adjudicating on prison offences but they also had the greatest motivation to attempt to discredit the authority of the prison staff. A petition from William George Bundy, dated 22 January 1896, criticised the limitations of the official reports and the judgements that were made on the strength of such superficial and reductionist material. He complained that,

> You do not know my mind, its inclinations and aversions; you do not know my life, its lights and solemn shadows. Little episodes viewed through a distorting medium are all you have to judge me by; yet you condemn and would utterly degrade me.[101]

A large proportion of the petitions that have been preserved in the Home Office records make accusations that convicts have been ill-treated, beaten, or even murdered by prison staff. Yet investigations into them tended to consist of a routine questioning of the staff involved and a generally unquestioned belief in their answers. The end result of this for the petitioner could be punishment for making false accusations. For his 'unfounded' accusations, in which he claimed that prisoners were being abused by prison officers, Bundy was sentenced to forfeit 540 marks, or in other words three months' remission. Such punishments were, Bundy commented sarcastically, 'no doubt intended to encourage convicts to tell the truth'.[102]

In a later petition to the Home Office, Bundy stated that 'at present you are powerless to ascertain the truth'.[103] While this prisoner was asserting that the truth of a petition could not be ascertained under existing procedures, the Directors were presenting Bundy as an example of the way in which prisoners abused the right of petition. In this case the Home Office upheld the right of petition but suggested that 'the Prison Officials need take

---

[99] Ibid., memorandum dated 4 August 1902.
[100] For example, PRO HO144/557/A59275, PRO HO144/558/A60074 and PRO HO144/564/A612219.
[101] PRO HO144/203/A47874.
[102] Ibid.
[103] Ibid., petition dated 14 April 1896.

no notice of any allegations in them . . . unless S of S [the Secretary of State] should think any inquiry necessary'.[104] Of course, the accusations made by Bundy may well have been unfounded, but given the cursory nature of investigations made into such complaints it is unlikely that this would have been discernible.

In addition to administrative checks and investigations, the severity of prison regimes might have been moderated by the formalisation of notions of prisoners' rights, or by a concept of the point at which unfairness or harshness could undermine the legitimacy of the authority that was imposing it. In this period any notions regarding prisoners' rights were undeveloped. The system of penal servitude imposed deprivations in order that convicts had to win their release from them; not even the provision of basic necessities was considered a right as these could be withdrawn as a punishment for disobedience or misbehaviour. One example of this principle was that from February 1876 all public works prisons imposed single-file, silent exercise for those on probation and in the third class. It was up to the individual convict to advance himself out of these classes through industry, self-discipline and good behaviour. When this silent rule was extended beyond the lowest classes, violating the principle that industry and good conduct should be rewarded, it met with some resistance from prisoners, which suggests that the inmates understood the principles under which their imprisonment was managed.[105] Such tactics for the management of prisoners proved resilient. In 1995, Sparks and Bottoms still referred to the 'historically received view that prisoners' goods and services should be regarded as "privileges", awarded or removed by discretion'.[106]

One of the main criticisms of prison has not been with reference to the loss of legal rights as a result of becoming a prisoner, but with reference to the 'forfeitures' imposed by administrative or organisational rules.[107] These have included the censorship of mail, mental and physical stagnation and, to use a more modern example, the lack of access to legal advice or representation.[108] Furthermore, in the light of the evidence of the abuses which prevailed in the public works prisons during this period, another type of 'forfeiture' would include freedom from assault or persecution by fellow prisoners or prison staff. Given the closed nature of the convict system, individual incidents of abuse or injustice rarely received attention outside prisons.

---

[104] Ibid.

[105] McConville, English Prison Administration, pp. 412–13.

[106] J.R. Sparks and A.E. Bottoms, 'Legitimacy and Order in Prisons', British Journal of Sociology 46, No. 1 (March 1995), p. 46.

[107] N. Walker, Punishment, Danger and Stigma: The Morality of Criminal Justice (Oxford: Blackwell, 1980), p. 173.

[108] For example, the first internal adjudication on a prison offence which allowed legal representation for the prisoner was in January 1984. See H. Woolf and S. Tumin Prison Disturbances April 1990 (London: HMSO, 1991), Cm 1456.3.

The prison authorities continued to cite the reformation of prisoners as an important, though not predominant, objective of imprisonment. This is evident in Du Cane's list of what he perceived to be the three main objects of prison labour. These were:

> Firstly, to create a deterrent effect on the prisoner himself, and on the criminal class; Secondly, to produce a reformatory effect on the prisoner himself; and, Thirdly, to recoup, as far as possible, the cost of maintaining the prison.[109]

The second and third objects worked to prevent a level of severity in the convict prisons that would impair the mental or physical health of large numbers of the convict population. As Lacey has suggested, 'the justifying aims or functions of punishment themselves incorporate certain limitations on their own pursuit or fulfilment'.[110] The object of behavioural reform may have permitted very harsh labour to be imposed to inculcate the habit of work in the convicts, but in principle would disallow overt physical cruelty since this would associate labour with brutality. The health of convicts had to be maintained not only to prevent public scandal but also so that they were physically able to labour to recoup some of the costs of their imprisonment. These principles, however, did not mitigate the kind of exemplary punishment carried out by Du Cane to try to stop the extreme forms of self-injury that occurred among the convicts at Chatham Convict Prison.

An organisational approach to preventing violence

The persistence of violent incidents in the public works prisons was decisive in the development of policies regarding the segregation of troublesome or vulnerable prisoners, policies which remain important in twenty-first-century prisons. One of the most difficult problems that faced the prison system after the decline of the use of transportation, and which continues to face it, was what to do with persistently violent or refractory prisoners. The use of segregation whether as a control or a protective mechanism has been indispensable to the development of classification and discipline in nineteenth-, twentieth- and twenty-first-century English prisons. While the form of segregation has varied, the basic principle has remained the same – the further marginalisation of a minority whose behaviour is unacceptable either to the prison authorities or to the main body of prisoners.

---

[109] Du Cane, *Account of Penal Servitude*, p. 42. Du Cane's claims of the extent to which prison labour defrayed the costs of the prison have been questioned by Radzinowicz and Hood, see *History of English Criminal Law*, p. 539.

[110] N. Lacey, *State Punishments, Political Principles and Community Values* (London: Routledge, 1988), p. 200.

Policy regarding segregation in the period covered by this chapter can be seen, for example, in the initial separate phase of penal servitude, in the punishment cells, in the separation of troublesome prisoners, and in the separation of the physically and mentally impaired. In the late twentieth century, similar strategies were reflected, for instance, in the use of special control units and of Rule 43. Control units were established in 1984 as a strategy to manage 'those prisoners who persistently present serious control problem in long-term prisons'.[111] Rule 43 entails the segregation of vulnerable prisoners, including sex offenders, informers and ex-police officers, from the rest of the prison population.[112] Vivian Stern, one-time Director of the National Association for the Care and Resettlement of Offenders, has asserted that the necessity to keep some prisoners apart under Rule 43, 'locked away in specially secure parts of prisons for protection, living an impoverished existence in fear of their lives', was partly a consequence of strong internal prison cultures which resulted in the intimidation of these offenders.[113]

McConville also makes a direct link between the control units utilised in the late twentieth century and the 'time-tested methods of separation and progressive stages' refined in the second half of the nineteenth century.[114] The nineteenth-century equivalent of attempts to segregate the more vulnerable prisoners was the introduction of a 'star' class in 1880 for convicts who were first-time offenders. The stated concern regarding 'star' class prisoners was, however, to prevent the contamination of first-time offenders, not to protect them against possible assault by other prisoners, as with the more modern Rule 43.

Thus, vulnerability during the nineteenth century was assessed under differing criteria than in the late twentieth century. Convicts guilty of 'unnatural' crimes or indecency were excluded from the first 'star' class at Chatham Convict Prison as being potentially contaminating.[115] But a large proportion of those segregated in modern prisons under Rule 43 are there

---

[111] A.K. Bottomley, 'What is Special about Special Units?', *Prison Service Journal* 92 (March 1994), p. 2. For criticism of control units see M. Fitzgerald, *Prisoners in Revolt* (London: Penguin, 1977), pp. 40–3.

[112] I. Heritage, 'The Politics of Rule 43', *Prison Service Journal* 94 (July 1994), pp. 14–19.

[113] V. Stern, 'An Open Letter to Lord Justice Woolf', *Prison Service Journal* 77 (1990), p. 11.

[114] McConville, 'The Victorian Prison', p. 155.

[115] *Report of the Commissioners Appointed to Inquire into the Workings of the Penal Servitude Acts*, BPP, 1878–9 (C.2368), XXXVII. This report recommended the introduction of a 'star' class. The Directors of the Convict Prisons felt, however, that providing space in the convict prisons for this classification might be a problem and also that many dangerous criminals might have no previous convictions. It was therefore decided that each convict should be investigated prior to being placed in this class. See *RDCP*, BPP, 1880 (C.2694), XXXVI.11.

precisely because of their vulnerability to assault from other prisoners due to the sexual nature of their offences. One aspect that both periods have in common is that the potential or presumed threat presented by the more serious long-term prisoners was used to justify some segregational practices. The need for segregational strategies in the second half of the nineteenth century was often seen to lie in the accumulation of incorrigible characters in the convict prisons since the ending of transportation. A hundred years later it has been asserted that segregation was needed to control the increasing numbers of prisoners serving very long sentences or even life. As Sparks and Bottoms have suggested, 'The long-term prisons proved amenable to being depicted as congregations of dangerous and violent men with nothing to lose.'[116]

One example of the historical segregation of particularly troublesome prisoners can be found in Portland Convict Prison. A decline in the number of assaults upon prison staff at Portland Prison in the late 1870s was attributed by the Directors to the introduction of a system of isolating selected inmates into a group called 'Party 57'.[117] Party 57 was a refinement of the existing classification of convicts and contained a group of prisoners who were considered to be trouble-makers or who had incited others to cause trouble. This party was first referred to in the report of the governor of Portland Prison for 1874. He stated that all convicts guilty of violent offences in prison had been formed into a separate party, 'placed under experienced officers, rigid discipline enforced, and a system of isolation on week days and Sundays carried out'. If these prisoners behaved well for three months they were allowed a fresh start on the public works with the main body of convicts.[118]

Conclusion

During the 1880s the quality and usefulness of the Reports of the Directors of the Convict Prisons deteriorated. Although statistical information was still given, any criticism or analysis of these statistics declined. It may be that incidences of the more serious forms of violence or self-injury declined. However, disciplinary strategies, among them better categorisation, had developed in order to prevent and manage such behaviour more effectively. Furthermore, the worst and most arduous labour on the public works was gradually replaced by industrial labour, and the use of some punishments,

---

[116] Sparks and Bottoms, 'Legitimacy and Order', p. 46. Sparks and Bottoms, however, go on to state that such an assertion could not be maintained after the mid-1980s following disturbances among remand prisoners.

[117] RDCP, BPP, 1878(C.2175), XLIII.383.

[118] RDCP, BPP, 1875(C.1346), XXXIX.351.

particularly corporal punishment and the use of restraints, was increasingly subject to regulation.[119] Forfeiture of marks and remission came to compose one of the main forms of punishment for prison offences. In addition, the gradual reduction in the size of the convict population alleviated the problems involved in organising such large groups of men. The Penal Servitude Act of 1891 reduced the minimum period of penal servitude to three years, and shorter sentences may also have had some impact upon the individual propensity towards violent or disruptive behaviour.[120]

The daily average number of prisoners of both sexes held in convict prisons during the year ending 31 March 1880 was 10,299; by 1890 this had declined to 5359, and by 1895, the year of Du Cane's retirement, to 3523.[121] This was partly a reflection of the reduction in crime rates identified by historians over the second half of the nineteenth century.[122] Radzinowicz and Hood suggest that the declining numbers of convicts actually allowed an increased control over them and more secrecy to surround the workings of the convict prisons. Any evidence of internal criticism has been wiped from the published reports, as have the signatures of the authors of the reports from individual prisons.[123]

This examination of violent prison offences presents the argument that there was an increase in the intensity of penal servitude under the administration of Du Cane. This was heralded by the changes in the system implemented as a consequence of the Penal Servitude Act of 1864. During the period covered by this chapter, it was the deterrent nature of penal servitude and the lack of in-built checks upon excess that produced among the most terrible acts of self-injury in the history of modern imprisonment in England. The deterrent system that Du Cane was prominent in operating was expressed in a meticulous and inexorable programme of progressive stages, with the recording of privileges and punishments in a character book. However, penal labour and diet were also intentionally designed to be a severe deterrent to those who became subject to them. It was the convicts

---

[119] *Royal Commission to Inquire into the Working of the Penal Servitude Acts*, BPP, 1878–9(2368), XXXVII.xlix–l. The Commission recommended that restraints should not be used as a form of punishment.

[120] *An Act to amend the Law relating to Penal Servitude and the Prevention of Crime*, PP 1891: 54 & 55 Vict., c.69.

[121] RCPDCP, BPP, 1896 (C.8200), XLIV.272.

[122] For example, V.A.C. Gatrell, 'The Decline of Theft and Violence in Victorian and Edwardian England', in *Crime and the Law: The Social History of Crime in Western Europe since 1500*, ed. V.A.C. Gatrell, B. Lenman and G. Parker (London: Europa Publications, 1980); Radzinowicz and Hood, *History of English Criminal Law*, pp. 113–17; Wiener, *Reconstructing the Criminal*, pp. 216–17.

[123] Radzinowicz and Hood, *History of English Criminal Law*, p. 568. The reports of individual governors, medical officers and chaplains no longer carried their signatures after 1878.

who refused to submit to the system who experienced the worst conditions, and who could be subject to segregation as well as repeated punishments and transfers between prisons.

Under the administration of Edmund Du Cane, some of the fundamental principles of modern imprisonment were developed and refined. These include the classification and segregation of the most troublesome or vulnerable prisoners, and the entrenchment of the principle that even basic necessities were not rights but could be designated by the prison authorities as privileges to be earned.[124] More overtly than ever, the behaviour of prisoners was to be regulated by a continuum of rewards and punishments. However, the increase in the deterrent value of penal servitude, particularly that portion of the sentence spent in the public works prisons, was not only the result of the domination of the prison system by Du Cane but of a much wider change in social attitudes towards the criminal. The hardened criminal character was increasingly perceived as primitive and unresponsive to reformatory opportunities, and therefore could be discouraged from crime only through the imposition of the most severe of punishments.

---

[124] Recent legislative changes in the Human Rights Act 1998, which came into force in Britain in October 2000, could instigate major changes in the prison system, see M. Cavadino and J. Dignan, *The Penal System: An Introduction*, 3rd edn (London: Sage, 2002). For example, the power of prison governors to adjudicate on internal prison offences has been overturned, see *Guardian*, 27 July 2002.

6

Change and resistance: from the Gladstone Committee to the war

The nature and extent of penal reform in the period 1895 to 1914 have been the subject of some debate. One of the main reasons for this is that the period has been seen as witnessing a pivotal transition in which classical ideas about punishment were seriously challenged by newer positivist ideas about criminality and the appropriate way to deal with offenders. To a large extent, this debate originated with the publication in 1985 of David Garland's *Punishment and Welfare: A History of Penal Strategies*, in which he suggests that this period witnessed the evolution of modern penal policy and practice. In a later publication Wiener interprets this period in a similar manner, albeit from a stance which emphasises the importance of more cultural and literary factors.[1]

Unlike previous chapters, local and convict prisons will be dealt with together in this chapter. This is in part because Garland's thesis encompasses both, but also because of the gradual convergence in administration and discipline which had been occurring in the two systems since nationalisation in 1877. As Edmund Du Cane, the chairman of the Prison Commission from 1877 to 1895 and of the Prison Directorate from 1869 to 1895, stated in his evidence to the Gladstone Committee, 'this process of welding the departments [local and convict] into one commenced as soon as the Prison Act, 1877, came into operation, and has been gradually extending ever since'.[2] The Prison Act of 1898 finally brought the offices of the Prison Commission and the Directors of the Convict Prisons together into one formal body. In addition, one aspect of the reform measures of this period involved the extending of practices instigated in the convict prisons prior to 1895 into the local prisons. For instance, convicts had been entitled to earn remission of their sentence as early as 1857, but it was not until 1898 that this opportunity was extended to local prisoners.[3] By 1905, the remission

---

[1] M.J. Wiener, *Reconstructing the Criminal: Culture, Law and Policy in England, 1830–1914* (Cambridge: Cambridge University Press, 1990).
[2] *Report from the Departmental Committee on Prisons* (Gladstone Committee), BPP, 1895(C.7702), LVI.422, qu.10,808. Du Cane described the original division as having been an 'accident of history'.
[3] See Chapter 3 of this publication for a discussion of the reintroduction of remission for convicts in 1857.

entitlement for local prisoners was three weeks for a sentence of nine months, six weeks for a twelve-month sentence and three months for a sentence of eighteen months.[4]

This chapter begins with an analysis of a serious disturbance which occurred in Wormwood Scrubs Prison in 1907 and examines the extent to which this revealed internal tensions produced by prison reform in the years from 1895 to 1914. The reform measures introduced will then be evaluated and considered in the context of the main pillars of Garland's thesis: that the role of the prison became increasingly to segregate rather than to correct offenders; that the prison shifted from the centre of penality towards a more coercive end point in penal alternatives; and that penal policy became increasingly influenced by positivist thinking. Finally, Garland's thesis will be questioned in the context of contributions to this debate by Victor Bailey and William Forsythe, who both deny the far-reaching influence of positivist criminology in penal practice which has been claimed by Garland.[5] Bailey argues that the changes in the structure of the criminal justice system were not only more limited than those suggested by Garland but were influenced much more by classical liberalism and humanitarianism than by positivist criminology. He also asserts that Garland does not address the full complexity of penal culture in this period and highlights what he sees as the most significant change of the period, 'the massive abatement of imprisonment'.[6] Hence Bailey maintains that,

> I am not convinced that a new positivist discourse, underwritten by the human sciences, dominated what could be seen, thought, and performed in the penal domain. I am not convinced that 'demoralization,' or a diminished faith in the efficacy of individual willpower, was as pronounced or advanced as Garland and Wiener contend.[7]

[4] PRO HO45/12905/116578, Penal Servitude and Imprisonment Memorandum.

[5] V. Bailey, 'English Prisons, Penal Culture, and the Abatement of Imprisonment, 1895–1922', *Journal of British Studies* 36 (July 1997), pp. 285–334; W.J. Forsythe, *Penal Discipline, Reformatory Projects and the English Prison Commission, 1895–1939* (Exeter: Exeter University Press, 1991); W.J. Forsythe, 'The Garland Thesis and the Origins of Modern English Prison Discipline: 1835–1939', *Howard Journal* 34, No. 3 (August 1995), pp. 259–73; W.J. Forsythe, 'National Socialists and the English Prisons Commission: The Berlin Penitentiary Congress of 1935', *International Journal of the Sociology of Law* 17, No. 2 (1989), pp. 131–45.

[6] Bailey, 'English Prisons 1895–1922', p. 293. The continued relaxation of prison conditions and decline in the prison population in England during the inter-war years have been described by Forsythe. See Forsythe, 'National Socialists and the English Prisons Commission', p. 143.

[7] Bailey, 'English Prisons, 1895–1922', p. 305.

This chapter joins the debate largely in support of Bailey's first assertion that alterations in the structure of the 'penal complex' have been exaggerated, and concentrates on the changes that occurred in the mainstream convict and local prisons. Fundamentally, the changes that were implemented constituted not a decisive shift in philosophy or penal practice but rather an amelioration of some existing practices and the development of others. Indeed, one element of the debate regarding the nature of reforms in this period that has received relatively little attention is the level of continuity with measures taken prior to 1895. This is important because the origins of many of the areas of resistance to change in the years from 1895 to 1914 can be located prior to 1895 and these served to slow the pace of reform.

The origins and causes of prison disturbances have been notoriously difficult to uncover for those seeking explanations. Despite the over-arching framework of prison rules and regulations, the complex intermixing of individual personalities and actions within the prison influences the character of each prison regime. In a late twentieth-century examination of prison culture, Finkelstein has shown that the culture and expectations of prison staff can significantly affect the discipline and attitudes within individual prisons to the extent that they present an obstacle to change. The principal argument of Finkelstein's research is that 'no matter how necessary or desirable change may be its management is subject to extreme social and cultural constraints within individual prisons many of which stem from the expectations of prison staff'. A further obstacle to change which he cites is the 'structural opposition constructed by the prison between prison officers and the prisoners'.[8]

A determining factor in the nature of a regime and in the extent of openness or resistance to change in the prisons was the attitudes and expectations of prison officers. Prison officers represented the sharp end of prison discipline and had to implement and administer the system on a day-to-day basis. Thomas has suggested that prison reforms introduced in this period were a major cause of the long-term isolation of prison officers from involvement in reformatory measures and from senior prison officials. This, he asserts, was instrumental in promoting militancy and resistance to change among prison officers.[9]

The alienation of prison officers that Thomas identifies was reflected in conflict situations with prisoners. It is, however, important to point out that overt combined physical conflict was not the norm, although individual assaults upon prison officers remained quite frequent. For example, during the year ending 31 March 1909 corporal punishment was inflicted on four

---

[8] E. Finkelstein, *Prison Culture: An Inside View* (Aldershot: Avebury, 1993), p. 1.
[9] J.E. Thomas, *The English Prison Officer since 1850: A Study in Conflict* (London: Routledge & Kegan Paul, 1972), pp. 117–22.

convicts in Dartmoor and five convicts in Portland for 'gross personal violence to an officer of the prison'.[10] In the following year, corporal punishment was inflicted on five offenders in each of these two prisons, also for assaults upon prison officers.[11] Individual conflict of this kind revealed the tensions that lay below the surface of day-to-day life in the prisons but rarely received much attention in the published reports of the prison authorities.

The disturbance at Wormwood Scrubs Prison in 1907 that will be examined here was no more typical of daily life in the prisons of this period than the occasional incidents of exceptional friendliness between prison officers and prisoners. One example of such friendliness is an episode in which two officers at Warwick Prison were given a severe reprimand and demoted because, while escorting a prisoner to the Police Court, they made a detour and went to a public house and had a drink with him.[12] Nevertheless, the investigation by the Prison Commissioners into the disturbance at Wormwood Scrubs Prison is valuable because of the survival of an in-depth report into the occurrence. This report suggests that there were tensions created by the nature of the changes in the prison system during this period.

An incident in Wormwood Scrubs Prison

At about 11.30 a.m. on 6 April 1907 a convict at Wormwood Scrubs Prison climbed up the stack pipe of 'C' hall on to the roof, breaking skylights and creating a disturbance. Because of this, the Saturday afternoon leave of all the prison officers was cancelled and extra officers were ordered into the hall. The prisoners in this hall became very excited, 'kicking at their doors, ringing their bells, using violent, abusive, and obscene language, encouraging the prisoner McCoy, who was up on the roof, and provoking the warders on duty'.[13] The Principal Warder in charge, Read, left the hall and did not return until the prisoner, McCoy, was down from the roof. During the time that McCoy was on the roof an 'unprecedented episode' occurred. 'C' hall had been left in the charge of Principal Warder Wall who ordered the prison officers in the hall to 'locate the disturbance' which, according to the investigation, was taken by some to mean 'quell the disturbance'. The quelling of the disturbance took the form of six to ten officers entering the

---

[10] RCPDCP, BPP, 1909 (Cd.4847), XLV.195.

[11] RCPDCP, BPP, 1910 (Cd.5360), XLV.337.

[12] PRO HO45/10609/193551, letter from Ruggles-Brise to the Under Secretary of State, dated 3 June 1910.

[13] PRO HO144/854/151885, report of the Prison Commission to the Under Secretary of State, dated 29 April 1907.

cells of some of the prisoners, 'who either provoked them by their abuse, or against whom they had old scores to pay off', and administering 'what they would call a "severe drubbing", probably with their fists, and also with the legs'; fourteen prisoners suffered wounds and bruises.[14]

The explanations that the officers gave for their behaviour, and the reaction of the investigators to them, are revealing in the context of this chapter. The officers claimed that they had taken matters into their own hands because

> they could not rely upon being supported by the Governor and Deputy Governor, when reports were preferred by them against prisoners for assault &c., and that such assaults were likely to be more numerous, and such support to be more necessary under the present condition of 'associated labour'.[15]

During this period both local and convict prisons were experiencing a relaxation in the extent of isolation imposed upon inmates. Part of the utility of the separate system, as indicated by the above quotation, was its value as an internal control mechanism as well as being a deterrent. The investigators accepted this explanation given by the officers, and in their report stated that, as a result of the efforts of the governor to deal leniently with prisoners, he had 'failed to realise his duty towards his staff' and the officers had lost confidence in his administration. They further stated that this loss of confidence had been exacerbated by the 'grievously inadequate' punishments given by the Visiting Committee to prisoners for prison offences.[16]

Significantly, the evidence against two of the officers included statements regarding suspected involvement in early attempts to establish a prison officers' union. Evidence recorded against one officer, Warder Twiggy, referred to a 'grave suspicion that this officer was closely connected with the movement'. Against another, Mills, it was stated that there 'is strong reason to believe that he is an active member of the movement'. Very few of the officers were willing to give any information and this frustrated the investigators and severely hampered the course of the investigation. However, it is clear that in some respects the investigators sympathised with the offending officers and acknowledged that they had been subject to some provocation. Indeed, Ruggles-Brise, the chairman of the Prison Commissioners and Directors, even referred to their actions as 'rough justice'. Despite this, the offending officers were punished harshly as a reminder to them of the standards that the prison authorities expected them to uphold in their position as prison officers and of their primary role in the maintenance

---

[14] Ibid.
[15] Ibid.
[16] Ibid.

of order and control. The behaviour of the officers was condemned as consti-tuting 'an unprecedented episode throwing a great slur and reproach not only on the prison itself, but also on the whole service'.[17]

The circumstances of this incident reflect some of the problems that arose as a consequence of prison reform during this period. The position of the prison officer became less clearly defined than under the previous overtly deterrent system. While still expected to continue his existing role in maintaining control, the prison officer could no longer rely upon the unquestioned support of the prison authorities in any conflict or dispute with prisoners. With the shift in emphasis towards reform, officers experienced some confusion of their role.[18]

Thomas asserts that the real blockage or resistance to reform has been that 'society has not defined this as the primary task of the prison system'.[19] The primary tasks of prison officers have remained control and security. This is why the basic hierarchical and paramilitary structure of the prison service has persisted.[20] The entrenchment of such a structure was fostered under Du Cane who encouraged the recruitment of ex-army men because he valued their 'habits of order and discipline, of rendering and enforcing strict obe-dience, and their aptitude in dealing with large bodies of men'.[21] Control and security remained the primary tasks of prison officers but such tasks became devalued during a period in which reform was a prominent subject of official debate.

Forsythe has commented that ordinary prison officers were not generally considered to be capable of playing a major role in reformatory projects.[22] Some prisoners noted this lack of confidence in the prison officers. For instance, Stephen Hobhouse, who was imprisoned for his conscientious objection to compulsory conscription during the First World War, observed that,

> The want of confidence in the prisoners is accompanied by a corresponding want of confidence in the warders. These officers are also spied upon by the Chief Warder and Governor; and such is the fear of collusion or bribery, that a warder is forbidden to engage in 'familiar' conversation with a prisoner, and is not supposed

---

[17] Ibid.

[18] Thomas, *English Prison Officer*, p. 42. Conflict between prison officers and prisoners has also been seen as indicating an uncertainty in the role of prison officers, increased militancy and resentment at their exclusion from rehabilitative efforts for prisoners during the 1970s. See M. Fitzgerald and J. Sim, *British Prisons* (Oxford: Basil Blackwell, 1979), pp. 11–15.

[19] Thomas, *English Prison Officer*, p. 50.

[20] Ibid., p. 8.

[21] E.F. Du Cane, *The Punishment and Prevention of Crime* (London: Macmillan, 1885), p. 188.

[22] Forsythe, *Penal Discipline, Reformatory Projects*, pp. 140–1.

to say anything to him that does not bear upon his work or the prison rules. This rule is largely disregarded, but, as warders themselves have complained to me, it makes it practically impossible for them to exercise a lasting reformative or uplifting influence on a prisoner.[23]

The prison rules themselves were contradictory in defining the ideal prison officer–prisoner relationship. In the prison rules published in 1903, Rule 108 stated that it was the duty of prison officers to 'treat prisoners with kindness, [and] to listen patiently and report their complaints or grievances' while also maintaining firm discipline. This rule also stated that prison officers should 'strive to acquire a moral influence over the prisoners'. Rule 114, however, ordered that an officer should not 'allow any familiarity on the part of a prisoner towards himself or any other officer or servant of the prison' nor should he even 'speak to a prisoner unnecessarily'.[24]

The lack of confidence in prison officers was an important factor in the expansion of the role of professionals within the prison; it was the prison medical officers, the prison visitors, and later the social welfare professions, that took on the task of reform in the prisons, a trend recognised by both Foucault and Garland.

According to Thomas, the early investigative committees appointed to consider the pay and conditions of prison officers revealed communications problems within the prisons between the different levels of staff. There was a reluctance to complain through prison governors or through the prison inspectors, indicating a lack of confidence and possible fear of retaliation in the light of the hostility that had been shown towards the organisation of prison officers.[25] Indeed, the Rosebery Committee, which published its report in 1883, declared that despite the prison officers having 'ample opportunities of making their grievances known to the Directors' they preferred the method of 'public agitation' to make their case.[26] The Reports of the Commissioners of Prisons and the Directors of Convict Prisons framed this in the best possible light. Their report for the year ending 31 March 1908 commented that the fact that 'so few officers avail themselves of the opportunity offered at each inspection to bring to the notice of the Inspector any request or grievance that they may wish to put forward is, in our opinion,

---

[23] S. Hobhouse, 'An English Prison from Within', *The Quarterly Review* 230 (July 1918), p. 29. Also see S. Hobhouse and A. Fenner Brockway, *English Prisons Today* (London: Longman, Green & Co., 1922), pp. 371–5.

[24] C.R. Henderson, *Modern Prison Systems: Their Organization and Regulation in Various Countries of Europe and America* (Washington: Government Printing Office, 1903), p. 116. The rules referred to here applied to both local and convict prisons.

[25] Thomas, *English Prison Officer*, pp. 91–119.

[26] PRO PCom7/603, Report of the Committee appointed to Enquire into the Position and Prospects of Convict Warders and Broadmoor Asylum Attendants, p. 12.

a testimony to their general conduct'.[27] But this lack of communication was a reflection of the gradual alienation of prison officers from before 1895.

Thomas comments that, 'As the reformative movement gathered momentum, so did the certainty among staff that the bonds between officers and governors were being weakened because of a strengthening relationship between governor grades and prisoners.'[28] Little in the way of reformative effort was directed towards prison officers who gained few concessions during the period.[29] This increased the resentment and obstructiveness of prison officers towards reformative efforts from which they were excluded. But if this was the case, how great were the reforms that were introduced and who benefited from them?

A changing philosophy

Garland maintains that prior to 1895 (the year of the publication of the Gladstone Committee Report) penal policy was dominated by classical ideas regarding deterrence, uniformity and a belief in a proper proportionality between an offence and its punishment.[30] During the period from 1895 to 1914, however, the Victorian penal system was transformed to the extent that the 'pattern of penal sanctioning which was established . . . with its new agencies, techniques, knowledges and institutions, amounted to a new structure of penality'.[31] Foucault, Garland contends, was mistaken to consider the expansion of surveillance, normalisation and individualisation, integral to the development of the prison as the primary method of punishment, as being achieved in the early nineteenth century. Garland asserts that,

> The legalistic insistence upon uniformity, equality of treatment and proportionality ensured a mass regime which could allow a marginal place to generalised, reformative practices, but which refused any serious concession to individualisation. The development of specific practices of normalisation, classification, categorisation and discrimination between criminal types simply did not occur in Britain until after 1895.[32]

The framework of classical thinking on crime and punishment had been outlined in what became one of the leading texts in classical criminology,

[27] RCPDCP, BPP, 1908 (Cd.4300), LII.476.
[28] Thomas, *English Prison Officer*, pp. 120–1.
[29] Ibid., ch. 7.
[30] D. Garland, *Punishment and Welfare: A History of Penal Strategies* (Aldershot: Gower, 1985), pp. 10–15.
[31] Ibid., p. 5.
[32] Ibid., p. 32.

On Crimes and Punishments by Cesare Beccaria. Beccaria stated that the purpose of punishment

> can only be to prevent the criminal from inflicting new injuries on its citizens and to deter others from similar acts. Always keeping due proportions, such punishments and such method of inflicting them ought to be chosen, therefore, which will make the strongest and most lasting impression on the minds of men, and inflict the least torment on the body of the criminal.[33]

Within this classical liberal viewpoint the seriousness of the crime was determined not by intent but by the harm to society.[34]

According to Garland, under the influence of positivist and neo-Darwinian discourses after 1895 the state began to intervene much more purposefully not only in prison reform but also in wider areas of social welfare.[35] Positivist science originated in a belief that the measurement, classification and observation of facts were an effective means of proving identifiable laws of human behaviour. This resulted in a deterministic approach to human motivation which concluded that 'since people were impelled to commit crime by constitutional and environmental forces beyond their control and, thus, were not responsible for their actions, treatment, not punishment, was the most appropriate legal response'.[36] One contemporary saw this as the strongest argument against this 'new school', because to accept it 'the doctrine of free-will must be abandoned. Yet without free-will there can be no personal responsibility, and the right to punish at once disappears.'[37]

It has been observed that the difference between Darwinism and neo-Darwinism is that the latter combined the importance placed by Darwin on the inheritance of characteristics, with older ideas regarding population pressure and the survival of the fittest. These ideas together produced an argument which maintained that intervention in the evolutionary process –

---

[33] C. Beccaria, *On Crimes and Punishments*, translated and introduced by H. Paolucci (Indianapolis: Bobbs-Merrill, 1963), pp. 42–3. Also see I. Taylor, P. Walton and J. Young, *The New Criminology: For a Theory of Deviance*, International Library of Sociology, ed. J. Rex (London: Routledge & Kegan Paul, 1973), ch. 1, and L. Radzinowicz, *Ideology and Crime: A Study of Crime in its Social and Historical Context* (London: Heinemann, 1966), ch. 1.

[34] Beccaria, *On Crimes and Punishments*, p. 65.

[35] Garland, *Punishment and Welfare*, ch. 3.

[36] Bailey, *English Prisons, 1895–1922*', p. 290. In a similar vein, Wiener suggests that positivist ideas had resulted in a 'diminishing sense of the power of the individual will into a new form; the criminal was no longer a wicked individual but rather a product of his environment and heredity'. See Wiener, *Reconstructing the Criminal*, p. 226.

[37] A. Griffiths, *Secrets of the Prison-House or Gaol Studies and Sketches, Vol. I* (London: Chapman and Hall, 1894), p. 37.

for instance, by segregating those considered to be genetically inferior or primitive – was justifiable.[38] Wiener contends that the diffusion of such ideas from the 1880s left two options for dealing with criminals:

> if neither moralization nor deterrence offered a solution, a different tack would be required. One could optimistically set about changing the environment, even the heredity, by social reform and eugenics, or one could pessimistically see little to be done beyond quarantine and perhaps gradual extinction.[39]

In his argument in support of the significance of positivist and neo-Darwinist ideas in this period, Garland cites increased individualisation as an important factor. He makes the distinction between the individualism existing in prisons prior to 1895 and the move towards individualisation which, he claims, 'alters the penal field fundamentally'.[40] He explains this by saying that the Victorian system went some way, through judicial discretion and the recognition of extenuating or aggravated circumstances, towards making the punishment appropriate to the individual offender. After 1895 there was a greater diversification in the range of penalties and sanctions available so that the appropriate treatment of each offender could be determined to a considerably greater extent. Therefore, according to Garland, the modern criminal justice system introduced after 1895 enabled offenders to be considered on the basis of 'specific characteristics', such as inebriety, youth or feeble-mindedness, which represented an individualisation. As a result of this change 'it became a respectable and established policy to disregard the formal equality of legal subjects and instead take account of their peculiarities as specific individuals'.[41]

Garland maintains that the ideological changes of the years from 1895 to 1914 were derived mainly from four origins, each of which sought to address the problem of social regulation and the proper role of the state. These he termed the 'criminological' programme, the 'eugenic' programme, the 'social security' programme, and the 'social work' programme.[42] The expansion of the science of criminology in the late nineteenth century had been remarkable and, according to Garland, brought to prominence an ideology in which the 'basis of crime no longer lay in sin or in faulty reasoning, but in an aberration or abnormality of the individual'. This change in ideology did not, however, represent a sudden break from classical to more positivist thought.

[38] W.J. Forsythe, *The Reform of Prisoners 1830–1900* (London: Croom Helm, 1987), pp. 173–5.
[39] Wiener, *Reconstructing the Criminal*, p. 228.
[40] Garland, *Punishment and Welfare*, p. 28.
[41] Ibid.
[42] Ibid., p. 74.

As Garland has suggested, the period between 1895 and 1914 witnessed the struggle between contesting discourses.[43]

The official rhetoric of the period does use the language of medical assessment and individualisation, but classical ideas about punishment remained prominent even within the same individuals. Evelyn Ruggles-Brise, Chairman of the Prison Commissioners and Directors from 1895 to 1921, displayed this parallel reasoning. In his history of the prison system published in 1921 he commented that it was 'only by the "individualisation of punishment" i.e., by a careful, and exact scientific system of preventive diagnosis that a true and correct assessment of criminal responsibility can be attained'.[44] Yet he also stated that the 'primary and fundamental purpose of punishment . . . must remain in its essence retributory and deterrent'.[45] To cite another prominent example, Winston Churchill, Home Secretary for eighteen months in 1910–11 and an enthusiastic prison reformer, stated in 1910 that 'we should have a regular series of scientifically graded institutions which would gradually and increasingly become adapted to the treatment of every variety of human weakness'.[46] Yet, as Bailey contends, Churchill was also firmly attached to a just proportionality between the offence and the punishment and was opposed to indeterminate sentencing.[47] According to Addison, one of Churchill's main concerns regarding preventive detention was that repetition of the offence rather than seriousness of the offence had been the main criterion for imposing it. During his time as Home Secretary, Churchill ordered that a circular be sent around the courts stressing that preventive detention should be reserved for only the worst offenders.[48]

In spite of ambiguities evident in the official rhetoric of the period, it is clear that the primacy of classical ideas, deterrence and uniformity, if not seriously challenged, was at least contended. One indication of this was public criticism of Du Cane and his administration towards the end of his career, as well as Du Cane's own bitterness at his increasing exclusion from the decision-making process.[49] In 1893, he complained about the way in which he was excluded from the discussion of matters relating to his own

---

[43] Ibid., p. 79.

[44] E. Ruggles-Brise, *The English Prison System* (London: Macmillan, 1921), pp. xv–xvi.

[45] Ibid., p. viii. Also see Forsythe, 'National Socialists and the English Prisons Commission', p. 136.

[46] Quoted in V. Bailey, 'Churchill as Home Secretary: Prison Reform', *History Today* 35 (March 1985), p. 10.

[47] Ibid., pp. 12–13. With regard to young offenders, for example, Churchill's main concern was that he felt they were often given sentences that were disproportionately severe relative to the crime they had committed. See P. Addison, *Churchill on the Home Front: 1900–1955* (London: Jonathan Cape, 1992), p. 114.

[48] Addison, *Churchill on the Home Front*, pp. 118–19.

[49] See S. McConville, *English Local Prisons 1860–1900: Next Only to Death* (London: Routledge & Kegan Paul, 1995), ch. 12.

department.[50] The charges made against Du Cane's regime in the closing years of his career reached their height in a series of articles in *The Daily Chronicle* entitled 'Our Dark Places'.[51] These articles included criticism of the militarist organisation of the prisons, insufficient workshop industry, the over-working of prison staff and the cruelty of the silent system. One over-arching accusation made by the self-appointed 'Special Commissioner' who wrote these articles was that the 'Men in our prisons are treated in the herd and the mass'.[52] Harding argues that reformers supporting a differing ideological standpoint from that of Du Cane exaggerated criticisms of the prison. This produced a convenient feeling of crisis which could be used to promote the need for change.[53]

A rather defensive Du Cane described the 1895 report of the Gladstone Committee as 'judge and jury to try the indictment, and the Prison Acts and the administration, considered as the subjects of the indictments'.[54] Although not critical of all the recommendations of the report, he saw in this much-heralded 'individualisation' dangers of anarchy, corruption and inequality.[55] What the Gladstone Committee Report did reveal was the mixing of a classical approach with elements of a contemporary, positivist criminology. The report concluded that both 'deterrence, and reformation' should be the 'primary and concurrent objects' of prison treatment.[56] It favoured a more 'elastic' system, 'more capable of being adopted to the special cases of individual prisoners'. The report also recommended a better system of classification to separate habituals, inebriates, the weak-minded and young offenders, with a consequent redistribution of prisoners to make it easier 'to apply to them the necessary special treatment'.[57] But the Committee also thought that a careful introduction of 'such reformatory influences as were brought to bear on convicts at Pentonville when first established' was worth considering, although this did not refer to the

---

[50] Du Cane Papers, Bodleian Library, Ms.Eng.hist.c.650/40, letter from Du Cane to Herbert Gladstone, Under Secretary of State, dated 20 August 1893.

[51] There is some disagreement about who actually wrote these articles. Forsythe, *Penal Discipline, Reformatory Projects*, p. 23 and Garland, *Punishment and Welfare*, p. 64 believe it was William Morrison, but McConville, *English Local Prisons*, p. 562 believes it was actually the editor of the newspaper, Massingham.

[52] Du Cane Papers, Bodleian Library, Ms.Eng.hist.c.650/89, memo regarding this series of articles; Ms.Eng.hist.c.650/91, cutting from *The Daily Chronicle* dated 25 January 1894; Ms.Eng.hist.c.650/92, cutting from *The Daily Chronicle* dated 29 January 1894.

[53] C. Harding, '"The Inevitable End of a Discredited System"? The Origins of the Gladstone Committee Report on Prisons, 1895', *Historical Journal* 31, No. 3 (1988), p. 601.

[54] E.F. Du Cane, 'The Prison Committee Report', *The Nineteenth Century* 38 (August 1895), p. 279.

[55] Ibid., pp. 288–9.

[56] Gladstone Committee Report, p. 22.

[57] Ibid., p. 12.

practice of an initial period in separate confinement, which they recommended should be reduced.[58]

Garland asserts that changes in penal policy increasingly enabled the determination of punishment to be based on the background and character of offenders, or in other words allowed a process of individualisation. In this process, it is suggested, the institution of the prison moved from the centre to the end of a range of penal options, and became a coercive last resort 'on an extended network of "alternatives to imprisonment" and special establishments'.[59] Garland maintains that although the prison remained an important coercive institution it was decentralised and reconstituted. The prison continued to be a sanction of major importance but was now used in a different manner. The increased use of non-custodial sanctions, primarily for the less serious types of offender, was enabled by the expansion of social welfare measures. In addition, the removal of some categories of offenders from the mainstream prisons into either more ostensibly treatment-oriented institutions or for preventive detention meant that the prison itself dealt increasingly with a narrower section of offenders.[60] According to Garland's thesis, therefore, the prison during the period from 1895 to 1914 operated to a greater extent as a kind of back-up sanction for other institutions.

Evidence of the diversion of offenders from the prisons reinforced another trend, which has been identified by Gatrell and Hadden in their examination of nineteenth-century criminal statistics – that of the reduction in the proportion of the general population who committed crime through dire need. Both these trends helped to reduce the prison population during the late Victorian and Edwardian eras. Gatrell and Hadden suggest that, as a result of the improving economic circumstances of the working classes from the 1860s, the prison population became more representative of the very lowest sections of society. They state that by the 1880s and 1890s,

> those who stole by habit or who had to steal to survive were more and more conspicuously the most depressed and the least literate in the population: and the increase in their average age and in the percentage who had past records suggests also that those who came before the courts were hard-core, confirmed criminals, in a new sense.[61]

[58] Ibid., p. 32.
[59] Garland, *Punishment and Welfare*, p. 28.
[60] Ibid.
[61] V.A.C. Gatrell and T.B. Hadden, 'Criminal Statistics and their Interpretation', in *Nineteenth Century Society*, ed. E.A. Wrigley (Cambridge: Cambridge University Press, 1972), p. 379

It is important to stress that the reduction in the prison population as a consequence of the improved economic position of the lower social classes began prior to the 1890s.

Garland maintains that, despite official rhetoric which often claimed the reverse, the role of the prison was displaced away from correction and reform and towards segregation as more specialised penal institutions expanded. What Garland calls 'the segregative sector' included the main-stream prisons, the state reformatories for inebriates and the feeble-minded, as well as the preventive detention institutions. These institutions 'operated as the coercive terminus for the whole penal network'.[62] Prison was, and remains, a means of segregating specified offenders from the rest of society. Certainly, Sykes has suggested, 'prison exists as a dramatic symbol of society's desire to segregate the criminal, whatever reasons may lie behind that desire'.[63]

A change in philosophy questioned

Debate about this period has, of course, concentrated upon the nature and extent of change; few would argue that this was not a time of institutional and welfare reform. Yet, as Bailey has pointed out, the mainstream prisons were 'still the mainstay of the criminal justice system in the early twentieth century'.[64] This questions the stress Garland places on the 'extended network of alternatives to the prison' and on specialisation within the penal complex. Change within differing penal institutions unfolded at varying speeds. In the years between 1895 and 1914 reform within the mainstream prisons was slow and the most significant changes were not implemented until after the First World War.

Despite the convergence in the administration of local and convict prisons, the two systems still presented differing problems inherent in the nature of the offenders they held. The Prison Commission was well aware of the marginal role of some of the more specialised new penal institutions and of the persistent problem of short-sentenced prisoners in local prisons. The Probation of Offenders Act 1907, which allowed for the probation of certain offenders as an alternative to a prison sentence, and the Criminal

---

[62] Garland, *Punishment and Welfare*, p. 242. The other two sectors that Garland identified were the 'normalising' sector, which included 'new, state-sponsored practices of probation, after-care and licensed supervision', and the 'correctional' sector, which included the various 'Borstals, reformatory schools, industrial schools and privately-run retreats and reformatories for the inebriate and the weak-minded', pp. 238–41.

[63] G.M. Sykes, *The Society of Captives: A Study of a Maximum Security Prison* (Princeton: Princeton University Press, 1958), p. 18.

[64] Bailey, 'English Prisons, 1895–1922', p. 318.

Justice Administration Act of 1914, which allowed magistrates to give time for offenders to pay fines, were clear attempts to divert petty offenders from a pattern of undergoing repeated short sentences.[65] Certainly, the Act of 1914 was a significant advance on the Prisons Act of 1898 by which offenders could pay any part of the fine and the same proportion of the prison sentence would be remitted, but which did not allow time to pay.[66]

The Prison Commissioners were clearly concerned to address what Ruggles-Brise referred to as the 'ceaseless tramp of this multitude of men, women and children, finding no rest behind prison walls, and only issuing thence to re-enter again', and the prison statistics suggest they achieved some considerable success.[67] According to the *Report of the Commissioners of Prisons and Directors of the Convict Prisons*, during the year ending 31 March 1905 the daily average population of the local prisons was 18,169.[68] By the year ending 31 March 1914 this had declined to 14,352.[69] A more rapid decline in the prison population was brought about by the effects of war and by the allowing of time for the payment of fines, so that the average daily population of the local prisons for the year ending 31 March 1919 was 7,073.[70]

The inmates of the local prisons in the early twentieth century were, however, still referred to as hopeless, even though a large proportion of these had offended against the newer regulatory laws introduced at the end of the nineteenth century. For example, in the year ending 31 March 1905 offences against police regulations and bye-laws composed 17 per cent of convictions.[71] The Prison Commissioners recognised that, to a large extent, the direction of prison reform was bypassing the majority of prisoners. In their report of 1912–13, they stated that if prison reform was to have any 'real meaning' it 'must be a question of how to deal effectively with the mass of persons, male and female, coming to prison under short sentences of a month or less'.[72]

With regard to local prisons, it is undeniable that the introduction of the classified prison sentence for prisoners after 1898 resulted in a more complex system of classification being made available within the criminal

---

[65] The Probation of Offenders Act 1907, 7 Edw.7.c.17. A sentence of probation was to be given with regard to 'the character, antecedents, age, health, or mental condition of the person charged, or to the trivial nature of the offence, or to extenuating circumstances'. The Criminal Justice Administration Act 1914, 4 & 5 Geo.5.c.58.

[66] The Prisons Act 1898, 40 & 41 Vict.c.21.s.2.

[67] Ruggles-Brise, *English Prison System*, p. xix.

[68] BPP, 1906(Cd.2723), L.9.

[69] RCPDCP, BPP, 1914 (Cd.7601), XLV.365.

[70] RCPDCP, BPP, 1919 (Cmd.374), XXVII.762.

[71] RCPDCP, BPP, 1906 (Cd.2723), L.14.

[72] RCPDCP, PP, 1912–13(Cd.6406), XLIII.352, report for the year ending 31 March 1912.

justice process. The 1898 Prison Act introduced three main classes for those not sentenced to penal servitude. Significantly, the decision with regard to individual classification was to be made by the courts. That the courts should classify prisoners was expected to be a move towards individualisation and rationalisation and away from the 'great evil' of stereotyped forms of prison sentencing.[73]

The first division was to correspond with the first division established, but little used, by the 1865 Prison Act. It was largely intended for offenders of conscience or of a political nature and imposed a relatively relaxed prison regime.[74] If the court gave no direction or gave a sentence with hard labour the prisoner was to be treated as an offender of the third division. However, the failure of the courts to take up this measure questions the extent of the diffusion of more positivist ideas regarding punishment. Furthermore, as Bailey points out, the criteria to be assessed by the courts included individualisation through attention to the character and antecedents of the offender, but also more classical considerations with regard to the nature of the crime and provocation.[75]

The resistance of a conservative judiciary circumvented the introduction of the classification of local prisoners. The Reports of the Prison Commissioners and the Directors of the Convict Prisons in the early twentieth century comment repeatedly that magistrates were not using the second division.[76] This division was intended to include first offenders and those without 'criminal habits' or those who were not guilty of offences of moral depravity.[77] The main objective of the second division was to keep these offenders away from the more criminal third division, although the actual conditions and regime of these two divisions were similar.[78] During the year ending 1901 only 2133, or 5 per cent, of those sentenced to imprisonment without hard labour had been placed in the second division, and only sixty had been placed in the first division.[79] The *Report of the Commissioners of Prisons and Directors of Convict Prisons* of 1907 referred to the 'sorry response' of the courts to implementing these divisions to the

---

[73] Ibid., 353.

[74] The Prison Act 1865, 28 & 29 Vict., c.126. Section 67 of this Act allowed misdemeanants to be divided into two classes. It was stated that 'a Misdemeanant of the First Division shall not be deemed to be a Criminal Prisoner within the Meaning of this Act'. Also see Forsythe, *Penal Discipline, Reformatory Projects*, pp. 98–9.

[75] Bailey, 'English Prisons, 1895–1922', p. 294. Also see the Prison Act 1898, 40 & 41 Vict., c.21.s.6.

[76] See RCPDCP, BPP, 1905 (Cd.2273), XXXVII.15; RCPDCP, BPP, 1906 (2723), L.20; RCPDCP, BPP, 1906 (Cd.3169), L.600; RCPDCP, BPP, 1909 (Cd.4847), XLV.144.

[77] RCPDCP, BPP, 1904 (1800), XXXV.25.

[78] Forsythe, *Penal Discipline, Reformatory Projects*, p. 98.

[79] RCPDCP, BPP, 1902 (Cd.804), XLV.9.

extent that 'What should be a judicial decision is now an administrative act *after* commitment on the part of the prison authorities.'[80]

The most consistent use to which the first division was put during this period was in dealing with the sentencing of suffragettes.[81] Indeed the suffragettes were to test to the full the differing status implied by the first division, but this will be examined in Chapter 7. Neglect of the second division meant that almost all local prisoners were going into the third division. What was required among the judiciary, according to one report, was 'a more modern conception of the nature and purpose of punishment'.[82] But to attempt to impose this would have required a far-reaching and politically controversial reform of the judiciary. Legislative changes alone were not sufficient to modify the entrenched classical ideology of the judiciary.

The classification system within the convict prisons was also modified. Three main classes were implemented under the administration of Ruggles-Brise: the star class, the intermediate class and the recidivist class. The aim was to separate what were considered to be the more criminal from the less criminal. Indeed, according to the Prison Commissioners, the star class, which was originally introduced as a result of the recommendations of a Royal Commission in 1877–8, was composed of offenders who they referred to as 'criminals by accident'. This was asserted because many of the offenders who were placed in this class belonged to higher social classes and would, the Commissioners maintained, have felt 'more keenly the disgrace of a conviction and the humiliation of penal servitude'.[83] Based on previous refinements in classification, these classes then provided the basis for some later changes – for instance, the reduction in the period of separation in 1899 to three months for stars, six months for intermediates and nine months for recidivists. This was further reduced in 1911 to one month for stars and intermediates and three months for recidivists.[84]

The successive reductions in the period of separation represent an important amelioration but one that was enjoyed only by the minority of offenders, that is those whose crimes were serious enough to merit a sentence of penal servitude. Furthermore, as Hobhouse and Fenner Brockway pointed out, the extension of classification in the local and convict prisons of this period was instigated by negative reasoning – a more effective prevention of

---

[80] *RCPDCP, BPP,* 1908 (Cd.3738), LII.12.

[81] Ibid., p. 13.

[82] *RCPDCP, BPP,* 1912–13(Cd.6406), XLIII.353.

[83] Ibid., p. 370.

[84] Ruggles-Brise, *English Prison System,* pp. 45–6. For an analysis of the role of the playwright and reformer, John Galsworthy, in bringing about the reductions in the period of separation, see M. Nellis, 'John Galsworthy's *Justice*', *British Journal of Criminology* 36, No. 1 (Winter 1996). Also see Forsythe, *Penal Discipline, Reformatory Projects,* pp. 63–7.

contamination, rather than, what they perceived as, the more important object of individual treatment.[85]

There was also increased specialisation within convict prisons during this period. For instance, Parkhurst specialised in physically and mentally weak male adults, Maidstone in star class convicts, Aylesbury in women convicts, Dartmoor and Portland in the most serious male offenders.[86] But much of this kind of specialisation had been developed and refined during the second half of the nineteenth century and very much as a result of concerns over contamination or control. The segregation of particular groups of convicts was implemented primarily from organisational and administrative motives, to facilitate supervision.

Imprisonment in this period continued to be a punitive experience and deterrence remained the primary justification for its imposition. The decline of labour on the public works and also of the use of unproductive treadwheel or crank labour in the local prisons resulted in an alleviation in the intensity of imprisonment, but alternative forms of hard labour were intended to be as exacting.[87] One indication of the concern that prison labour should continue to be arduous was the tightening up of the regulation of task labour in the local prisons.

In their report for the year ending 31 March 1905, the Prison Commissioners observed that there had been an increase in the number of punishments given in local prisons. The total number of offences by male prisoners for that year was 44,092 as compared with 26,437 in the previous year. They explained that the increase was due to a tightening up of the labour task of oakum picking, undergone in the first month of hard labour. The tasking of prisoners with reference to the quality of the oakum junk and the capacity of the workers had previously been at the discretion of the governors of individual local prisons, and this had resulted in considerable variations in practice. More definite rules regarding tasks and punishment for non-completion were, therefore, prescribed by the Commissioners.[88] Eight years later, this was still given as the cause of the increase in prison punishments. The continued increase in punishments was attributed to an initial 'difficulty in making prisoners realise that under the new system of marking, idleness would be detected and punished. Now that they are realizing it there is every reason to think that punishments will revert to the normal level of former years.'[89]

[85] Hobhouse and Fenner Brockway, *English Prisons Today*, p. 216.
[86] Forsythe, *Penal Discipline, Reformatory Projects*, p. 63.
[87] By May 1902 there remained only five treadwheels in use in the local prisons. PRO PCom7/332, memo from Ruggles-Brise to the Home Office, dated 1 May 1902.
[88] *RCPDCP*, BPP, 1906(Cd.2723), L.25.
[89] *RCPDCP*, BPP, 1914(Cd.7092), XLV.29.

The diverting of sectors of the criminal population into tributary institutions, such as Borstals, inebriate reformatories and preventive detention institutions, was one of the most obvious indications that more complex considerations than guilt were coming into play within the criminal justice system. But the actual numbers of offenders that were directed after conviction into the new specialised institutions were limited. For example, from a total of 151,329 offenders committed in the year ending 30 March 1914 only 487 were sentenced to Borstal imprisonment and 59 to preventive detention, while 150,045 were sentenced to ordinary imprisonment and 797 to penal servitude.[90] The daily average population of the local prisons in this year was 14,352 whereas the average population of the Borstals was 928. The daily average population in the preventive detention prisons was 171, and in state inebriate reformatories, 81.[91]

In addition to the limited number of prisoners actually diverted to the new penal institutions, one of the most obvious points to make with regard to the expansion of penal specialisation is the early failure of the inebriate reformatories established under the Inebriates Act of 1898.[92] Radzinowicz and Hood have suggested that these reformatories were set up with unrealistic expectations of being able to cure their inmates through extended confinement and medical treatment.[93] They also state that the regulations drawn up for this treatment were little more than 'an exercise in fantasy'.[94] The ambiguity of the term 'inebriate' and the reluctance of the judiciary to view this as a disease seriously affected the supply of inmates to the state and private reformatories. Furthermore, as Bailey has highlighted, a high proportion of the inmates of these institutions were women, which reflected moral rather than medical priorities.[95] Control problems and the failure to cure brought about an increasing reliance upon the kinds of disciplinary techniques used in the prisons. This undermined claims that the inebriate reformatories offered distinctive and individualised treatment. By 1921, all

---

[90] Ibid., p. 364. These figures include offenders imprisoned as debtors and in default of sureties but exclude military offenders.

[91] Ibid., p. 365.

[92] Inebriates Act 1898, 61 & 62 Vict., c.60. For objections to closure of one local inebriate reformatory see W.J. Collins, 'The Treatment of Inebriates, Municipal Reformers and the Farm Field Reformatory', *The Nineteenth Century and After* 74 (October 1913), pp. 764–73.

[93] L. Radzinowicz and R. Hood, *A History of English Criminal Law and its Administration from 1750*, Vol. 5 (London: Stevens, 1986), pp. 307–15.

[94] Ibid., p. 307. In the 1920s Mary Gordon, the first female inspector, claimed with regard to the inebriate reformatories that 'from the material that presently filled them, it became evident that cure was out of the question'. See M. Gordon, *Prison Discipline* (London: Routledge and Sons, 1922), p. 58.

[95] Bailey, 'English Prisons, 1895–1922', pp. 303–4.

of the inebriate reformatories were closed and the inmates integrated back into the mainstream penal system.[96]

Another new specialised penal institution which proved less than successful was preventive detention. Bailey points out that the 1908 Prevention of Crime Act, which allowed the preventive detention of offenders, represented a 'dual track' system which was an 'awkward alliance of classicism and positivism'.[97] Habitual offenders were first to undergo a sentence of penal servitude and then afterwards were to be detained in a preventive detention institution for between five and ten years. Release would be at the discretion of an Advisory Board, with a possibility of earlier discharge on licence.[98] According to Bailey, judges were nervous about such 'double sentencing' and were, therefore, reluctant to impose it. Churchill, who as Home Secretary tried to confine the use of preventive detention to the dangerous habitual criminal, did not improve this situation.[99]

Forsythe has also commented on the inadequacies of the system of preventive detention as well as on its eventual abolition in 1967.[100] Like Bailey, he concludes that preventive detention 'failed as a penal project because of judicial dislike of both indeterminacy and double sentencing'. This institution, he continues, exemplified the character of the modern penality of which Garland writes, combining segregation, indeterminacy and eugenic theory, and yet it was precisely these factors which undermined its operation.[101] The failure of preventive detention again demonstrates that changes in legislation alone were insufficient to overcome entrenched attitudes and practices in long-standing bodies such as the judiciary. Garland's thesis, with its concentration upon the discourses of the period, does not take full account of the rift between official rhetoric, legislation and penal practice.

Uncertainty regarding the philosophy upon which preventive detention was based was also reflected in disturbances by the inmates at the preventive detention institution on the Isle of Wight, Camp Hill. Soon after the opening of this institution the dissatisfaction of the prisoners became evident. The Church of England chaplain at the prison believed that the unrest at the prison, which constituted a combined refusal to obey orders, was partly caused by the 'uncertainty surrounding the date of discharge' that was

---

[96] Radzinowicz and Hood, History of English Criminal Law, pp. 308–9.
[97] Bailey, 'English Prisons, 1895–1922', p. 302.
[98] The Prevention of Crime Act 1908, 8 Edward.7.c.59. For a full account of the implementation and workings of this Act see Radzinowicz and Hood, History of English Criminal Law, pp. 268–87
[99] Bailey, 'English Prisons, 1895–1922', p. 302.
[100] This was, however, not the last incarnation of preventive detention. For example, the Mental Health Bill of 2002 signals the possible return of a form of preventive detention for individuals described as having serious personality disorders.
[101] Forsythe, Penal Discipline, Reformatory Projects, pp. 90–1.

inherent in a sentence of preventive detention. The Roman Catholic chaplain claimed that the disturbance was caused by disappointment. Some prisoners claimed that the judge who had sentenced them had said that at Camp Hill 'they would have all they desired except liberty'. The prisoners even claimed 'rights'. The Roman Catholic chaplain went on to explain that because 'they were not treated with severity several of them thought they had a right to complete relaxation of discipline'. As a result, those who were considered to be the leaders of the disturbance were transferred back to convict prisons. The remainder were 'made' to realise that 'they are prisoners under strict discipline until, by good conduct, they rise to a certain grade'.[102] Therefore, in the face of disobedience from the prisoners undergoing preventive detention, the prison authorities relied upon tried and tested control methods: strict discipline and transferring troublesome prisoners.

The selecting of groups of offenders for different treatment does not necessarily imply the predominance of positivist principles of individualisation and medical treatment. The mentally ill, juveniles, inebriates and even, on occasion, habitual criminals were considered less able to make, or incapable of making, moral choices. For these offenders the prison authorities were willing to explore outside the established prison system for alternative methods of control and reform. As Bailey has suggested, it was only for these groups that Ruggles-Brise was 'willing to waive the application of culpability, punishment, and moral reformation. Ruggles-Brise still perceived the attainment of obedience, discipline, order and habits of industry to be the most important aims of the prison system.'[103]

In the years from 1895 to 1914 there was, therefore, resistance to any shift away from adherence to classical ideas regarding punishment. Even in the face of existing variations in sentencing practices the courts were reluctant to relate the conditions and length of imprisonment primarily to the character or background of the offender rather than to the nature of the offence. Aside from the inherent conservatism of the judiciary this reluctance was in part a consequence of the difficulties in defining terms such as inebriate, mental defective and habitual criminal. Continuing disagreements within the prison medical service did little to alleviate these difficulties. One prominent argument was waged between Dr Charles Goring, the deputy medical officer at Parkhurst who had been encouraged by the Prison Commission to investigate the physical and mental condition of prisoners, and Dr Horatio Donkin, a retired Prison Medical Commissioner.[104] This argument highlighted the basic disagreements between those who believed in the primacy of hereditarily

---

[102] RCPDCP, BPP, 1914(Cd.7092), XLV.27–8 & 291–8.
[103] Bailey, 'English Prisons, 1895–1922', p. 315.
[104] Forsythe, Penal Discipline, Reformatory Projects, pp. 153–5. Also see PRO HO45/10563/172511, Dr C. Goring, The English Convict, 1913.

transmitted inferiority and those, like Donkin, who believed in the primacy of environmental factors.

Another important issue which provoked considerable debate in this period was the enforcement of silence in both local and convict prisons. The Gladstone Committee had cautiously suggested reform of the silent system, commenting that,

> the privilege of talking might be given after a certain period as a reward for good conduct on certain days for a limited time, and under reasonable supervision, to all long-sentenced prisoners, local as well as convict, who have conducted themselves well, and who are not deemed unsuitable for the privilege.[105]

A long-sentenced division was established for those convicts who had earned marks representing a ten-year sentence; sufficient marks could actually be earned in seven and a half years through good conduct. In this division, meals could be taken in association and conversation was allowed at exercise and meals.[106] The existing system had offered no further privileges after the first four years of a convict's penal servitude until the last year of their sentence, at which point they entered the special class. After four years convicts had, therefore, merely 'marked time'.[107] The only incentive in the intervening period was the negative one of losing privileges that had already been earned.

Both the Prison Commissioners and staff within the individual prisons were resistant and most refused to use their discretion to allow talking at exercise even for long-sentenced, well-behaved convicts.[108] Ruggles-Brise went so far as to attribute disturbances at Parkhurst and Dartmoor to a relaxation of the 'so-called' silent system – so-called because many governors believed that it did not curtail talking at all.[109] By 1907, only one local prison governor allowed the talking privilege, although the situation in the convict prisons was somewhat better.[110]

The perceived need to control communications between prisoners, and the possible consequences of the failure to do this effectively, were at the heart of resistance to reform by prison staff at all levels of the prison system. Du Cane could not have been alone in the fears he had expressed about the dangers of unequal treatment leading to 'anarchy'. In a letter to the Under Secretary of State (5 December 1901), Ruggles-Brise commented

---

[105] Gladstone Committee Report, p. 29, para. 73.
[106] Forsythe, *Penal Discipline, Reformatory Projects*, p. 63.
[107] RCPDCP, BPP, 1906 (Cd.3169), L.610–11.
[108] RCPDCP, BPP, 1902 (Cd.1278), XLV.17. The rule regarding talking was actually changed in 1899.
[109] PRO HO45/10048/A62416/3.
[110] Thomas, *English Prison Officer*, p. 130.

that a 'discretionary power works very badly in Convict Prisons'; as convicts were transferred from prison to prison any inequalities in treatment would be a cause of discontent. Dissatisfaction through feelings of relative deprivation was seen as a potential cause of discontent and conflict.[111]

Resistance to the breaking down of the silent system was due to the caution common in the face of all reforms, that of creating a precedent that could not be withdrawn without possible conflict. Officials commented on the tendency for privileges gained by prisoners to be taken for granted and almost immediately considered a right to be defended. With regard to the convicts in the long-sentenced division, for example, the governor of Dartmoor commented that they appreciated the extra privileges they were allowed, but it was 'characteristic of the English convict that a few have been dissatisfied at not getting more; for what is granted as an indulgence soon comes to be regarded as an elementary right'.[112] Thomas cites Sykes, describing the transition from a situation where rewards are given for good behaviour, to one where inmates perceive these as a right. Once this has occurred, the rewards lose value as a means of control.[113] Thomas fails, however, to consider that improvement in the treatment of prisoners through the giving of privileges might, depending upon the particular circumstances, alleviate the original or potential causes of prison disorder.

A further area of criticism of Garland's thesis has been that he fails to take sufficient account of penal developments before the retrenchment of the second half of the nineteenth century. Thus, Forsythe has criticised Garland's thesis for failing to take adequate account of reformatory projects that existed prior to the 1860s.[114] Forsythe maintains that reformatory aims were inherent not only in the 'techniques of admonition, sermonising, education, assessment, [and] behavioural conditioning' which had been introduced in the period between 1800 and 1865, but in the very principles of the architecture of the separate prisons.[115] Although Chapter 3 of this publication maintains that the local take-up of these reformatory projects varied considerably, there is little doubt that the prison system did become more organised and those who operated it more skilled in methods of control. Forsythe believes, however, that the reformatory projects inherent in the separate system prior to 1865 were aimed at an individualistic and

---

[111] See W.G. Runciman, *Relative Deprivation and Social Justice: A Study of Attitudes to Social Inequality in the Twentieth Century* (London: Routledge & Kegan Paul, 1972).

[112] RCPDCP, BPP, 1906 (Cd.3169), l.1131.

[113] Thomas, *English Prison Officer*, pp. 131–2. Also see Sykes, *Society of Captives*, ch. 3.

[114] Forsythe, 'The Garland Thesis', pp. 259–73.

[115] Ibid., p. 261. Also see R. Evans, *The Fabrication of Virtue: English Prison Architecture 1750–1840* (Cambridge: Cambridge University Press, 1982), p. 5. Evans identifies a 'profound belief in the transforming powers of architecture'.

'permanent alteration of attitude and conduct from vice, wickedness and lawlessness to virtue, religion and obedience to law'.[116]

According to Forsythe, the treatment of offenders in the penal institutions of the mid-nineteenth century was operated on an individual basis with meticulous reports of prison offences and punishments being kept on each offender. Forsythe also emphasises the accumulation of case study-type material on prisoners during this period.[117] Therefore, it is important to recognise that, although the recording of behaviour may have become more efficient after 1895, reflecting the growing concern with individual reform, the organised keeping of records on prisoners had been common practice in both local and convict prisons as far back as the first half of the nineteenth century. This was one of the factors that enabled Foucault to assert that by the 1840s the modern prison had been established.

Forsythe presents the deterrent period from 1865 to 1895 as witnessing the dismembering of the reformatory projects of the first half of the nineteenth century. He also maintains that Garland's lack of consideration of prison reform implemented prior to the 1860s explains his over-estimation of the achievements of positivist and neo-Darwinist ideology between 1895 and 1914. Therefore, Forsythe suggests that 'Garland picked up on a system which had become deliberately and overwhelmingly deterrent as a flight from the earlier interventive reformative aim of punishment.'[118]

One of the main changes Garland identifies in the mainstream prisons from 1895 to 1914 was the increase in rewards, as opposed to what he describes as 'the older purely negative system of punishment for mis-behaviour'.[119] Under this he places the discretionary granting of permission to talk, the mark system of gratuities and a new system of remission extended to local prisons. Despite the resistance to the talking privilege, reward mechanisms were certainly extended in this period, most notably to the local prisons. Nevertheless, even at the height of deterrence in convict prison administration between the mid-1860s and the 1890s marks were used as an inherent and crucial part of the progressive stage system as well as of the procedures for earning remission and gratuities. The use of a continuum of both reward and punishment mechanisms in the control and regulation of the behaviour of convict prisoners had become standard practice in the public works convict prisons well before the 1890s. The importance of developments in the prison system prior to the 1890s was acknowledged by the Prison System Enquiry Committee, which compiled the publication, *English Prisons Today* (1922). They stated that the

---

[116] Forsythe, 'The Garland Thesis', p. 261.
[117] Ibid., p. 262.
[118] Ibid., p. 266.
[119] Garland, *Punishment and Welfare*, p. 24.

new rules introduced under the 1898 Prison Act did not constitute anything approaching to a revolution in the system . . . but rather were a development, on less repressive lines, of the older system of discipline, which is intimately associated with the name of Sir Edmund Du Cane.[120]

Conclusion

There were clearly changes in the regimes in the convict and local prisons in this period. Many of these were considered by the prisoners and prison officials to be improvements or alleviations. During her fifteen years in women's convict prisons from 1889 to 1904, Florence Maybrick identified several improvements for women. Among these she listed the obtaining of a night-dress, a floor mat, a wooden stool, toothbrushes, tea substituted for cocoa, white bread instead of wholemeal, and the decline in solitary from nine months to four months. She also commented on prisoners being allowed an increased number of letters and visits.[121]

It was largely the longer-sentenced prisoners who benefited from such reforms in the mainstream prisons in this period. One of the most important steps for local prisoners was the eligibility, from September 1907, to earn remission of up to a sixth of their sentence after serving one month.[122] But this still effectively excluded a large proportion of short-sentenced prisoners. Of 205,000 committals to prison in 1909, for instance, 61 per cent were for periods of a fortnight or less.[123] The final demise of the treadwheel and the crank and the significant reduction of oakum picking after 1895 were of both real and symbolic importance. All treadwheels and cranks were abolished in local prisons by 1901.[124] Changes in the convict prisons were diverse. The period of initial separation was successively reduced and the system of classification refined. In addition, the *Report of the Commissioners of Prisons and Directors of Convict Prisons* for the year ending 31 March 1911 announced that definite arrangements had been made for two lectures and two musical entertainments per year at each convict prison.[125] The same report also announced the extension of the red-collar system, whereby 'trustworthy prisoners are employed away from immediate supervision', from convict to

---

[120] Hobhouse and Fenner Brockway, *English Prisons Today*, p. 73. Also see Sean McConville's assessment of the very limited achievements of the 1898 Prisons Act, *English Local Prisons*, ch. 17.

[121] F. Maybrick, *My Fifteen Years Lost* (New York: Funk & Wagnalls, 1905), pp. 134–6.

[122] RCPDCP, BPP, 1908 (Cd.4300), LII.469.

[123] Addison, *Churchill on the Home Front*, p. 116.

[124] RCPDCP, PP, 1902(Cd.804), XLV.26.

[125] RCPDCP, PP, 1911(Cd.5891), XXXIX.259.

local prisons.[126] These changes certainly amounted to an alleviation in the intensity and severity of imprisonment in the period from 1895 to 1914.

In the mainstream prisons, the pace of reform was restrained by long-standing and entrenched administrative and control mechanisms. Predominant among these was the hierarchical and militaristic structure of the prison staff. Under the administration of Du Cane, prison officers had enjoyed largely unquestioned support of their day-to-day authority over the prisoners, which was particularly evident in the, often cursory, investigation of the complaints of prisoners against prison staff.[127] By the late nineteenth century, this was less evident and more emphasis was given to reformatory measures. Even though the actual extent of reform in the mainstream prisons during this period was limited, this exacerbated prison officers' resentment given the hostility that had been shown by the prison authorities to agitation by prison officers to improve their pay and conditions and to establish a prison officers' union. This was also partly due to the fact that the reforms that were implemented in the marginal penal institutions – the Borstals, inebriate reformatories and the preventive detention institution – received an amount of attention in the official reports out of proportion to their importance, certainly in terms of the number of prisoners they held. Furthermore, with regard to the reforms that were implemented, little confidence was shown in the suitability of prison officers to play a constructive role. This not only alienated the prison officers further but also reinforced the restriction of their role to the maintenance of custody and security.

The ideology behind the reforms in the criminal justice system in the years from 1895 to 1914 and the nature of the changes that were implemented were complex. The predominance of classical ideology in guiding penal policy was challenged. But this was not an easy conquest and Garland accepts that the extension of positivism was afflicted by the 'resistances, contradictions, limitations and failures, which ensure that no complex strategy is ever a total success'.[128] Despite this acceptance, and as Bailey suggests, Garland underestimates the tenacity of a classical ideology which remained the main conceptual pillar of the English criminal justice system.[129] Certainly, the resistance of an inherently conservative judiciary has played

---

[126] Ibid., 265. These prisoners were identified by a band on their left arm.

[127] See Chapter 5.

[128] Garland, *Punishment and Welfare*, p. 257.

[129] For example, it has been pointed out that the British delegates to the Berlin Penitentiary Congress of 1935 adhered to the classical view 'that criminality, whilst effected by heredity and environment, was primarily the result of free moral choice'. This was in contrast to the approach of the delegates from Germany who emphasised a eugenic approach to criminality which 'favoured such methods as sterilization, permanent segregation and execution'. See Forsythe, 'National Socialists and the English Prison

an important part in ensuring the continued predominance of classical principles.

The repeated references to 'individualisation' by contemporaries of this period serve to confuse attempts to perceive the motivations behind reform. Supporters of both classical and more positivist ideologies could quite consistently make use of this concept since it was often not defined. Individualisation could mean a belief in the rational choice of the prisoner and therefore the establishment of a system of meticulously recorded rewards and punishments. Alternatively individualisation could mean the critical assessment of the mental condition and physical environment of the offender to determine the correct 'treatment' for him or her.

The failure of both preventive detention and the state inebriate reformatories leaves only the mainstream prisons in Garland's 'segregative sector'. The local prisons, especially, continued to provide the symbolic backbone of the criminal justice system. Nevertheless, as Bailey asserts, one of the most significant achievements of this period was 'the reduction in the number [of offenders] passing through the prison turnstile', in the context of a 'profound scepticism' about the effectiveness and purpose of imprisonment prior to the First World War.[130] Despite reforms, the purposes of the prison remained unchanged as the long-standing formula of retribution, deterrence and reformation. The Prison Commissioners continued to assert that any inversion of these factors of punishment would 'be fatal'.

Reform in the local and convict prisons was not far-reaching, nor did it significantly alter the fundamentally deterrent character of the prison discipline. Indeed,

> the ameliorations introduced by Ruggles-Brise and the Home Office did not – nor were ever intended to – alter the basic purposes of penal servitude which were severe punishment, deterrence and the demonstration of the awesome power of the state over those who defied its laws.[131]

Cross has commented that the changes to prison conditions in this period were in no sense spectacular. The convict's head was still cropped, prison clothes were still an ill-fitting 'dress of shame, bespattered with broad arrows, work might be in association, but there was very little recreation in association, and as much as seventeen hours out of twenty-four might be spent in the cell (more still on Sundays)'.[132] Nevertheless, gradual reform was in the spirit of the age and further reforms were implemented after the

Commission', p. 132; also see pp. 133–7 for discussion of the beliefs of members of the English Prison Commission 1914–35.
[130] Bailey, 'English Prisons, 1895–1922', pp. 318–20.
[131] Forsythe, *Penal Discipline, Reformatory Projects*, p. 70.
[132] R. Cross, *Punishment, Prison and the Public* (London: Stevens, 1971), p. 17.

First World War. This was partly a result of the accumulation of pressure from political prisoners who had experienced the inside of the prison walls over the previous ten years. In 1921, the close cropping of convicts' hair was abolished, and from March 1922 older prison uniforms were gradually phased out; the new ones had the broad arrow stencilled on the inside.[133] In 1922, the initial period of separation for convicts was suspended, and in 1931 it was formally abolished.[134]

---

[133] B.2.15, *Among the Broad-Arrow Men: A Plain Account of English Prison Life* (London: A & C Black, 1924), p. 183. On the hesitant nature of prison reform in the period after the First World War, see Bailey, 'English Prisons, 1895–1922', pp. 299–300.

[134] Nellis, 'John Galsworthy's *Justice*', p. 81. Also see Bailey 'English Prisons, 1895–1922', p. 301. Bailey states that for those imprisoned with hard labour the preliminary period of separate confinement still existed until 1931.

7

Political prisoners and prisoners of conscience, 1850 to 1920

It is clear from Chapter 6 that the criminal justice system continued to be based fundamentally on classical principles which related the level of punishment principally to the seriousness of the offence, although provocation, mitigating circumstances and insanity could also be considered.[1] There was, however, one type of offender that seriously challenged the association between the level of punishment and the seriousness of the offence: these were offenders who were often referred to as political prisoners, or prisoners of conscience, even in official documentation. These prisoners posed moral conundrums in a liberal society, especially for Liberal politicians. Certainly, offenders who committed politically motivated crimes were able repeatedly to force concessions from governments. It was asserted in Parliament in 1912 that 'motive must be a strong element in our moral judgement upon the crime, and that motive ought to be taken into account by the judge in passing sentence' upon such offenders, in this case suffragettes. However, successive British governments never accepted this as a rule, nor has a generic definition been established in law.[2]

The groups of political offenders that were imprisoned during the period from the 1850s until 1920 were extremely diverse and included Irish nationalists, suffragettes, conscientious objectors to compulsory conscription, socialists, members of the Salvation Army and anti-compulsory

---

[1] For an account of the legislation and practice with regard to the criminally insane during the nineteenth century see J. Saunders, 'Institutionalised Offenders: A Study of the Victorian Institution and its Inmates with Special Reference to Late Nineteenth Century Warwickshire', Ph.D. thesis, Warwick University, 1983, pp. 220–4.

[2] *Hansard's Parliamentary Debates*, vol. 38, col. 2028, 22 May 1912, McKenna, the Home Secretary, 'Suffragist Prosecutions, Sentences'. McKenna also stated that motive should be taken into account when 'advising upon the exercise of the prerogative of mercy. On all those points all my predecessors in office on both sides of the House would agree.' It is important to note one exception to the lack of legal recognition of political prisoners. As Radzinowicz and Hood explain, the Prison Act of 1877 stipulated that offenders convicted of sedition should be accorded separate treatment under the rules for firstclass misdemeanants. However, by the last quarter of the nineteenth century prosecution for sedition was rare and the offence had been rendered largely obsolete by the creation in 1848 of the crime of treason-felony. See L. Radzinowicz and R. Hood, 'The Status of Political Prisoners in England: The Struggle for Recognition', *Virginia Law Review* 65, No. 8 (1979).

vaccinationists. The crimes for which they were committed to prison were also diverse. These ranged from obstruction and assault to criminal damage, conspiring to subvert the government and refusal to obey military regulations.

To give a definition to encompass such diverse groups of 'political prisoners' is far from straightforward, and a broad meaning is taken here. It is recognised that given the limited space that can be devoted to such a complex area, any definition of these groups must be an over-simplification. The definition used here is also one predicated upon the English experience. Nevertheless, a common factor which defines these groups as political is that they were involved in resistance, passive or active, that was deemed by the state (represented by official bodies such as the courts) to be either against the law or a threat to law and order. Resistance was justified by such political groups on the basis of a lack of, or deprivation of, certain rights or liberties claimed by them. These specified actual or potential rights or liberties were within the realms of the power of the state to maintain, withhold or establish. The contested areas of what constituted a 'political' act and what constituted the law, the breaking of the law or a threat to the law, meant that the subject of political prisoners attracted considerable ideological debate. This is a much broader definition than, for instance, that adhered to by Amnesty International which includes only prisoners of conscience, that is those imprisoned for their own views or associations and who have neither used nor advocated violence.[3] In some cases, political offenders sought imprisonment. Imprisonment entailed the expropriation of citizenship rights and brought the offender effectively down to the level of the criminal or the mentally ill. Political offenders perceived this as an attempt to degrade them. It was also perceived as a coercive technique that highlighted the injustice or inequality that they maintained required political action to resolve, and which justified their illegal actions.

Harding has suggested that there were three main categories of political prisoners in this period. In the first category he locates those who committed conventional criminal acts but from political motivations. This category would include the Irish dynamiters of the 1880s and some suffragettes. In his second category he places those who have broken the law through passive resistance or whose offences are breaches of public order only. The most prominent group of offenders in this category would be conscientious objectors to compulsory military service during the First World War, although this would also include groups such as objectors to vaccination and some suffragettes. Harding's third category of political prisoners contains those who were detained in times of emergency although they have, in most cases,

---

[3] A. Neier, 'Confining Dissent, The Political Prison', in *The Oxford History of the Prison: The Practice of Punishment in Western Society*, ed. N. Morris and D.J. Rothman (Oxford: Oxford University Press, 1995), p. 392.

committed no criminal offence. This last category would include prisoners of war detained in internment camps in England during the First World War and also Irish nationalists detained in May 1918. Both groups were detained under the Defence of the Realm Act (DORA), August 1914 (amended November 1914 and March 1915).

This chapter deals with prisoners who come within all three of Harding's categories but with one important exception. This exception takes into account the exceptional circumstances of wartime Britain (1914–18). During the First World War, some prisoners were openly recognised as being political, that is they were recognised as prisoners of war. Other prisoners regarded themselves as prisoners of war but were not legally recognised as such, namely the Irish nationalists imprisoned in May 1918. An important and defining consequence of this difference was that legally recognised prisoners of war were detained under the shared or ultimate authority of the War Office – for example, enemy alien civilians interned in Britain.[4] Irish nationalists imprisoned without trial under the Defence of the Realm Act were, for the most part, under the authority of the Home Office during their imprisonment, the same authority that dealt with ordinary criminals. This chapter refers only to those political prisoners that were predominantly under the control of the Home Office.

Historical research regarding political prisoners of this period has often been undertaken as only one element of a wider examination of the movements to which they belonged. A couple of examples of such work for the period around the First World War are John Rae's account of conscientious objectors and Stephen Hartley's consideration of the Irish question in terms of British foreign policy.[5] The subject matter covered by this chapter is both narrower and broader than much of this research. It is narrower in the sense that it concentrates predominantly on the prison experiences of these offenders and on the strategies developed by government and prison authorities to cope with them. It is broader in the sense that it does not examine the experiences of only one group of 'politicals' but of several, although the range of the groups included has been limited to enable concentration on the most significant challenges to the prison system. The most prominent similar approach to this subject

---

[4] See J.C. Bird, *Control of Enemy Alien Civilians in Great Britain 1914–1918* (New York: Garland Publishing, 1986), pp. 12, 49 and 132–3. To be precise, several government departments shared practical responsibility for different aspects of the problems posed by interned enemy alien civilians. For example, responsibility for the internment camps at Knockaloe and Douglas on the Isle of Man was divided between the Home Office and the War Office

[5] J. Rae, *Conscience and Politics: The British Government and the Conscientious Objector to Military Service 1916–1919* (London: Oxford University Press, 1970); S. Hartley, *The Irish Question as a Problem in British Foreign Policy 1914–1918* (London: Macmillan Press, 1987).

has been by Leon Radzinowicz and Roger Hood who have also directly addressed the historical confinement of political offenders in English prisons.[6]

Those offenders who perceived themselves to have acted from political motives often sought recognition from government by obtaining treatment different from that meted out to ordinary prisoners. Acknowledgement of status as political prisoners would lend them public credibility. In contrast to the majority of ordinary prisoners, political offenders were often members of organisations that were able to give support and publicise their treatment. Public knowledge did not, however, necessarily correlate with public sympathy; for example, the mood of the public remained largely against conscientious objectors for most of the war.[7] Many political offenders were wealthier and better educated than the average prisoner. Leading suffragettes had friends and relatives among the Members of Parliament sitting to decide which strategies to adopt in dealing with the 'tactical creativity' of the suffragettes both inside and outside of prison.[8] June Purvis believes that historians have too readily assumed that suffragettes were 'bourgeois'.[9] However, the leaders of these movements were often from wealthy and influential families.

There were three main groups of political prisoners who made their presence felt in English prisons between 1850 and 1920: Irish nationalists, suffragettes, and conscientious objectors to compulsory military service. These groups of prisoners were a prominent cause of disorder – disorder which sometimes spread to ordinary prisoners. For a prison system that had developed primarily to deal with inmates who had little influence and who often originated from the lowest classes of society, the presence of political prisoners brought particular problems. The public attention they attracted through their activities and their political influence and connections placed both the prison authorities and the prison staff under considerable pressure. As Thomas has suggested, the three main groups of political prisoners 'were the subject of confused and ambivalent feelings on the part of the public and Parliament, and all three presented prison staff with very difficult problems of control'.[10]

---

[6] Radzinowicz and Hood, 'Status of Political Prisoners', pp. 1421–81.

[7] T.C. Kennedy, 'Public Opinion and the Conscientious Objector, 1915–1919', *Journal of British Studies* 12, No. 2 (May 1973), p. 108.

[8] I.C. Fletcher, '"A Star Chamber of the Twentieth Century": Suffragettes, Liberals, and the 1908 "Rush the Commons" Case', *Journal of British Studies* 35 (October 1996), p. 508.

[9] J. Purvis, 'The Prison Experiences of Suffragettes in Edwardian England', *Women's History Review* 4, No. 1 (1995), pp. 103–33.

[10] J.E. Thomas, *The English Prison Officer since 1850: A Study in Conflict* (London: Routledge & Kegan Paul, 1972), p. 136.

During the second half of the nineteenth century the increasing centralisation of the prison system meant that central government had more direct influence over the treatment of political prisoners. An important step in determining the length of sentence as well as the treatment which political offenders received was the passing in 1848 of the Treason Felony Act, which introduced the crime of treason-felony. Prior to this, two pieces of legislation had been generally applied, but were perceived by the government to be insufficient to deal with the last Chartist uprising of 1848 and, more especially, the Fenian rebellion of the same year. High treason was too narrowly defined and juries were reluctant to convict given the very severe penalty that was imposed for this offence, the 'severing of the head and quartering'.[11] In addition, speech could not be treasonable and the alternative crime of sedition was only a misdemeanour. The new offence, treason-felony, made treason a felony which could be punished by trans-portation or penal servitude within the country. It also aimed to deprive political offenders of prestige by treating them like ordinary convicts.[12]

Irish nationalists

Most of the Irish nationalists imprisoned in England in this period were Fenians. The name 'Fenian' had been taken from a legendary band of pre-Christian warriors who stood for high ideals, chivalry and Irish nation-hood.[13] In its late usage the word 'Fenian' referred to the members of the Irish Republican Brotherhood (IRB), established in 1858, or to the Fenian Brotherhood in America. By the mid-1860s the word was used widely as a generic term for all Irish nationalists.[14] During the second half of the nineteenth century, and again after the Easter Rising of 1916, large numbers of Fenians became subject to the treason-felony legislation introduced in 1848. Sinn Fein, which had links with the IRB, also had large numbers of its members imprisoned in England.[15] Sinn Fein was a Republican group established in 1902 by Arthur Griffith, who was imprisoned in England in 1916 and 1918.

[11] Radzinowicz and Hood, 'Status of Political Prisoners', pp. 1436–7.
[12] Ibid.
[13] P. Quinlivan and P. Rose, *The Fenians in England* (London: John Calder, 1982), p. 1.
[14] For a summarised account of the events surrounding the establishment of the Irish Republican Brotherhood see J. Lee, *The Modernisation of Irish Society 1848–1919* (Dublin: Gill & Macmillan), pp. 53–9. Also see Quinlivan and Rose, *Fenians in England*, pp. 1–5.
[15] For instance, de Valera, who in October 1917 became President of Sinn Fein, had been a member of the IRB in 1916, and by 1918 Michael Collins, as well as being Director of Organisation in the Volunteers, was a leading members of the IRB. See P. Colum, *Arthur Griffith* (Dublin: Gill & Macmillan, 1959), p. 175.

There were several waves of Irish nationalist activity and imprisonment between 1850 and 1920. The first wave of prisoners was confined as a result of Fenian activity during the 1860s and 1870s, including an attempted insurrection in Ireland in March 1867. This period witnessed some events that rocked contemporary public opinion and increased prejudice against the Irish.[16] The blowing up of the boundary wall of Clerkenwell Prison was perhaps the most sensational of these events. During a failed attempt to rescue two imprisoned Fenians in December 1867, one of them a leader in the movement, a row of houses opposite Clerkenwell Prison was blown up killing three people and injuring over a hundred. *The Times* referred to the Clerkenwell explosion as 'an act of wholesale and deliberate murder' and 'the worst crime of modern English history'.[17]

The second wave of Irish nationalist activity was broadly between 1880 and 1887 and was the earliest development of terrorist activities in Britain. The money and much of the personnel came from two Irish-American organisations, O'Donovan Rossa's Skirmishers and Clan na Gael.[18] Terrorist attacks in the form of dynamite attacks on public buildings intentionally made use of violence to further the aims of the Republican movement. The violence ended due to the continued opposition of the IRB to the use of dynamite and also the threat of the withdrawal of American sanctuary.[19]

Two waves of imprisonment of Irish nationalists also occurred during the First World War. The first followed the Easter Rising which began on 24 April 1916, and the second was in May 1918 under the Defence of the Realm Act. During the Easter Rising a republic was proclaimed which declared 'the right of the people of Ireland to the ownership of Ireland, and to the unfettered control of Irish destinies to be sovereign and indefeasible'.[20] The rebels were defeated within a week and fourteen were executed, including Thomas Clarke, who had served fifteen years' penal servitude between 1883 and 1898 for his Fenian activities and was also the first signatory of the proclamation of 1916.[21] The execution of the rebels changed the initial public confusion in Ireland over the events into overt hostility towards the British government.

---

[16] N. McCord, 'The Fenians and Public Opinion in Great Britain', in *Fenians and Fenianism*, ed. M. Harmon (Dublin: Scepter Books, 1970).

[17] *The Times*, 16 December 1867, p. 8, col. e.

[18] K.R.M. Short, *The Dynamite War: Irish-American Bombers in Victorian Britain* (Dublin: Gill & Macmillan), p. 1.

[19] Short, *The Dynamite War*, pp. 225–7.

[20] *The Sinn Fein Rebellion Handbook*, compiled by *The Weekly Irish Times*, 1916 (2nd edition). This publication claimed to be a 'Complete and Connected Narrative of the Rising'.

[21] T. Clarke, *Glimpses of an Irish Felon's Prison Life*, introduction by P.S. O'Hegarty (Dublin: Maunsel & Roberts, 1922), p. xiii. O'Hegarty refers to Clarke as 'the embodiment of Fenianism'.

Eamon de Valera was reprieved for his role in the Rising partly, it has been claimed, due to his American citizenship. He was sentenced to penal servitude for life.[22] Those seriously implicated in the rebellion were treated as convicts and imprisoned in England. Those against whom there was no direct charge, over 1500, were interned at Frongoch in Wales.[23] All those imprisoned as a result of the Rising were released by June 1917. Although the Easter Rising had been the work of the IRB, the press and the British government attributed it to Sinn Fein and inadvertently gave the faltering organisation an enormously increased notoriety.[24]

The fact that the imprisonment of Sinn Fein leaders in May 1918, as well as the internment of enemy aliens, was brought about under the Defence of the Realm Act caused some concern in England regarding what was seen as the side-lining of the due process of the law. It was pointed out in *The Times* that the Defence of the Realm Act enabled imprisonment without either a charge or a trial. It was feared that one of the main guarantees of individual freedom was being destroyed. Nevertheless, while the country was at war, the public were not likely 'to quarrel with the thoroughness in the Defence of the Realm, even though it should mean an occasional act of hardship or injustice to individuals'.[25] The Sinn Fein leaders detained in May 1918 were imprisoned without trial on the pretext that they had been involved in a 'German Plot'. The actual reason for their detention may have been Sinn Fein's opposition to the introduction of compulsory conscription in Ireland.[26] Some individuals were imprisoned in both 1916 and 1918, most prominently Eamon de Valera who later became head of Sinn Fein. Indeed, the imprisonment of the leaders of the IRB in 1916 and of Sinn Fein in 1918 played an instrumental role in determining the organisation of Sinn Fein and enhancing the vote-winning power of the party.[27] In the election of December 1918 Sinn Fein won seventy-three seats; of these seventy-three members, forty-three were in various prisons.[28]

---

[22] Hartley, *The Irish Question*, p. 61.

[23] Colum, *Arthur Griffith*, p. 161.

[24] Ibid., p. 171. Also see J.J. Lee, *Ireland 1912–1985, Politics and Society* (Cambridge: Cambridge University Press, 1989), p. 38. A further example of the attributing of the Easter Rising to Sinn Fein was in a publication by *The Weekly Irish Times* in 1916 entitled the *Sinn Fein Rebellion Handbook* which claimed to be a complete account of the rebellion.

[25] *The Times*, 10 February 1916, p. 9, col. c.

[26] F.S.L. Lyons, *Ireland Since the Famine* (London: Weidenfeld and Nicolson, 1971), pp. 390–7.

[27] M. Laffan, 'The Unification of Sinn Fein in 1917', *Irish Historical Studies* 17 (1970–1), pp. 373–9. Also see Lee, *Ireland 1912–1985*, p. 40. Lee states that the British government's miscalculation in arresting the Sinn Fein leaders in 1918 allowed the more overt advocates of physical force to rise to prominence within the party.

[28] Colum, *Arthur Griffith*, p. 184.

Suffragettes

The Women's Social and Political Union (WSPU) was formed by Emmeline and Christabel Pankhurst in 1903 to actively campaign for votes for women. It was this organisation, together with some members of the less militant Women's Freedom League, which split from the WSPU in 1907, that supplied the bulk of suffragette prisoners. From 1905 until the outbreak of the First World War about one thousand women and forty men were imprisoned as a result of their suffrage activities.[29] The WSPU began on a fairly moderate scale using such tactics as public demonstrations, petitioning Members of Parliament and attempting to get a Private Member's Bill on suffrage through the House. However, they soon became impatient with conventional lobbying tactics, which had been used by constitutional suffrage associations since the 1860s. In the face of successive failures to secure any measure of female enfranchisement and the opposition of prominent members of the Liberal government, particularly Asquith, WSPU tactics became increasingly aggressive. Militant suffragettes harassed Liberal MPs, were prepared to incite public disorder, attacked public buildings and art treasures, and committed arson.[30] In 1909, Winston Churchill was assailed at Bristol railway station by Theresa Garnett brandishing a dog whip, although he was able to deprive her of the whip before he was struck.[31]

In some cases, militant suffragettes actively sought imprisonment by refusing to pay fines or give sureties for their good behaviour. Their tactics became so violent that Monaghan has made a convincing case for describing these militant tactics as terrorism. She maintains that militant suffragettes can be defined as terrorists because, amongst other factors, they used violence or the threat of violence to terrorise for a political motive. They also selected representative targets, initially government buildings, with the aim of modifying government behaviour.[32]

---

[29] J. Purvis, 'Doing Feminist Women's History: Researching the Lives of Women in the Suffragette Movement in Edwardian England', in *Researching Women's Lives from a Feminist Perspective*, ed. M. Maynard and J. Purvis (London: Taylor & Francis, 1994), p. 169. At no point in this article is it suggested that information regarding the imprisonment of suffragettes might be obtained from the records of the Home Office or the Prison Commission.
[30] S.S. Holton, 'In Sorrowful Wrath: Suffragette Militancy and the Romantic Feminism of Emmeline Pankhurst', in *British Feminism in the Twentieth Century*, ed. H.L. Smith (Aldershot: Elgar, 1990), p. 8.
[31] P. Addison, *Churchill on the Home Front: 1900–1955* (London: Jonathan Cape, 1992), p. 130.
[32] R. Monaghan, '"Votes for Women": An Analysis of the Militant Campaign', *Terrorism and Political Violence* 9, No. 2 (Summer 1997), pp. 65–78.

The increasing aggressiveness of WSPU tactics had a momentum propelled by the need to maintain public and media interest and by the persistence of government opposition to giving women the vote. Holton agrees with Brian Harrison that militant suffragettes realised that militancy had an internal motivation and that the demands made by the leadership upon its members could only intensify, even to the point of self-destruction.[33] Holton suggests that Emmeline Pankhurst's philosophy, as evident in her biography My Own Story, can be located in the romantic tradition. Her 'pole star' was 'revolution, social rupture, and the dependence of social regeneration on the exertions of noble individual authenticity on a passionate, not merely reasoned, engagement with society'.[34] Her motto was 'deeds not words' and she fought against what she perceived to be the appalling double standards of male society.[35] As Emmeline Pankhurst asserted, 'They [men] have decided that for men to remain silently quiescent while tyrannical rulers impose bonds of slavery upon them is cowardly and dishonourable, but that for women to do the same thing is not cowardly and dishonourable but merely respectable.'[36] This reasoning, and the importance of the struggle itself, as well as the morality of their actions, can be seen in the strategy that the suffragettes adopted in prison.

Conscientious objectors

Between January 1916 and August 1919, conscientious objectors to compulsory military service proved to be an intractable problem for the British government. The experience of dealing with the anti-compulsory vaccination movement in the late nineteenth and early twentieth centuries had highlighted the difficulties of legislating to allow for individual conscience.[37] In 1907, an Act had been passed which ended compulsory vaccination and merely required objectors to make a 'statutory declaration' of their objection.[38] On that occasion the government gave way to public pressure for the maintenance of individual freedom in such matters. However, within a year the numbers of certificates of conscientious objection issued had doubled. In the light of this experience it was the conservative view which prevailed in 1916, and exemptions on the grounds of

---

[33] Holton, 'In Sorrowful Wrath', p. 10.
[34] Ibid., p. 11.
[35] E. Pankhurst, My Own Story (London: Nash, 1914), p. 38.
[36] Ibid.
[37] R.M. MacLeod, 'Law, Medicine and Public Opinion: The Resistance to Compulsory Health Legislation 1870–1907', Part 1 and Part II, Public Law (Summer–Autumn 1967), pp. 107–28 and 189–211.
[38] An Act to substitute a Statutory Declaration for the Certificate required under section two of the Vaccination Act, 1898, of Conscientious Objection, 1907: 7 Edw.7., c.31.

conscientious objection were to be decided by local tribunals established under the Military Service Acts of January and May 1916.[39]

In practice, the definition of a conscientious objector came to be determined through the operation of the tribunals. As Rae has suggested:

> Though imperfect, the most useful definition is the one that came to be accepted by the governments of the day: conscientious objectors were men whose bona fides was established by a tribunal, or who, having failed to satisfy or appear before a tribunal, still refused combatant service on conscientious grounds.[40]

If the local Recruiting Officer contested an application for exemption or postponement of call-up he sent a Military Representative to the meeting of the local tribunal. In addition, the War Office appointed Advisory Committees of men with local knowledge and experience to examine applications and instruct the Military Representative. Even the tribunals which made genuine attempts to be fair, and some were openly prejudiced against those claiming exemption on conscientious grounds, were reluctant to reject the opinion of both the Recruiting Officer and his Advisory Committee. Despite this, it has been estimated that some form of exemption was given to over 80 per cent of the objectors who applied to them. There were, however, additional problems as a result of the initial confusion over the types of exemptions the local tribunals could give.[41]

There were actually three main categories of conscientious objector: those who accepted non-combatant service under the military, those who accepted alternative service under civilian authority, and those absolutists who would perform no service at all and who in many cases refused to appear before tribunals.[42] There were 5944 conscientious objectors who either refused to accept the decision of the tribunals or refused to apply to them;

---

[39] Rae, *Conscience and Politics*, pp. 43–4. The Act of 27 January 1916, An Act to make provision with respect to Military Service in connexion [sic] with the present War, 1916: 5 & 6 Geo.5., c.104, introduced compulsory conscription for all unmarried men or widowers between the ages of 18 and 41 who were without dependent children, unless otherwise exempt. The Act of 25 May 1916, An Act to make further provision with respect to Military Service during the present War, 1916: 6 & 7.Geo.5., c.15, introduced compulsory conscription for all men between the ages of 18 and 41, unless otherwise exempt.

[40] Rae, *Conscience and Politics*, p. 70.

[41] Ibid., pp. 18 and 94–133. Also see Kennedy, 'Public Opinion', pp. 108–9. Kennedy states that, 'Chiefly composed of unpaid, middle-aged patriots without legal training who had previously been prominent in recruiting activities, these tribunals were more likely to reflect popular attitudes than Government intentions.'

[42] Ibid., p. 87, and also pp. 47–51 for discussion of the problems with the conscience clause.

most of these were Christian pacifists although many others were socialists.[43] Absolutists, as they were called, proved to be a particularly difficult administrative and moral problem. They became subject to a cycle of arrest, conscription into the military, court martial for failing to obey orders and then imprisonment. After completion of their sentence they were subject to the same cycle repeatedly, and the problem of what to do with them passed from the tribunals to the military and on to the unwilling prison authorities. By June 1917, the number of conscientious objectors serving their second or further sentence was 600.[44] This situation was exacerbated by the constant traffic between serving men who became conscientious through service and conscientious objectors who renounced their objection.[45]

Three main groups, therefore, supplied the bulk of the political prisoners who experienced the inside of England's prisons during the second half of the nineteenth century and the early part of the twentieth century. These were Irish nationalists, suffragettes and conscientious objectors to compulsory military service. The goals for which they fought and the activities that resulted in their imprisonment differed considerably, but there were many similarities in the ways in which they perceived their struggle and also in their motivations for pursuing it.

Conscience, morality and the political offender

The existence of political pressure groups was facilitated by their belief in political legitimacy – that power was only legitimate if it was to some extent conferred from below, by the people who were subject to it.[46] The problem with this, as O'Sullivan points out, is how to define 'the people'.[47] In practice, political groups defined their own concept of 'the people' on whose immediate behalf they believed they were acting, and to whom they primarily directed their propaganda. Irish nationalists, suffragettes and conscientious objectors defined the issues upon which they would confer legitimacy: an independent Ireland, votes for women, or the abolition of compulsory conscription. To justify their illegal activities it was necessary for such organisations to claim that the achievement of their objectives would result in benefits accruing to a much wider section of society than that represented by their own activists and supporters.

---

[43] P. Priestly, *Jail Journeys: The English Prison Experience since 1918: Modern Prison Writings* (London: Methuen, 1989), p. 2. Also see Rae, *Conscience and Politics*, p. 70.
[44] Rae, *Conscience and Politics*, p. 207.
[45] Ibid., p. 120.
[46] N. O'Sullivan, *Terrorism, Ideology and Revolution* (Sussex: Wheatsheaf Books, 1986), p. 9.
[47] Ibid.

The confinement of those who broke the law, or in some cases only threatened the law, for reasons of principle rather than personal gain raised questions about the purpose of imprisonment and also about the treatment and conditions imposed within prison walls. These groups publicly represented prison as an instrument of state control and repression. The imprisonment of people who might otherwise conventionally be seen as law-abiding and moral had the potential to undermine the stigmatising and labelling effect of the prison and indeed turn it into the reverse, as according a mark of martyrdom. However, those who would otherwise provide a moral lead for society might instead actually encourage lawlessness. In documentation which was produced to enable the Secretary of State to answer a Parliamentary question of March 1910, it was stated that,

> the law does not punish a man in proportion to the immorality of his conduct but rather in proportion to the public harm his conduct involves. On the whole the offender who has broken the law from a good motive is likely to be more harmful to the public than an ordinary offender, because he is likely to encourage others to follow his example and there is something to be said for punishing him more severely than others.[48]

Nevertheless, the treatment of political prisoners as criminals sat uneasily with England's liberal image and traditions, particularly when the state sanctioned such methods as the forcible feeding of hunger strikers.

Ideologically a liberal state does have the right to take action against those seeking to undermine law and order; indeed this is one of the main purposes of liberal government. Lacey points out that the existence of a liberal state does not preclude the punishment of offenders whose morality conflicts with that of the state. The state must 'vindicate its own public judgement of the justice of its criminal law by treating her [the political offender] as an offender (though perhaps also by mitigating her punishment) if the social benefits of the system as a whole are not to be diminished'. The crux of the problem lay in the principle that 'a just system will be such as to leave the citizen a real possibility of putting her own conscientiously held beliefs before her publicly acknowledged social responsibilities'.[49] The argument that, accepting the protection of certain basic freedoms, decisive measures were required to maintain law and order was common in contemporary statements by officials and in the media. In a letter dated 19 August 1909, the Secretary of State commented, 'complete liberty of speech and meeting being allowed, neither the Constitution nor the law contemplates the immunity from the ordinary process of law of those who deliberately choose to break the law

---

[48] PRO HO144/1042/183256/18.
[49] N. Lacey, *State Punishments, Political Principles and Community Values* (London: Routledge, 1988), p. 134.

for the purposes of political propaganda'.[50] In 1916, *The Times* pointed out what it saw as the dangers of conscience and maintained, 'it is obvious that if conscience were allowed to justify conduct society could not exist at all'. There was, *The Times* observed, a difference between the 'liberty to hold opinions as individuals and liberty to act upon them as members of a community'; individual obligations to the state should take precedence.[51]

Many of the arguments regarding politically motivated offences concerned the balance between the obligations of the individual to the state and to their own conscience.[52] This view presupposed an existing, pre-eminent loyalty to the state owed by one of its citizens, a view that was challenged by Irish nationalists who denied the primacy of their loyalty to England over Ireland. Once an individual or group had given precedence to conscience in a manner that came into conflict with the law, and was then punished for this, further issues emerged. If these offenders considered a law unjust, the punishment given for the breaking of this law was also, for them, unjust. A few political prisoners who published accounts of their experiences quoted from Thoreau, stating that 'under a government which imprisons any unjustly, the true place for a just man is also in prison'.[53] The symbol of the prison as a place of confinement for the 'bad' or 'evil' in society was reversed by political offenders, and imprisonment in their eyes became instead a stamp of moral conviction.

Cohen believes that the manner in which political prisoners are punished is a reflection of the 'sophistication and humaneness' of the community.[54] The treatment of political prisoners in England during this period revealed at times a definite lack of both these qualities.

The motivations and objectives of political prisoners

England might force me to associate with the dregs raked in from the gutters, might shave my head like theirs, and stamp the Government broad arrow all over me; humiliation might be heaped on to me with an unsparing hand, and punishments-diabolically brutal measured out for years, but never for one moment did I forget I was an Irish Political Prisoner, and in spite of it all, never felt any degradation. On the contrary, I wore that convict garb with a certain amount of

---

[50] PRO HO144/1033/175878.

[51] 8 April 1916, p. 9, col. b.

[52] See, for instance, J.E.C. Welldon, 'Conscience and the Conscientious Objector', *Nineteenth Century and After* 79 (May 1916), pp. 977–87.

[53] Cited, for instance, in J.S. Duckers, *'Handed-Over': The Prison Experiences of Mr. J. Scott Duckers, solicitor, of Chancery Lane, under the Military Service Act*, introduced by T. Edmund Harvey (London: Daniel, 1917), p. vii.

[54] C. Cohen, *Civil Disobedience, Conscience, Tactics and the Law* (New York: Columbia University Press, 1971), p. 86.

pride, and took satisfaction in the thought that all her laws and with all her power this great England could not force me one of the mere units of the Irish rank and file to regard myself as one of the criminal class any more than I could ever be forced to regard myself as English.[55]

The above quotation, perhaps written with posterity in mind, was taken from an account of convict prison life in the 1880s and 1890s written by a Fenian, Thomas Clarke. It provides a good example of the pride and bitterness often inherent in the conflict between political prisoners and the prison authorities and government. The quotation also indicates the importance of political status to these prisoners and shows the use of language steeped in righteousness and often also in militarism. O'Hegarty asserted that Clarke 'always regarded himself as a soldier of the Irish Republic, to whom prison and suffering were the day's work: he nerved himself against prison and bore it, largely because of his proud consciousness of the cause he stood for', he wanted nothing less than the complete separation of Ireland from England.[56]

Many political offenders continued to agitate for their specific causes in prison. Within the existing highly controlled prison environment, however, there was limited room for manoeuvre. Whether political prisoners were intentionally challenging the prison authorities or were venting their frustration at the constraints of prison discipline, they came directly into conflict with the prison staff. Prison staff were often perceived as representing the power of the state against which they struggled in one form or another. In many cases this intensified the hardships of prison life for political prisoners and also the difficulties faced by prison staff in controlling such prisoners. Behind every confrontation, no matter how small, lay the political relations and circumstances that had brought political offenders into prison, whether that was male domination, militarism and state compulsion, or the rule of the British state over Ireland. On the other hand, these internal tensions could be exploited to gain publicity and further their cause outside of the prisons. When Emmeline Pankhurst stated that, 'We press our cause in such a way as to give the Government but two alternatives – either to do us justice or to do us violence', she recognised the representational value of the prison, the influence that public opinion could have upon political policy and the way these could be manipulated.[57]

Other political offenders were also aware of the representational value of the prison as well as the power of individual suffering to mitigate public prejudice. With regard to the opposition faced by conscientious objectors during the First World War, T. Edmund Harvey MP stated that,

---

[55] Clarke, *Irish Felon's Prison Life*, p. 62.
[56] Ibid., pp. xv–xvi.
[57] Cited in C. Lytton, *Prisons and Prisoners* (London: Heinemann, 1914), p. 36.

'in the end the clamour of the Press, the outcry of the platform and the eloquence of the pulpit cannot prevail against the still, small voice of truth in prison'.[58] He wrote this in his introduction to the account of the experiences of J. Scott Duckers. Duckers was a prominent member of the No-Conscription Fellowship and Stop-the-War, who had not appeared before a tribunal because he refused to recognise that it had the right to try his conscience.[59]

As long as political prisoners had an organised body of support outside the prison, and were able to communicate with it, their plight could be used to publicise their particular cause and attempt to gain public sympathy. In many cases such publicity could also be used to pressurise the government into allowing a mitigation of their sentence or treatment. Such campaigning was, however, often unsuccessful. For instance, despite prolonged pressure from his friends and from the Irish Political Prisoners Amnesty Association during the 1890s, the government never accepted that Thomas Gallagher, one of the Irish dynamiters, was insane. He was finally released in August 1896 and spent the rest of his life in an insane asylum. Alfred White was released at the same time; he had also gone insane after thirteen years' imprisonment.[60]

Political offenders used the symbol of the prison as a place not only of punishment but also of shame and degradation to highlight their devotion to their cause. A sentence of imprisonment conferred upon political prisoners a stamp of conviction, commitment and even martyrdom, a martyrdom which, according to *The Times*, was obtained cheaply.[61] But it was cheap only in the sense that for most, but not all, political prisoners it was a punishment short of death. In the two years after 1868, for example, 'seven Fenians died in gaol, four committed suicide, and four went completely mad'.[62] Nine conscientious objectors to compulsory conscription died in prison and an estimated sixty others died later in consequence of the treatment they had received in prison.[63]

---

[58] Duckers, 'Handed Over', p. viii.

[59] For an inside account of conscientious objection to the war and specifically of the activities of the No-Conscription Fellowship see W.J. Chamberlain, *Fighting for Peace: The Story of the War Resistance Movement* (London: No More War, 1928).

[60] Short, *The Dynamite War*, p. 235. The circumstances of the Irish 'dynamiters', numbering fourteen in 1893, were frequently discussed in Parliament where Irish MPs, including John Redmond, head of the Parliamentary Party, and Michael Davitt, pressed for an amnesty to be given. See *Hansard's Parliamentary Debates*, 4th ser., vol. 8 (1892), cols 915–1000; vol. 9 (1892), cols 313–14; vol. 16 (1893), cols 1106–7 and 1357–8; vol. 22 (1894), cols 221–41; vol. 34 (1895), col. 238; vol. 40 (1896), cols 1441 and 1570.

[61] 5 March 1912, p. 9, col. e.

[62] Quinlivan and Rose, *Fenians in England*, p. 139.

[63] Rae, *Conscience and Politics*, p. 226.

Political prisoners suffered for their cause and were subjected, in some cases, to illegal punishments, assaults and forcible feeding. There was, however, a certain pride in such endurance that was evident in the accounts of political prisoners. A. Fenner Brockway, a socialist imprisoned for his conscientious objection to compulsory conscription, was proud to undergo imprisonment 'as a witness to our anti-war convictions and . . . accepted punishment gladly as an honour in the cause'.[64] Another conscientious objector questioned, 'What greater glory can one have than to be in prison for an ideal?'[65] Perhaps more than for suffragettes or conscientious objectors, the nationalist fight for an independent Ireland encouraged the attitude that 'In order to achieve anything, men must be prepared for suffering.'[66]

Political offenders perceived their cause in varying ways. Purvis claims that for many suffragettes their cause was like a religion that was cemented by the community spirit and supportive networks that, she suggests, were created by suffragettes in prison.[67] Stephen Hobhouse, a conscientious objector to compulsory conscription, also saw his stance in spiritual terms and maintained a faith in the righteous and Christian character of conscientious objection.[68] For Irish nationalists and suffragettes in particular, the fight for their cause was referred to as a war. Thus military language and the classification of themselves as prisoners of war appear frequently in the personal accounts of their experiences. Emmeline Pankhurst described the WSPU as being 'simply a suffrage army in the field' adopting 'revolutionary methods' and 'guerilla warfare against the Government through injury to private property'.[69]

In the context of a liberal political tradition in England, suffragettes and conscientious objectors justified their actions in terms that highlighted the extent to which the rhetoric of liberalism had never been achieved in practice. It was they, and not the government, who were asserting important traditional moral values and individual freedoms. Emmeline Pankhurst was expansive on this subject. She asserted that, 'We never went to prison in order to be martyrs. We went there in order that we might obtain the rights of citizenship.'[70] She went on to explain that,

---

[64] A. Fenner Brockway, *Inside the Left: Thirty Years of Platform, Press, Prison and Parliament* (London: George Allen & Unwin, 1947), p. 91.

[65] E. Williamson Mason, *Made Free in Prison* (London: George Allen & Unwin, 1918), p. 181.

[66] J. O'Donovan Rossa, *Irish Rebels in English Prisons* (New York: Sadleir, 1882), p. 19. This view persisted in the writings of twentieth-century Irish nationalists. See T.P. Coogan, *On the Blanket, The H-Block Story* (Dublin: Ward River Press, 1980), ch. 2.

[67] Purvis, 'Prison Experiences of Suffragettes', p. 111.

[68] S. Hobhouse, 'An English Prison from Within', *Quarterly Review* 229 (July 1918), pp. 21–37.

[69] Pankhurst, *My Own Story*, pp. 59 and 280–1.

[70] Ibid., pp. 187–8.

If it were the custom to treat political offenders as ordinary offenders against the well-being of society . . . we should not have complained if we were treated like that; but it is not the international custom to do so, for the dignity of the women of the country, and for the sake of the consciences of the men of the country, and for the sake of our nation amongst the nations of the earth, we are not going to allow the Liberal government to treat us like ordinary law-breakers in future.'[71]

J. Scott Duckers perceived his campaign in terms of a fight for freedoms which, he said, could only be preserved by individuals.[72] A pamphlet protesting against the treatment of political prisoners in Britain accused the government of hypocrisy: 'We know that Liberal heart now, so enraged at an opponent's tyranny, so enthusiastic over distant struggles for liberty, so callous in its own brutality, and so indifferent to the cry of freedom at its door.'[73] In a similar vein, one publication suggested that what had been required during the First World War was not a Defence of the Realm Act but a 'Defence of the People's Act, in defiance of the realm'.[74]

Imprisonment was not generally actively courted by political groups, although many members of the WSPU did so by refusing to pay fines or to give sureties for their good behaviour. Suffragettes who committed particularly destructive acts did not give themselves up for arrest, nor did conscientious objectors, although they seem to have viewed prison as the inevitable consequence of their passive resistance.[75] Suffragettes and conscientious objectors generally accepted punishment as a part of the process of civil disobedience. With regard to the Sinn Fein leaders who were detained in May 1918, one account maintains that they were forewarned but chose to await arrest in their homes rather than attempt to escape. The reasons given for this were that there would be others to take their place while they were in prison and also that their internment might arouse the country. In addition, Arthur Griffith, the founder of Sinn Fein, had been put forward as an electoral candidate in East Cavan, an Ulster constituency, and it was hoped that his arrest would increase support for him. The detentions prior to the election would, Padraic Colum maintained, 'swing the country away from the Parliamentary Party, for, with its founder in gaol, Sinn Fein would be unbeatable'.[76] This

---

[71] Ibid., p. 135.
[72] Duckers, 'Handed Over', p. 151.
[73] G. Sigerson, 'Custodia Honesta': Treatment of Political Prisoners in Great Britain, introduced by H.W. Nevison (London: Liberal Women's Press, 1913), p. 7.
[74] C. Gilbert Cole, The Objectors to Conscription and War (Manchester: Co-operative Printing Society, 1936), p. 12.
[75] Monaghan, '"Votes for Women"', pp. 72–3.
[76] Colum, Arthur Griffith, pp. 182–3.

calculation proved correct and Griffiths won a decisive election victory in East Cavan.[77]

For many political prisoners in local prisons the first step to obtain some recognition of their status was to serve their sentence in the first division. This division had been specified by the Prison Act of 1865 as being for non-criminal prisoners. Conditions in the first division were also markedly better than those in either the second or third divisions established under the 1898 Prison Act.[78] Hobhouse and Brockway described the differences between the divisions in local prisons in their publication, *English Prisons Today*. This publication was the product of an inquiry established by the Executive of the Labour Research Department and was in part a consequence of the imprisonment of conscientious objectors, including the two authors, during the First World War.

Above those privileges given to a prisoner in the third division a prisoner in the first division was allowed to wear his own clothes, to have such books and newspapers as were not considered objectionable by the authorities, and to arrange to have their own food supplied from outside. In addition, prisoners in the first division were not required to work, could hire another prisoner to do their cleaning duties and could receive and write one letter a fortnight.

In contrast, the privileges allowed to a second division prisoner above those in the third division were that they might on application to the governor be released from the requirement to have a bath on reception and also could have a pint of tea in lieu of porridge for breakfast. They could not be compelled to clean any part of the prison except their own utensils, although this was not always observed, were not compelled to sleep on a bare board for the first fourteen days of their sentence and could only be employed on work of an industrial or manufacturing nature. Furthermore, they were allowed a visit and a letter, in and out, every four weeks instead of having to wait eight weeks for the first and six weeks for the second.[79] Prisoners in each of the three divisions in local prisons were supposed to be kept separate, in part to avoid moral contamination. It was therefore the first division status and privileges that were the main issue for political prisoners held in local prisons during this period.

For political prisoners confined in convict prisons, privileges were based predominantly upon conduct and the extent to which convicts had

---

[77] Lyons, *Ireland Since the Famine*, p. 394.

[78] Radzinowicz and Hood, 'Status of Political Prisoners', pp. 1458–9.

[79] S. Hobhouse and A. Fenner Brockway, *English Prisons Today* (New York: Longman, Green & Co., 1922), pp. 216–22. Also see Priestly, *Jail Journeys*, p. 2. Priestly refers to this report as 'magisterial in scope and meticulous in detail – a picture of society's most coercive institution taken at an instant of profound crisis in the national life'.

progressed through their sentence within the progressive stage system. Jeremiah O'Donovan Rossa, a Fenian who was given a life sentence in 1865 but was released on ticket-of-leave in 1871, repeatedly complained about being made to associate with convicts, which he interpreted as an attempt by the prison authorities to degrade him. This was not, he explained, because he preferred to be alone rather than mix with convicts but rather to kick against the prison authorities. He went on to say that this resistance actually cost him in personal terms, suggesting that, 'If you who shudder at the thought of contact with the vilest of human beings come to test the strength of your horror and sense of contamination by two or three years of solitary confinement, you may change.'[80]

Within the Home Office fears were expressed that if political prisoners were able to determine the terms of their own imprisonment this would cause disobedience among ordinary prisoners and undermine discipline generally. Furthermore, if political prisoners in local prisons were automatically detained in the first division, such preferential treatment might increase the number of candidates for 'easy martyrdom'. One prison governor was surprised by the assertiveness of two suffragettes received into his prison who told him 'with the most refreshing candour that, unless they were treated as 1st Division prisoners & political offenders, they would break every prison rule in existence & take no food'.[81] Defiance of this kind was by no means unusual. The prison authorities and the Home Office were concerned that imprisonment would 'become meaningless' under the stress of the competing demands to diffuse or placate defiance on such a large scale while maintaining prison discipline.[82]

The strategies of political prisoners

Recognition of political status was a primary aim for all three of the groups of political prisoners featured in this chapter. In association with this objective, political prisoners resisted the elements of prison discipline that were fundamental to the process of making an individual into a prisoner. These were also aspects which had symbolic value for political prisoners and which were identified in the public mind with the degradation and powerlessness of the prisoner as well as the relative authority of the state. If

---

[80] O'Donovan Rossa, *Irish Rebels*, p. 92.
[81] PRO HO144/552/185732, November 1909. Also see PRO HO144/904/176114/5, report of the governor of Holloway Prison, dated 25 February 1909, regarding the imprisonment of Mrs Pethick Lawrence and Constance Lytton who stated that they would create trouble only if their demands were not met.
[82] PRO HO144/552/185732.

control over these aspects of the prison could be wrested from the prison authorities then a defeat over the power of the state could be achieved which had not been achieved outside the prison.

In many respects the resistance of political prisoners took the same form as that of ordinary prisoners. Most complaints made by ordinary prisoners focused on the quality and quantity of prison food, and political prisoners also complained about this. Both ordinary and political prisoners complained about being punished too harshly or for no reason. The significant difference in the resistance of political prisoners was that their actions were more often part of a conscious overall strategy, albeit that this strategy was subject to continual modification and individual innovation. On one level, therefore, resistance was integral to the fight of political prisoners for a recognition of status, but on a more personal level it was a coping strategy and a protest against some of the prison rules and regulations – what Brockway experienced as an 'intellectual revolt'.[83]

The rule of silence, the authority of the prison staff, prison dress and labour were all assailed so that at times it seemed to the prison authorities that there was 'a general conspiracy against prison discipline'.[84] However, the differing conditions and treatment that political prisoners received meant that they were not affected evenly by these aspects of the prison, nor did political prisoners target them evenly. The Irish detained in 1918 had not been convicted of any crime and were therefore officially internees. As internees the regulations regarding them directed that they were to be kept separate, were to retain their own clothes, did not have to work and were allowed to buy extra food and clothing, although these regulations were not always adhered to.[85]

A small group of political prisoners at Liverpool Prison during the First World War, including three anarchists and Brockway, told the governor of the prison that they would refuse to abide by the rule of silence and other inhuman rules. Part of his plan, Brockway maintained, was to 'create public discussion not only of the position of the C.O.s [conscientious objectors] but of the barbarities of the prison system'. As a result of this they were moved to the remand hall, but the example they had given soon spread to the rest of the conscientious objectors, as well as to the ordinary prisoners in the same hall. The other conscientious objectors were put in the punishment cells. The next day those who had been dispersed to the remand hall and to the

---

[83] Brockway, *Inside the Left*, p. 107.

[84] PRO HO144/1042/183256/17, memorandum dated 14 October 1909 from Evelyn Ruggles-Brise, the Chairman of the Prison Commissioners and Directors, to E. Troup, Permanent Under Secretary of State, regarding suffragette prisoners.

[85] PRO HO144/1496/362269/163, *Regulations for the treatment of Persons other than Aliens interned in Prison under the Defense of the Realm Act*. Because they were allowed to wear their own clothing, for instance, these prisoners obviously had no need to object to prison dress.

punishment cells were returned to the conscientious objectors' hall because, according to Brockway, the prison authorities feared that the indiscipline would spread to the rest of the prison. This allowed the conscientious objectors to organise further. A committee was elected and new prison rules and a revised timetable agreed upon. Taking back control over their daily lives meant for Brockway that they 'had become individuals again'.[86]

After ten days the leaders of this 'revolt' were transferred to other prisons, while the remainder who continued their resistance were given three days' bread and water. In an attempt to regain control some of them went on hunger strike. Brockway refused to go on hunger strike for two reasons: because he felt that as a pacifist he was not justified in forcing liberation by threatening his own life, and because he believed that the prison authorities would feed them forcibly and so entirely defeat them. This was how the conflict ended, he stated, 'My companions were forcibly fed – and they gave up resistance altogether.'[87]

The 'revolt' by Brockway and his companions was non-violent but there were occasions when the resistance of political prisoners took the form of outright verbal or physical attack against the prison staff. In the 1860s, Jeremiah O'Donovan Rossa had displayed general insubordination towards the convict prison governors that he came into contact with. This included verbal abuse, refusing to salute and, in one prison, refusing to go before the governor to receive sentences for prison offences.[88] Claims of brutality on the part of prison staff were also frequently made by political prisoners, and in some cases, but certainly not all, were false or exaggerated. Two suffragettes, Selina Martin and Leslie Hall, maintained that they had been treated with brutality while on remand in Walton Street Prison, Liverpool, in 1909. Their claims, or an exaggerated version of them, were published in 'Votes for Women' under the heading 'Atrocities in an English Prison'. Accusations were made against the prison authorities that they were 'the tools of Government, and act as they are bidden by the Home Office'. At the investigation which followed these allegations, however, Selina Martin gave a very toned down version of events and Leslie Hall refused to make any complaint.[89]

The labelling of prison staff as instruments of officialdom also emerged from an altercation between Emmeline Pankhurst and a prison matron in 1914 which was taken before the Visiting Committee at Holloway Prison. According to the matron, Mrs Pankhurst had said to her:

[86] Brockway, *Inside the Left*, pp. 108–12.
[87] Ibid.
[88] O'Donovan Rossa, *Irish Rebels*, pp. 95, 137–8 and 144.
[89] PRO HO144/1052/187234.

Why don't you be a woman, and not a tool of this filthy Government. Why don't you go on to the streets and get a living; it would be more honest than assisting in torturing women who are working to better your conditions; you are no better than a woman who walks the streets for a living. You prostitute yourself daily.[90]

In her defence Mrs Pankhurst denied using such language but did not deny the content of her outburst. It was a harsh judgement upon the matron for which Mrs Pankhurst later apologised. Certainly, her outburst had occurred under the stress of her repeated imprisonment under the Prisoners (Temporary Discharge for Ill Health) Act of 1913, commonly known as the Cat and Mouse Act. This altercation occurred after she had been re-arrested for the eleventh time. Mrs Pankhurst perceived herself to be working and suffering for the welfare of all women, but in prison it was women who helped to operate a prison system that not only denied suffragettes political prisoner status but also forcibly fed them. This must have presented a frustrating state of affairs for her.[91]

The indignity and anonymity of wearing prison dress was another aspect of imprisonment that was rebelled against. An inquiry into prison dress that reported in 1889 indicated the emotiveness of this issue. It was largely the imprisonment of members of the Salvation Army, usually for obstruction offences, that instigated this investigation.[92] From the evidence of witnesses from the Salvation Army as well as anti-vaccinationists who had spent short terms in prison, it is clear that they regarded the wearing of prison dress and also the cropping of their hair as a form of punishment. The evidence shows the repulsion experienced by some at having to wear and use objects tainted by criminals. One anti-vaccinationist complained to the Committee that when

[I] went to take my gruel in the gaol, they handed me half a wooden spoon, and I wondered what murderers mouth that had been in. I have never forgotten it

---

[90] PRO HO144/1254/234646/149, report of the proceedings of the Visiting Committee at Holloway Prison on 10 July 1914 in which Mrs Pankhurst was charged with 'unseemly language and violence'.

[91] Also see A. Brown, 'Conflicting Objectives: Suffragette Prisoners and Female Prison Staff in Edwardian England', *Women's Studies: An Interdisciplinary Journal* 31, No. 5 (2002), pp. 627–44.

[92] *Report of the Committee of Inquiry as to the Rules Concerning the Wearing of Prison Dress*, BPP, 1889 (C.5759), LXI.271–8. For an account of the circumstances which resulted in the imprisonment of members of the Salvation Army see V. Bailey, 'Salvation Army Riots, The "Skeleton Army" and Legal Authority in the Provincial Town', in *Social Control in Nineteenth Century Britain*, ed. A.P. Donojgrodzki (London: Croom Helm, 1977).

from that day to this, and I never shall, to think that I had committed no crime, and yet should be submitted to such indignity.[93]

Not only were prison clothes tainted but they made these prisoners look the same as criminals, as did the close cropped hair.

The investigating committee accepted that the advantages of prison dress and hair clipping were disciplinary as well as sanitary. Prison dress was necessary to ensure safe custody, which was 'a leading axiom in prison management'.[94] However, it was also admitted that those imprisoned for offences relating to health, education and highways legislation were exposed to a 'painful trial' in being forced to put on prison dress. But to allow some prisoners to wear their own clothing would 'introduce an invidious and irritating class distinction, which would greatly add to administrative difficulties' as well as tending 'to confuse the sense of moral guilt'.[95]

Prison labour was an element of discipline that was commonly heralded as reformative and as offering a training to enable discharged prisoners to obtain work. Historically, prison labour has often been characterised by useless make-work tasks or hard manual labour such as that on the dockyards. For many conscientious objectors it was seen as an arm of the militarism they were rejecting and they therefore refused to work. Brockway posed the question, 'We had refused to obey orders in the army as a protest against the military regime. Should we not refuse to obey orders in prison as a protest against the penal regime?'[96] The extent of the absolutists' rejection of militarism was shown when, in August 1918, the government transferred those who had served an equivalent of two years' imprisonment to Wakefield Prison. There they were to enjoy the better conditions experienced by men under preventive detention, including the right to wear their own clothes and to mix and talk after working hours. However, the absolutists continued to refuse to work and within two months discipline had collapsed and they were returned to normal prisons.[97]

The Prison Commissioners found the absolutist conscientious objectors intractable and a source of constant conflict. Upon their refusal to do work of national importance conscientious objectors were given ordinary prison sentences, usually hard labour in the third division, although they usually refused to work. It was not until the end of 1917, under considerable pressure from the press, that the government allowed some extra privileges to those conscientious objectors who had been in prison at least twelve months. Of

---

[93] *Report of the Committee as to the Rules Concerning the Wearing of Prison Dress*, BPP, 1889 (C.5759), LXI.343, qu.1959.
[94] Ibid., 273.
[95] Ibid., 275.
[96] Brockway, *Inside the Left*, p. 105.
[97] Rae, *Conscience and Politics*, pp. 228–30. Rae refers to this action by the government as an 'astonishing failure to grasp the essentials of the absolutists' position'.

these privileges, the only ones Stephen Hobhouse deemed to be of value were the permission to have books sent in and the allowance of two daily periods of exercise, at which talking in pairs was permitted.[98]

In some cases political prisoners used their own health as a weapon to exploit the defensiveness of the prison authorities. The most consistent use of this tactic was made by suffragettes who went on hunger, and in some cases thirst, strike. This was seen as a means to coerce the government into giving women the vote by subverting imprisonment. Since the death of a suffragette in prison would be roundly and publicly criticised, the government was forced to release hunger-striking suffragettes before the end of their sentence. In 1913 Annie Kenney, a prominent member of the WSPU, declared, 'We say, "let us die", we are prepared to die'. She went on to say that 'they know perfectly well that if one women dies in prison those women who do not approve of militancy today will come out to be militant tomorrow'.[99] On at least one occasion members of the WSPU smuggled drugs into prison in order to induce vomiting and make hunger-strike tactics more effective in the face of forcible feeding.[100]

In May 1912, when Emmeline Pankhurst and the Pethick Lawrences were sentenced to nine months in the second division, for 'conspiring to incite certain persons to commit malicious damage to property', they proclaimed their intention of hunger striking unless they were transferred to the first division. Five days later, at a WSPU meeting, Mabel Tuke declared that if all seventy-five members currently in prison were not transferred to the first division, including the leaders, they would all go on hunger strike. After a week Mrs Pankhurst and the Pethick Lawrences were transferred to the first division but not the others. The threatened hunger strike began on 19 June and by 6 July 1912 all the hunger strikers had been released, although without gaining the first division.[101]

Irish nationalist and conscientious objectors also used hunger strike tactics to great effect and, as with suffragettes, prison officials resorted to forcible feeding to prevent early release and the circumvention of the power of the state to impose punishment upon them. Despite several official denials,

[98] Hobhouse, 'An English Prison from Within', p. 22. Other privileges introduced included permission to wear their own clothes and to pay another prisoner to clean their cell. See Hobhouse and Brockway, English Prisons Today, pp. 223–4.

[99] HO144/1254/234646, clipping from The Times, 25 February 1913 – 'ARREST OF MRS PANKHURST'.

[100] PRO HO144/1320/252950. This documentation also records that the WSPU had accused the prison authorities of drugging suffragettes. This accusation had previously been made in 1890 by a Fenian prisoner, John Duff. His allegation was dismissed as 'preposterous'. Report as to the Treatment of Certain Prisoners Convicted of Treason-Felony, BPP, 1890 (C.6016), XXXVII.79, para. 11.

[101] Purvis, 'Prison Experiences of Suffragettes', pp. 121–2. Also see Pankhurst, My Own Story, pp. 221–55.

it became evident that forcible feeding was potentially dangerous. One conscientious objector, Edward Burns, died in Hull Prison in March 1918. The coroner's investigation recorded a verdict of 'Death accelerated by the inhalation of some fluid food during forcible feeding'.[102] This was not the only death as a result of forced feeding. A comment in a Home Office memorandum refers to the death of a 'Sinn Feiner' in the same way. It was observed that 'Public opinion in Ireland was greatly excited by the death of a Sinn Feiner as the result of artificial feeding, and the recent death in Hull Prison is likely to excite much sympathy among those sharing the views of the Conscientious Objector.'[103] At this time the Home Office was ever conscious of public opinion in Ireland, of the sensitive nature of England's relations with Ireland and of the possible repercussions upon Anglo-American relations during wartime.[104]

Following the Armistice a large number of imprisoned conscientious objectors went on hunger strike in order to pressurise the government into releasing them. The government was reluctant to release them until all of those in the military forces had been demobilised. In February 1919 conscientious objectors were on hunger strike in Wandsworth, Newcastle, Winchester, Maidstone, Hull, Leeds, Ipswich, Pentonville, Manchester and Wormwood Scrubs prisons.[105] During the first three months of 1919, 130 conscientious objectors were released under the 'Cat and Mouse Act' after being forcibly fed. The Prison Commission were aware that such tactics put the prison staff in a very difficult position and could spread to ordinary prisoners.[106] The Prison Commission had already registered its opposition to the forced feeding of prisoners, because 'while throwing an enormous and almost intolerable strain on the medical and discipline staff' it brought 'the law into contempt', and in 1919 they reiterated this view. They maintained that there was little justice in the factors determining the use of forcible feeding in prison. Whether prisoners, in this case conscientious objectors, were forcibly fed or released depended upon the availability of trained staff and upon the health of the prisoner.[107]

---

[102] *Hull Daily Mail*, 22 March 1918 – 'CO'S DEATH IN PRISON, HULL VERDICT: NO NEGLECT'.
[103] PRO HO144/1490/356124.
[104] See Hartley, *The Irish Question*. Also see J.M. McEwan, 'The Liberal Party and the Irish Question During the First World War', *Journal of British Studies* 12, No. 2 (May 1973), pp. 109–31.
[105] PRO HO144/1514/377015/2, letter from Ruggles-Brise to the Under Secretary of State, dated 20 February 1919.
[106] Ibid. Ruggles-Brise states that two military prisoners were already following the example provided by the conscientious objectors and had gone on hunger strike in the hope of early release. He asserted that hunger striking on such a large scale would 'be disastrous to the general prison population'.
[107] PCom7/355, letter regarding suffragette hunger strikers to the Under Secretary of

Despite any support network political prisoners were able to build in prison, they faced forced feeding alone. Suffragette Helen Gordon Liddle ascribed a superior morality to hunger striking because the dire consequences of it would finally be visited upon herself. She argued that the refusal of suffragettes to submit to injustice heightened the guilt of those using force against them. Her description of being forcibly fed is an indication of the suffering that these prisoners endured for their causes:

> A short quick thrust and her mouth is gagged again – the prisoner tries to control herself – her sobs increase – her breathlessness also – there is nothing but the pain and the relentless forcing of food down her throat – her choking despair, and the bitter draught of tonic and digestive medicine which is also poured down her throat.[108]

Irish nationalists imprisoned during the war often had experience of military training and took a directly aggressive stance towards the prison authorities. Prison officials were plainly anxious as to whether they would be able to contain such men with a depleted wartime prison service and only slight support from the military. In January 1919, the governor of Usk Prison reported to the Prison Commission that Irish internees in his charge were dissatisfied, and had submitted a list of complaints directly to the Chief Secretary of Ireland and to the Secretary of State. These men, he stated, 'undoubtedly have the impression that they can force from the Authorities by violence concessions which "constitutional" methods have failed to secure. That, they say, is their experience.' The internees at Usk demanded, as prisoners of war, the same privileges as those given to the prisoners at Frongoch in 1916, including greater freedom of movement and intercourse, and greater facilities for exercise and for the purchase of luxuries. A similarly threatening petition was submitted in Reading Prison, which demanded 'release or immediate trial, otherwise there would be trouble'.[109] There was genuine fear that large-scale violence might break out. Indeed the Home Office made it clear that in the event of an outbreak the difficulties that prison staff had experienced managing these prisoners would be taken into account.[110]

The government's response to the petitioning of the Irish internees was to give way on a few, usually smaller, points and to deploy delaying tactics

State dated 7 January 1913. Also see a memorandum dated 10 March 1919 recommending forced feeding be abandoned for conscientious objectors.
[108] H. Gordon Liddle, *The Prisoner: An Experience of Forcible Feeding by a Suffragette* (Letchworth: Garden City Press, 1911), pp. 46 and 51.
[109] PRO HO144/1496/362269/155.
[110] PRO HO 144/1496/362269/172.

for other demands, particularly those related to a defining of status.[111] Giving in to all the demands of the internees, or to none at all, would have provoked a collapse of discipline or direct, possibly violent, confrontation; in this way, an escalation of existing tensions could be avoided, at least in the short term. However, this strategy left the prison staff to cope with the frustration of the prisoners on a day-to-day basis. By 1919, the strain caused by the continued detention of Irish nationalists and also of conscientious objectors was mounting. In a memo to the Prison Commission in February 1919 the governor of Reading Prison asserted that the position had become insufferable: 'either the Prison must rule the Irish or it becomes, to people accustomed to discipline, intolerable'. The staff, he claimed, were at the end of their patience: 'Whatever is done for these men is simply looked upon as weakness and they demand more.'[112]

In February 1919, conscientious objectors at Wandsworth Prison were blamed for the disaffection of the military prisoners there, including the violent conduct of a few. The cause of this dissatisfaction was put down to the fact that the military prisoners received fewer privileges than conscientious objectors. However, it was also clear that these prisoners were disappointed at not being liberated following the Armistice.[113] As a consequence, the governor at Wandsworth was replaced; however, the unruly behaviour of some anarchist conscientious objectors at Wandsworth Prison, and the intolerance of the new acting governor, Blake, towards them, caused conflict, which resulted in a government inquiry.[114] In January 1919, responsibility for conscientious objectors was passed to the War Office under Winston Churchill who wanted to be rid of them. The release of all conscientious objectors who had served a minimum of twenty months was decided upon in early April 1919 and by August of the same year all of them had been released.[115] With regard to the Sinn Fein leaders, in February 1919 de Valera escaped from Lincoln Prison with the help of Michael Collins and Harry

---

[111] PRO HO144/1496/362269/155, letter from S.M. Power at the Irish Office regarding the Reading petition stating that they had dealt with most of the points but with regard to status he recommended waiting until the men asked again and then saying that the matter had been brought to the attention of the proper authorities.
[112] PRO HO144/1496/362269/171, memo from Governor Morgan, dated 2 February 1919.
[113] HO144/1514/377015.
[114] Report by Mr Albion Richardson, C.B.E., M.P., on an Inquiry held into the Allegations made against the Acting Governor of Wandsworth Prison concerning his Action against certain Disorderly Prisoners, BPP, 1919 (Cmd.131), XXVII. Blake described these prisoners as 'Bolsheviks' who, he declared, should be 'metaphorically hit straight between the eyes, and not patted on the back otherwise the future condition of this country will be serious indeed'. Also see HO144/1514/377015/3 and Rae, Conscience and Politics, pp. 230-3. For Blake's account see W. Blake, Quod (London: Hodder & Stoughton, 1927).
[115] See Rae, Conscience and Politics, pp. 232-3. Also HO144/1514/377015/2.

Boland. Soon afterwards, in March, partly in consequence of an influenza epidemic, the remaining Sinn Fein prisoners were released.[116]

The strategies used in the management of political prisoners

Local and convict prison systems had been developed to deal with the types of offenders that generally made up the prison population: those from the lowest sections of society who generally had little money, education, influence, or organisation. There was considerable discretion available within the system, but the routine structures of the prison were slow to change and the timetable and mechanical nature of prison life, as suggested in Chapter 2, had an internal momentum that was difficult to redirect. Upon receipt of significant numbers of political prisoners the prison system came under considerable stress. This was particularly the case during and immediately after the First World War in the context of a reduced prison staff, large numbers of military prisoners, and severely limited resources. Political prisoners exploited the weaknesses in the system to obtain concessions, but the fact that political prisoner status was never officially conceded is evidence that the balance of power within the prisons did not lie with political prisoners.

There were three Commissions appointed during the second half of the nineteenth century to investigate the treatment of Fenian prisoners in English convict prisons. The terms of reference of all three avoided political issues and the Commissions themselves made this explicit. For example, the 1867 *Report of the Commissioners on the Treatment of Treason-Felony Convicts in English Convict Prisons* emphasised that, 'As convicts we found them, and as convicts we have thought of them throughout.'[117] The Devon Commission (1871) did, however, recommend that less penal regulations be applied to Irish political prisoners.[118] When a new wave of Irish nationalists was received into English convict prisons during the 1880s, Du Cane initially suggested that they be imprisoned under this recommendation. But the Secretary of State, Harcourt, refused, saying 'I do not think there will be any difficulty in treating these men as ordinary prisoners and I do not desire at present that any difference should be made.'[119]

The small concessions made to the Irish dynamiters in the 1880s were largely due to the sensitiveness of the Liberals to their Irish supporters and tended to be justified on medical or security grounds. A Commission that

---

[116] Lyons, *Ireland Since the Famine*, pp. 402–3.
[117] BPP, 1867 (3880), XXXV.695.
[118] *Report of the Commissioners appointed to inquire into the Treatment of Treason-Felony Convicts in English Prisons* (Devon Commission), BPP, 1871 (C.319), XXXII.28.
[119] Radzinowicz and Hood, 'Status of Political Prisoners', pp. 1454–5. Also see PRO HO45/9624/A19541.

reported in 1878–9 had confirmed the view that such prisoners did not require separating from ordinary prisoners. The Kimberly Commission, established to inquire into the working of the Penal Servitude Acts, concluded that,

> we see no reason to believe that increased deterrent effect is given to the sentence of treason-felony by associating prisoners convicted of that crime with other convicts, whilst the grant to them of exceptional indulgences, tends to disturb the minds of the other prisoners, and to interfere with the orderly administration of the prison.[120]

The official stance was that treason-felony convicts were not to be treated differently from other convicts. In effect this condemned many of these Irish prisoners to a more harsh confinement than ordinary convicts. All three of these Commissions recorded the complaints of treason-felony convicts that they were constantly subjected to prejudicial treatment by prison staff. This included more rigorous and frequent searching, their sleep being interrupted during the night, and verbal and physical abuse. Thomas Clarke claimed that rules which served to protect ordinary prisoners were set aside for them, and that Fenians were subjected to 'a scientific system of perpetual and persistent harassing, which gave the officers in charge of us a free hand to persecute us just as they pleased'.[121] Paradoxically, but perhaps understandably given the nature of their complaints, Thomas Clarke and two of his imprisoned companions, Daly and Egan, did not primarily demand political status but merely an end to such negative discrimination.[122] The majority of these claims of prejudicial treatment were dismissed outright by the nineteenth-century Commissions, although one notorious exception to this concerned Jeremiah O'Donovan Rossa.

The defiance of O'Donovan Rossa and the unsympathetic attitude of the prison staff towards him appeared to have developed into a spiral of resistance and punishment. This culminated in O'Donovan Rossa being illegally kept in handcuffs for thirty-five consecutive days for throwing the contents of his chamber pot over the governor of Chatham Convict Prison.[123] The

---

[120] *Report of the Commissioners Appointed to Inquire into the Working of the Penal Servitude Acts* (Kimberly Commission), BPP, 1878–9 (C.2368), XXXVII.31.

[121] Clarke, *Irish Felon's Prison Life*, p. 6. For further criticism of the treatment of these Fenian convicts see F.H. O'Donnell, 'Fenianism – Past and Present', *Contemporary Review* 43 (May 1883), pp. 747–66.

[122] Radzinowicz and Hood, 'Status of Political Prisoners', p. 1456.

[123] O'Donovan Rossa, *Irish Rebels*, pp. 197–8. Also see Devon Commission, 14–16. According to an article in *The Saturday Review*, 7 January 1971, O'Donovan Rossa had been treated lightly and should have been flogged. It is clear that some Irish nationalist prisoners objected to such resistance by their companions. For instance, John Boyle O'Reilly, who was in the penal class in Millbank at the same time as O'Donovan Rossa,

Devon Commission recognised this, and stated that, 'finding himself a marked man from the first, and branded as a bad character when he was unconscious of deserving it, he was led to assume an independent, not to say defiant, attitude, and thus became involved in a protracted struggle with the prison authorities'.[124]

O'Donovan Rossa claimed that he was able to identify trends in what he described as government strategy. According to O'Donovan Rossa, the government's tactics towards the Fenian convicts imprisoned at this time entailed constant punishment and harassment over work. However, these methods were changed during the period in which questions were being asked about the Fenian prisoners in Parliament and during the setting up of the 1867 Commission appointed to investigate their treatment. At this time, Fenians were kept in isolation and were prevented from communicating with each other and with friends on the outside.[125]

There was one sense in which O'Donovan Rossa and the treason-felony convicts imprisoned with him did receive special treatment, and that was in their early release. O'Donovan Rossa served only five years and four months of his life sentence and was released in 1871 on the condition that he went to America and did not return. Early release and other selective treatment were at the discretion of the government. It seems, for example, that the Irish dynamiters did not receive such favourable treatment. Apart from three cases of mercy on medical grounds, they served close to their full terms.[126] Indeed the Home Secretary, Asquith, had stated his determination with regard to the dynamiters that,

> So long as I hold the position I do . . . there is not one of them who shall receive any different treatment, or whose sentence shall be any sooner interfered with, than that of any other criminal now lying in her Majesty's gaols.[127]

Government and the prison authorities had the discretion to determine the specific conditions of imprisonment for individuals and made full use of it to grant preferential treatment to selected prisoners. Michael Davitt, for instance, was convicted in 1870 of conspiracy to rebellion and sentenced to fifteen years' penal servitude. Following a clemency campaign he was released in 1877 on a ticket-of-leave which was revoked in 1881 because

---

later stated that 'I entirely disagreed with the course of conduct that he [O'Donovan Rossa] and many other political prisoners pursued – of giving reason to prison *subordinates* to punish them.' See W. O'Brien and D. Ryan, eds, *Devoy's Post Bag 1871–1928*, introduced by P.S. O'Hegarty (Dublin: C.J. Fallon, 1948), p. 38.

[124] Devon Commission, 16.

[125] Ibid., 215. Also see Quinlivan and Rose, *Fenians in England*, p. 29, and D.B. Cashman, *The Life of Michael Davitt* (Glasgow: Cameron, Fergusson, n.d.), pp. 20–3.

[126] Radzinowicz and Hood, 'Status of Political Prisoners', p. 1456.

[127] *Hansard's Parliamentary Debates*, 4th ser., vol. 8 (1892), col. 954.

of his continued agitation. Davitt was by this time a prominent figure in the Land League and on his return to prison he received very favourable treatment compared to his previous confinement. He was allowed a separate cell in the infirmary, a special diet and to work in the garden. He also had the unprecedented privilege of being able to write his manuscript to be published on discharge.[128]

Another example of a public figure who received favourable prison treatment was Bertrand Russell. In 1918 he was sentenced to six months' imprisonment in consequence of an article he wrote for the No-Conscription Fellowship's weekly magazine. His class connections and the personal intervention of Arthur Balfour, the Foreign Secretary, assured him first division treatment. He even commented in his autobiography that he found prison 'in many ways quite agreeable', although he did accept that for 'anybody not in the first division, especially for a person accustomed to reading and writing, prison is a severe and terrible punishment'.[129]

The prison authorities and the government had another important source of power with regard to political as well as other prisoners, and that was control over transfers between prisons. In 1918 the Irish internees deported to England under section 14B of the Defence of the Realm Act were initially dispersed between Reading, Durham, Birmingham, Brixton, Gloucester, Lincoln and Usk prisons.[130] Upon transfer to other prisons they found that they had to re-establish their position, treatment and conditions. When Darrel Figgis and other members of Sinn Fein were transferred from Gloucester to Lincoln Prison, the conditions that had been agreed to at Gloucester were withdrawn and the internees were forced to fight for them again. According to Figgis, the only privileges that were given initially were the right to associate at exercise and the fact that their own bags were not examined.[131] This was a process in which the government endeavoured to maintain the upper hand and withhold privileges as a source of bargaining power, although disorganisation and lack of communications within the prison system must also have played a part. Figgis complained that 'Nothing

---

[128] S. McConville, *English Local Prisons 1860–1900: Next Only to Death* (London: Routledge & Kegan Paul, 1995), p. 712, n.69. Also see M. Davitt, *Leaves from a Prison Diary, or Lectures to a 'Solitary' Audience*, introduced by T.W. Moody (Shannon: Irish University Press, 1972), pp. viii–xi and *Hansard's Parliamentary Debates*, 3rd ser., vol. 258 (1881), cols 260–1 and 500–1.

[129] Neier, 'Confining Dissent', pp. 399–400. A further example can be found with regard to Stephen Hobhouse and Clifford Allen who were among the first to be released under government concessions to conscientious objectors who were seriously ill. Many absolutists who were more seriously ill remained in prison. See Kennedy, 'Public Opinion', pp. 116–17.

[130] D. Figgis, *A Second Chronicle of Jails* (Dublin: Talbot Press, 1919), p. 60. Also see PRO HO144/1496/362269/1a.

[131] Figgis, *Second Chronicle of Jails*, p. 60.

was acknowledged as a right. Each point had to be won through bitterness, unpleasant and continuous struggle.'[132]

Following the Easter Rising of 1916, 122 men and one woman were sentenced to penal servitude and also eighteen men to terms of imprisonment. After six months these Fenians were given privileges regarding visits, letters, association and facilities for 'literary work'; they were also kept separate from other prisoners. However, the Prison Commissioners made it clear that these privileges were not given because they were political prisoners. They referred to a statement made by the Secretary of State in Parliament which affirmed that 'men having been convicted of criminal offences were not entitled to any special treatment on the ground that their offences were alleged to be of a political nature'.[133]

The privileges accorded to political prisoners were granted on the same terms as those to ordinary prisoners. They were conditional on good behaviour and could be withdrawn by the prison authorities at any time. Even the privileges accorded in the regulations to the Sinn Fein internees in 1918 were subject to variation from prison to prison.[134] Following the Easter Rising, a serious combined disturbance occurred among Fenian prisoners in Lewes Prison. According to the Prison Commissioners, the prisoners had claimed that they would refuse to give up their disobedience until the government acknowledged their status as prisoners of war. This resulted in these prisoners being transferred to other prisons and having all special privileges rescinded.

The *Report of the Commissioners of Prisons and Directors of Convict Prisons* of 1917–18 insisted that the privileges the Lewes prisoners had been granted were strictly conditional on good conduct, and implied that the failure to behave themselves constituted a lack of honour on their part. It 'was hoped rather than believed', the Commissioners maintained, 'that they would be grateful for the steps taken to segregate them from other convicts, and for the indulgences not shared by other convicts, and feel honourably bound, so long as they remained in prison, to conform to the rules'.[135]

The prison authorities had attempted to nurture the kind of harsh paternalism that was operated on ordinary prisoners. If the discretion to award a privilege or impose a punishment lay with the prison authorities then this power could be used to encourage fear or gratitude in prisoners. A significant obstacle to the operation of this mechanism, however, was the existence of strong subcultural relationships within the groups of political prisoners, which reinforced their struggle to gain privileges.

---

[132] Ibid., p. 75.
[133] *Report of the Commissioners and Directors of Prisons*, BPP, 1917–18 (Cd.8764), XVIII.119–20.
[134] See footnote 93.
[135] BPP, 1917–18 (Cd.8764), XVIII.119–20.

Political prisoners were united by their ideology and by their experience of confinement and this was particularly evident when they were imprisoned together in large numbers. In the prison, resistance to the authorities usually took precedence over disagreements between prisoners. There even seems to have been some common bond between different groups of political prisoners. One Sinn Feiner expressed sympathy with the plight of the conscientious objectors who were held in the same prison, stating that they 'had suffered for their ideals as we had not suffered for ours; and whereas we had behind us the support of our nation, theirs was a lonely war'.[136] Brockway, for example, was able to receive a regular supply of newspapers from the Sinn Feiners in the same prison.[137]

The prison authorities were understandably cautious about overuse of the power to grant privileges, especially if it seemed that this would achieve little in return. The aggressive stance of Irish nationalist prisoners and the importance to them of status increased the meaning of the privileges they obtained beyond their actual material value. This was observed by the Devon Commission as early as 1871 when it reported that the 'treason-felony convicts have, in fact, never ceased to protest against being classed with criminals, as a moral degradation, and every privilege, however trifling, which they have succeeded in obtaining, has but confirmed their belief in the justice of this demand'.[138]

Manipulation of the use of privileges was more complex than merely allowing or withdrawing them in attempts to maintain order. For example, one of the Irish internees highlighted what he interpreted as a tactic of the prison authorities and the government of 'intentionally awarding privileges which in practice were not carried out'.[139] He claimed that, although the Irish internees in Durham were supposed to receive English and Irish newspapers, the Irish newspapers were never sent to the censor and were destroyed. Figgis resented what he saw as calculated deception on the part of the government. Regarding the right to send and receive mail he commented that,

> Had the right been refused, we, and our friends at home, would have known just where we stood. Such action would have been brutal; but it would have been honest. Instead the right was formally granted; publicly it could not be maintained that it had been denied to us; but it was so carefully administered that it turned to ashes in the eating.[140]

---

[136] Figgis, *Second Chronicle of Jails*, p. 84.
[137] Brockway, *Inside the Left*, pp. 112–13.
[138] BPP, 1871 (C.319), XXXII.27, para. 207.
[139] Figgis, *Second Chronicle of Jails*, pp. 74–5.
[140] Ibid.

After these matters appeared in the Irish press the internees received a pledge that their mail would not be delayed in the censor's office for more than twenty-four hours, and they also began to receive certain Irish newspapers. In the context of the administrative and manpower problems caused by the war it is difficult to determine to what extent the delays complained of by Irish internees were simply due to bureaucratic inefficiency. However, the option to be flexible or inflexible in the treatment of political prisoners did enable the government to maintain a fluid strategy in answer to the changing tactics of each group of political prisoners.

It is clear that the government revealed a 'strategic adaptability' in their dealings with political prisoners.[141] In 1910, Churchill introduced a new rule, 243A, which effectively divided the second division in the local prisons into two. One part of the second division allowed the better conditions that were detailed under Rule 243A. The conditions of the new rule detailed that,

> In the case of any offender of the second or third division where previous character is good, and who has been convicted of, or committed to prison for, an offence not involving dishonesty, cruelty, indecency, or serious violence, the Prison Commissioners may allow such amelioration of the condition prescribed in the foregoing rules as the Secretary of State may approve in respect of prison clothing, bathing, hair-cutting, cleaning of cells, employment, exercise, books and otherwise. Provided that no such amelioration shall be greater than that granted under the Rules for Offenders of the First Division.[142]

This rule was introduced specifically to deal with suffragettes, but was also an attempt to solve the problem of the political prisoner in local prisons. In essence, it enabled the government to separate two aspects of political prisoner status that had previously been closely linked: status and conditions.

Rule 243A allowed those under it to be given significantly better conditions than previously allowed in division two without accepting their political status. No concessions were made to the demands of suffragettes for political status and the benefits of Rule 243A could be withdrawn in the event of misconduct. The Home Office stated that this proposal gave the Secretary of State the 'power to deal elastically with a certain class of prisoners without coming into conflict with a Court of Law and straining the Prerogative by transferring prisoners from one division to another'.[143]

A later measure, the Prisoners (Temporary Discharge for Ill-Health) Act of 1913, or the Cat and Mouse Act as it became popularly known, was a

---

[141] Radzinowicz and Hood, 'Status of Political Prisoners', p. 1460.
[142] PRO HO144/1042/183256/17. It was also pointed out, however, that the mere fact that the government felt the need to introduce such a measure could be interpreted as a victory for the suffragettes.
[143] Ibid.

measure introduced to deal with the hunger strike tactics of suffragettes and to avoid the possibility that a death might occur in prison. Awareness of the potential dangerousness of forcible feeding had been raised in March 1913 after Lillian Lenton was found seriously ill with pleurisy hours after being force-fed.[144] This Act enabled the government to release a hunger-striking suffragette from prison to recover her health and then re-arrest her. Only the time actually spent in prison would be counted as time served from her sentence.

The Home Office recognised that suffragettes would not obey the conditions of this Act. In practice it came to be used as a form of suspended sentence since efforts were made only to re-arrest those suffragettes who renewed their suffrage activities.[145] Such a policy brought an element of surveillance and coercion into the operation of the Act and introduced an additional and flexible method to control the agitation of political offenders outside of the prison.[146] The most famous example of the workings of the Cat and Mouse Act was that of Mrs Pankhurst. On the 3rd of April 1913 she was sentenced to three years' penal servitude for counselling persons to place gunpowder in a house being built for Lloyd George at Walton Heath. She was in and out of prison repeatedly and in the first five months she served less than three weeks of her sentence. The contest of wills ended only with the outbreak of war.[147]

Conclusion

The subject of political prisoners in the period 1850 to 1920 offers the researcher a very large and unwieldy array of sources. The quantity of evidence on political prisoners is related to factors such as the numbers of people from each political group that were imprisoned, their crime, the social class from which they were derived, and the extent of trouble they caused the prison authorities. Therefore, the largest, most contentious, and most militant groups of political prisoners tend to dominate not only the historical sources but also the writing on this subject. Such emphasis reflects the contemporary political and public attention these groups attracted and also, in some cases, the tenacity of the political problems they highlighted. This is particularly evident on the subject of British rule in Ireland, and also in the antagonism between individual conscience and the law that has been evident in the expansion of political pressure groups in the 1990s.

---

[144] PRO HO144/1255/234788.
[145] PRO HO45/10699/234800.
[146] Radzinowicz and Hood, 'Status of Political Prisoners', p. 1479.
[147] Ibid., p. 1478. Also see PRO HO144/1254/234646 which gives an account of the repeated detentions of Mrs Pankhurst and the lengths to which the police went to apprehend her.

In addition, the official sources reveal the differing experience of prison by groups that were much more influential and more vocal than ordinary prisoners. The same is true of the personal accounts left by some political prisoners which indicate the pride, the bitterness and the self-righteousness that was often inherent in such conflict. Political prisoners did not regard themselves as criminals and they therefore resisted the elements of the prison that transformed an individual into a prisoner, such as the rule of silence, the authority of the prison staff, and prison dress and labour. However, due to the fact that the treatment of political prisoners varied, both over time and between groups, these elements of the prison were not necessarily resisted to the same extent or in the same way.

The issue of political prisoners raises questions about the role of the prison as a coercive institution and the extent to which this has been manipulated by both the state and political groups. Imprisonment intensified the conflict between the government and these political groups. Insight can therefore be obtained into the organisational strategies of political prisoners, the prison authorities, and the government. Inside the prison, the power of political prisoners was in large part dictated by their numbers and by their organisation and co-ordination. Using these strengths, political prisoners could pressurise individual prison governors, the Prison Commissioners and the Home Office into granting incremental privileges. These privileges could increase the opportunity or ability of political offenders to pressurise for further concessions. This was a danger of which the Prison Commissioners were aware but which they were sometimes unable to prevent.

A flexible strategy was adopted to contend with the tactical creativity of the political prisoners. Such flexibility was shown, for instance, in the speed of the implementation of the Cat and Mouse Act. However, the extent of official flexibility was limited by the institutionalised structures of the prison which have historically been slow to change. In attempting to keep disobedience to a minimum, the prison authorities utilised existing techniques regarding the transfer of prisoners and the use of rewards and punishments. This achieved mixed results in the face of strong group subcultures among political prisoners. The imprisonment of political offenders was primarily a holding action by the government to prevent them committing further crimes or working to expand support for their cause, although it was, of course, also a punitive measure and many of these offenders suffered considerably and even died in prison.

One important factor to note is that some of the reactions of political prisoners to the prison were similar to those of non-political prisoners from higher social classes. The repulsion or rejection of ordinary criminals, seen as inherently different from themselves, is a testament to the success of the prison in labelling offenders as a distinct class, and also in imprisoning, to a large extent, the poorest, the least educated and sometimes the mentally and physically ill.

The importance of status to the political prisoner is perhaps what marks them out the most from other prisoners. For some political prisoners the quest for status and the pursuit of their cause overrode priorities of personal health and welfare. This begs recognition of their commitment without having to enter into judgements regarding the principles and methods of their organisations. To have allowed political prisoner status would have given these groups rights and privileges that could not easily be withdrawn. This would effectively have removed one of the main powers of the prison authorities to maintain order. In addition, the status of political prisoner would have lent official credibility to their organisations outside of the prisons. On the other hand, for political prisoners to have accepted the status of the criminal would have been to undermine the causes for which they had fought outside.

8

Conclusion: prison disturbances, structure and policy

The historical examination of disturbances in English prisons suggests that they have partly been an expression of a continual struggle over power. The struggle for power in the prison was constantly being waged between the prisoners, the prison staff and the prison authorities in the context of penal policy and discipline. Even the smallest offences against the prison rules and regulations by inmates could be a means of empowerment in this struggle. An illicit conversation or a forbidden item kept secret in a cell could constitute a successful challenge to the prison rules and regulations even if they became subject to punishment. The constraints of prison discipline and the authority of those who operated it necessitated the development of coping strategies by prisoners. In such circumstances, prison disturbances have also been an expression of frustration or desperation by prisoners in response to their environment. Therefore, an analysis of prison disturbances requires a broad examination of the structure, policy and internal dynamics of the prison.

The Woolf Report stated in 1991 that the serious disturbance of prison rioting could not be dismissed as one-off, purely local incidents, but that it was 'symptomatic of a series of serious underlying difficulties in the prison system'.[1] The report also went on to stress the importance of maintaining a correct balance between security, custody and justice and to emphasise the importance of ensuring that relations within the prison system were based on 'respect and responsibility'.[2] These comments indicated the complexity of the problems raised by prison disorder.

Woolf's observations considered the purpose and consequences of imprisonment as well as the distance between policy and its practical implementation in a prison system that had evolved over the previous 200 years. Historically, the prison authorities have retained a degree of autonomy and independence which has facilitated remoteness from other areas of government and from public scrutiny. The extent of official debate regarding the prison has in fact disguised the actual slow pace of change within the institution. Garland has drawn attention to this phenomenon and has

---

[1] H. Woolf and S. Tumin, *Prison Disturbances April 1990* (London: HMSO, 1991), Cm 1456, 16.

[2] Ibid.

observed that 'penal discourse is as much concerned with its projected image, public representation and legitimacy as it is with organising the practice of regulations'.[3] In a similar vein, Vivian Stern, one-time Director of the National Association for the Care and Resettlement of Offenders, described the history of Britain's prisons since 1945 as being dominated by a system which has defeated many dedicated people trying to improve it and in which 'the processes, procedures, rules, Standing Orders and Circular Instructions take on a life of their own, and gradually block out the consciousness that it is people not numbers being locked up'.[4] By approaching an analysis of the prison from the angle of disturbances that have occurred within it, the fact of the prison confining 'people not numbers' has remained predominant in this study.

The momentum of institutional routine and organisation and its effects upon those subject to it, as well as the imbalance between the amount of official debate and the amount of official action, has been an important aspect of this study of prison disturbances. This book has placed emphasis on particular themes to highlight the factors that were important in producing disorder not only at the specific historical stage in the development of the prison but often over the longer term. The basic themes explored in each chapter were not, however, isolated issues or the only determinants of particular disturbances; each prison disturbance was the consequence of a complex interaction of both personal and environmental factors.

Chapter 2 has highlighted the personal consequences of the structure and organisation of the prison, which resulted in a rigid routine and a monotonous and meaningless way of life for those subject to it. The distorted perception of time that resulted from this was a theme which appeared often in the personal accounts left by ex-prisoners and gives insight into the way in which prisoners tried to understand and cope with their environment. The externally determined routine and dependence of prison life simpli-fied existence to that of a child. This had repercussions for the dynamics of relationships between the prisoners and prison officers and for the identity and status of prisoners.

An examination of time in a highly regulated institution illustrated the existence of different perceptions of time, as opposed to that determined only by the clock. The development of an extended sense of the present was an inherent part of a sentence of long-term imprisonment and was, to a large extent, the intended consequence of prison policy. Empty time and long hours spent alone in their cells reinforced prisoners' perceptions regarding the institutional momentum of prison discipline and compounded the experience of prison time as personally isolating, or as dominated by the times

---

[3] D. Garland, *Punishment and Welfare: A History of Penal Strategies* (Aldershot: Gower, 1985), p. 261.
[4] V. Stern, *Bricks of Shame: Britain's Prisons* (Harmondsworth: Penguin, 1987), p. 267.

for food, sleep and work. One consequence of this was increased frustration and tension within the prison, which increased the likelihood of prison disturbances. In addition, the perception of an extended present also resulted in a distortion of the past and the future. The past gradually became stale and less useful as a source of identity and individual independence. Thought of the future was either to be avoided or was an avenue of escape into something imaginary and constructed.

Chapter 3 dealt with another factor that increased tension within the prison, the lack of belief by inmates in the legitimacy of the conditions and treatment that it imposed. Furthermore, the shifts in penal philosophy and policy over the period covered by this publication suggest that the prison had also failed to establish its legitimacy in the eyes of wider society. The evidence regarding the outbreak in Chatham Convict Prison in 1861 highlighted the unfairness that existed in the convict prison system and also the way in which the frustration caused by such unfairness could ignite into a large-scale conflict. Wilsnack has suggested that prison riots have been predominantly an expression of frustration at prisoners' lack of power rather than a demonstration of their force.[5] Such disturbances also highlighted the extent to which co-operation of inmates was necessary to maintain order in prison, although the reality of the convicts' position was that under no circumstances could the prison authorities allow inmates to gain the upper hand and retain it. Custody and security were the fundamental purposes of the prison.

Some of the causes of the Chatham Convict Prison outbreak, one of the largest prison disturbances in English history, were left behind in the 1860s. The remnants of the poor discipline and the brutality of the prisoners and prison staff who had been transferred from the hulks were gradually worked through the system. Convicts were organised into smaller groups on public works, and the obvious unfairness of penal legislation with regard to remission was amended. Nevertheless, evidence suggests that abuse of prison rules and regulations with regard to the fair and non-violent treatment of prisoners continued. Unofficial compromises and accommodations within the prisons also continued and have become part of the mechanisms that can maintain order in prisons, although the unpredictability and inequality of such compromises can also be a source of disorder. The unofficial side to the organisation and inter-relations that operated the prisons did not contribute to the establishment of fairness in the prison or mitigate the prison's legitimacy deficit. The outbreaks which occurred in the public works prisons during the late 1850s and early 1860s served to exacerbate public fears at the prospect of retaining serious criminals within the country following

---

[5] R.W. Wilsnack, 'Explaining Collective Violence in Prisons: Problems and Possibilities', in *Prison Violence*, ed. A.K. Cohen, G.F. Cole and R.G. Bailey (Lexington, Mass.: D.C. Heath, 1976), p. 73.

the running down of transportation. In addition, such disturbances hardened public opinion against convicts and highlighted the inadequacies of the penal system. This influenced the shift towards a more overtly deterrent philosophy from the mid-1860s.

An important aspect of the existence of unofficial compromises and accommodations in prison has been the persistence of inmate subcultures. Chapter 4 contended that inmate subcultures survived even after discipline within local prisons was tightened up and made increasingly uniform during the nineteenth century. Local prisons in particular were never the picture of organisation, rigour and discipline presented by revisionist writers such as Michel Foucault and Michael Ignatieff. Indeed, the rate of reform in local prisons varied considerably in the face of competing local priorities and pessimism with regard to the potential to reform short-sentenced prisoners. The United Gaol and House of Correction in Kingston-upon-Hull provided evidence of the slow rate of change and the direct interference that was, on occasion, required to force local authorities to invest in prison building and reform.

Inmate subcultures were significant in shaping the nature of internal relationships within individual prisons and in determining the extent of disobedience to prison rules and regulations. By their nature as an illicit part of the operation of the prison, inmate subcultures have rarely appeared in official records and if mention is made of this side of prison life it has tended to be implicit rather than explicit. The existence of inmate subcultures may well have helped to maintain a degree of order since the organisation of the prison was the framework within which inmate society was able to exist and establish an internal hierarchy. However, inmate society also constituted an undercurrent of continuous struggle with prison rules and regulations to probe the limits of operation and influence. Of course, the continuity and inclusiveness of this aspect of the prison should not be over-estimated; evidence of intimidation, theft and assault among prisoners would suggest that inmate subcultures also produced conflict between prisoners and could be as exclusive as they were inclusive.

The period from the mid-1860s to the end of the century was the most deterrent in the history of the modern prison. Historical writing has often laid much of the blame for this severity at the door of Edmund Du Cane, but the shift towards a more deterrent prison policy and practice was also the result of a change in wider public and Parliamentary opinion. The repeat offender especially was increasingly perceived as primitive and unresponsive to reformatory efforts and as a section of the population which would be discouraged from crime only by the deterrent example and experience of severe punishment. The deterrent prison system under Du Cane became expressed particularly in a more meticulous system of progressive stages. Rewards and privileges were recorded in a character book, and progress was determined by a system of accounting using marks earned by industry accompanied by good conduct.

The consequences of the increased intensity and deterrence of penal servitude during the period under Du Cane's administration were reflected in extreme forms of self-injury committed by convicts. Self-destructive behaviour was one means by which prisoners could call attention to their distress. This distress and helplessness were exacerbated by the lack of administrative checks to curb excesses within the prison rules and regulations, or abuses which occurred in contravention of them. Significantly, this period also witnessed the refinement of control methods, such as more sophisticated classification and segregation systems, as well as the entrenchment of a principle that remained largely unchallenged until the late twentieth century: that prisoners have no rights. Under this principle, even basic necessities could be designated by the prison authorities as privileges that had to be earned.

Chapter 6 made it clear that prison inmates were not responsible for all prison disturbances. Indeed, in 1907 a major and combined breach of prison rules and regulations was committed by a group of prison officers at Wormwood Scrubs Prison. An inmate had climbed on to the roof of one of the prison halls and created some disorder and excitement among the rest of the prisoners who were in their cells. In response, and after the principal officer had left the hall, a group of prison officers proceeded to enter individual cells and assault the occupants. One of the causes of the behaviour of these prison officers was that they felt alienated from prison reforms that were then taking place. These reforms were reflective of wider changes being implemented throughout the prison system.

Reforms of the period from 1895 to 1914 have been seen as representing a pivotal transition from penal policy dominated by classical ideas towards policy significantly influenced by newer positivist ideas about criminality and the appropriate way to treat offenders. The evidence regarding the major disturbance in Wormwood Scrubs certainly suggests that changes of a fundamentally different nature to those that had been introduced in the preceding decades were being implemented. However, given the limited nature of reforms in the direction of alleviating the condition of imprisonment, the reaction of prison warders must be explained more by the nature of reforms rather than their extent. Among the explanations given by the prison officers for their assaults upon prisoners in Wormwood Scrubs Prison in 1907 was that they could no longer rely upon being supported by the governor or deputy governor when reports were made against them by prisoners. Here can be seen a gradual alleviation of intensity in the prison punishments of the second half of the nineteenth century.

The entrenched militaristic and hierarchical structure of prison staff meant that they resisted the ameliorative measures that were gradually being introduced for the benefit of prisoners. The resentment that this caused was exacerbated by the resistance of prison authorities to the establishment of an independent prison officers' union and to agitation for an improvement of their pay and conditions. There was also considerable resistance to ameliorative change from senior prison staff. An autobiography published in 1932 provides a good example of the attitudes behind such resistance. This was written by Colonel Rich, an ex-prison governor, who worked in English prisons during the early twentieth century.[6] Rich objected to official interference in the running of prisons, particularly by those who had little or no experience, and saw this as one of the ways in which 'impractical idealists' had been allowed to undermine prison discipline.[7] He saw no reformative value in 'giving concerts to the bandits and other desperate characters' that inhabited the prisons, and instead declared that 'The 'cat' [cat-o'-nine-tails] would have cured the majority of them but a system of classes, visitors, concerts, lectures and similar amenities had not the slightest influence to keep them out of prison.' According to Colonel Rich, 'it was merely weakness to try to buy good conduct by a scheme of privilege'.[8]

Many of the penal innovations that were implemented in the period from 1895 to the First World War were in marginal institutions outside of the mainstream local and convict prisons. These marginal institutions, such as the inebriate reformatories and the preventive detention institution on the Isle of Wight, which were the most overt examples of the influence of positivist ideas, proved to be complete or partial failures. These failures were in part due to the continued strength of classical ideas regarding punishment, particularly among the judiciary, but also to the impracticability or immaturity of positivist theories. The mainstream local and convict prisons continued to provide the symbolic backbone of the English prison system. Indeed, the most significant reforms of penal policy during this period served to prevent more offenders from entering prison in the first place rather than to significantly improve their conditions once incarcerated.

Chapter 7 dealt with a cause of disorder in English prisons which resulted in a considerable amount of publicity and criticism of the prison authorities – the confinement of political offenders. Throughout the period covered by this publication, the prison was used to incarcerate those members of political groups who resorted to breaking the law to forward their campaigns. Members of political groups were also imprisoned during the First World War because they were considered to be of hostile association or intent. The imprisonment of political offenders was imposed to enforce the law and to uphold the principle, which has since been retained, that no exemption from the criminal law should be given on grounds of political motive or objectives.

Political prisoners were often more organised and more educated than ordinary prisoners and also had the support and co-ordinated efforts of their

---

[6] Lieutenant Colonel C.E.F. Rich, *Recollections of a Prison Governor* (London: Hurst and Blackett, 1932), p. 48.
[7] Ibid., pp. 128 and 46.
[8] Ibid., p. 274.

political groups outside of the prison. In such circumstances, the experiences of imprisoned members of political groups – such as Irish nationalists, suffragettes and conscientious objectors to compulsory conscription – were publicised in attempts to attain a kind of martyrdom for them and to further their cause. The issue of political prisoners raised questions about the role of the prison and also the extent to which the symbol of the prison could be manipulated both by the state and by political groups. Certainly, prison intensified the conflict both physically and philosophically between government and these groups. Much of the debate surrounding suffragettes and conscientious objectors concerned the liberal conundrum about the balance between the obligations of the individual to the state and to their own conscience.

Political prisoners did not see themselves as criminal and they therefore resisted the elements of prison that transformed an individual into a prisoner. These included the rule of silence, the authority of the prison staff, and prison labour and dress. Political prisoners were, in many cases, successful in using their strength and unity to pressurise the government and the prison authorities into awarding concessions. Overall, the government was able to adopt a measure of flexibility in answer to the fluid strategies employed by the groups of political prisoners. This flexibility on the part of the government was most clearly indicated by the passing of the Temporary Discharge for Ill-Health Act in 1913. However, institutional factors limited the amount of flexibility open to the government and, therefore, tried and tested methods of control were often used in dealing with these prisoners who were subject, for instance, to being transferred between prisons and to the continuum of rewards and punishments. The government was also able to exploit its informal influence over the judiciary. Nevertheless, such methods achieved mixed results in the face of strong group subcultures among these prisoners.

The importance of status to many political prisoners during this period was perhaps what marked them out most from other prisoners. The desire for recognition as being different, superior and more entitled to have a voice in the nature of their own imprisonment than the general run of prisoners was at the root of much of the disorder that they created. However, for the government to have recognised their political status would have given these prisoners the grounds to demand rights and privileges that could not easily be withdrawn.

The history of the prison in England has been regularly marked by disturbances. Such disturbances were both a consequence and a determinant of the organisation and structure of the prison. The nature and extent of prisoner resistance and disorder were however also a reflection of the prison and its inmates as a part of British society. The sometimes quite rigorous reception procedures were unable to cleave the prisoner from their past nor from their need for independent action or communication no matter how small. This is most explicit with regard to political prisoners whose challenges have left much greater historical reverberations than other prisoners, but can also be seen in the revolving door of local imprisonment. For convicts undergoing long sentences, the prison was closer to the total institutions depicted by Foucault and others, but still incoming inmates brought news, convicts sometimes worked, and trafficked, with civilians on the public works and on occasion newspapers could be smuggled in. In the convict prisons especially, large-scale disturbances, violent assaults and severe cases of self-injury reflected isolation and powerlessness and were a means of eliciting support, or at least acknowledgement, from outside the prison.

Throughout the period from the mid-nineteenth century to the 1920s, reformers, prison officials and the press promoted the idea that a better organised, more deterrent, better resourced, more rehabilitative or fairer prison would produce a desired impact on crime: deter it, prevent it, reform those who committed it, etc. Despite recognition of the defects of the prison, a basic faith in the power of an 'ideal' prison institution has persisted. In this sense the 'real' prison will never be legitimate but will always have a social role.[9]

---

[9] Currently the prison population seem to be rising inexorably. For example, in November 2002 there were 72,424 inmates in the prisons of England and Wales, an increase of 6 per cent on the previous year. See www.homeoffice.gov.uk/rds/pdfs2/prisnov02.pdf

Bibliography

Archives and libraries

Beverley Local Studies Library, East Yorkshire.
British Library Newspaper Archive, Colindale
Carnarvon Papers: British Library.
Du Cane Papers: Bodleian Library.
Hull City Record Office.
Hull Local Studies Library.
Jebb Papers: British Library of Social and Political Science.
Leeds Central Library.
Manchester Central Library.
Prison Service Library, Wakefield (now in Rugby).
Public Record Office.
Ruggles-Brise Papers: Chelmsford Record Office.
University of Hull Brynmor Jones Library.

Parliamentary papers

Statutes

Gaols Act, 1823: 4 Geo.IV, c.64.
Prisons Act, 1835: 5 & 6 Will.IV, c.38.
Prisons Act, 1839: 2 & 3 Vict., c.56.
Convicted Prisoners Removal Act, 1853: 16 & 17 Vict., c.43.
Penal Servitude Act, 1857: 20 & 21 Vict., c.3.
Security from Violence Act, 1863: 26 & 27 Vict., c.44.
Prison Ministers Act, 1863: 26 & 27 Vict., c.79.
Penal Servitude Act, 1864: 26 & 27 Vict., c.47.
Prison Act, 1865: 28 & 29 Vict., c.126.
Prevention of Crimes Act, 1871: 34 & 35 Vict., c.112.
Prison Act, 1877: 40 & 41 Vict., c.21.
Summary Jurisdiction Act, 1879: 42 & 43 Vict., c.49.
Prevention of Crime Act, 1879: 42 & 43 Vict., c.55.
Central Criminal Court (Prisons) Act, 1881: 44 & 45 Vict., c.64.
Penal Servitude Act, 1891: 54 & 55 Vict., c.69.
Prison Act, 1898: 61 & 62 Vict., c.41.

Inebriates Act, 1898: 61 & 62 Vict., c.60.
Vaccination Act, 1898: 61 & 62 Vict., c.49.
The Probation of Offenders Act, 1907: 7 Edw.7.c.17.
Vaccination Act, 1907: 7 Edw.7.c.31.
The Prevention of Crime Act, 1908: 8 Edw.7.c.59.
Temporary Discharge for Ill-Health Act, 1913: 3 Geo.5.c.4.
Defence of the Realm Act, 1914: 4 & 5 Geo.5.c.30.
Defence of the Realm Amendment Act, 1914: 5 Geo.5.c.8.
Defence of the Realm Act, 1915: 5 Geo.5.c.34.
The Criminal Justice Administration Act, 1914: 4 & 5 Geo.5.c.58.
Military Service Act, 1916: 5 & 6 Geo.5.c.104.
Military Service Amendment Act, 1916: 6 & 7 Geo.5.c.15.

Annual reports

First Report of the Inspectors of Prisons (NE), 1836(117–1), XXXV.161.
Second Report of the Inspectors of Prisons (NE), 1837(89), XXXII.499.
Third Report of the Inspectors of Prisons (NE), 1837–8(141), XXXI.1.
Fourth Report of the Inspectors of Prisons (NE), 1839(199), XXII.1.
Fifth Report of the Inspectors of Prisons (NE), 1840(258), XXV.565.
Sixth Report of the Inspectors of Prisons (NE), 1841 s.2 (339), V.1.
Seventh Report of the Inspectors of Prisons (NE), 1836(117–1), XXXV.161.
Eighth Report of the Inspectors of Prisons (NE), 1843(517), XXV & XXVI. 249.
Ninth Report of the Inspectors of Prisons (NE), 1844(595), XXIX.227.
Tenth Report of the Inspectors of Prisons (NE), 1845(675), XXIV.1.
Eleventh Report of the Inspectors of Prisons (NE), 1846(754), XXI.483.
Thirteenth Report of the Inspectors of Prisons (NE), 1847–8(997), XXXVI.361.
Fourteenth Report of the Inspectors of Prisons (NE), 1849(1055), XXVI.167.
Fifteenth Report of the Inspectors of Prisons (NE), 1850(1167), XXVIII.291.
Sixteenth Report of the Inspectors of Prisons (NE), 1851(1355), XXVII.461.
Seventeenth Report of the Inspectors of Prisons (NE), 1852–3(1600), LII.1.
Eighteenth Report of the Inspectors of Prisons (NE), 1856(2129), XXXIII.1.
Nineteenth Report of the Inspectors of Prisons (NE), 1856(2102), XXXIII.385.
Twentieth Report of the Inspectors of Prisons (NE), 1857 s.1 (2204), VII.313.
Twenty-first Report of the Inspectors of Prisons (NE), 1857 s.2 (2250), XXIII.1.
Twenty-second Report of the Inspectors of Prisons (NE), 1857–8(2373), XXIX.1.
Twenty-third Report of the Inspectors of Prisons (NE), 1857–8(2328), XXIX.209.
Twenty-fourth Report of the Inspectors of Prisons (NE), 1859 s.1 (2471), XI.213.
Twenty-fifth Report of the Inspectors of Prisons (NE), 1860(2645), XXXV.381.
Twenty-sixth Report of the Inspectors of Prisons (NE), 1862(2941), XXV.1.
Twenty-seventh Report of the Inspectors of Prisons (NE), 1862(2941–1), XXV.237.

Twenty-eighth Report of the Inspectors of Prisons (NE), 1863(3234), XXIII.109.
Twenty-ninth Report of the Inspectors of Prisons (NE), 1864(3326), XXVI.89.
Thirtieth Report of the Inspectors of Prisons (NE), 1865(3520), XXIII.257.
Thirty-first Report of the Inspectors of Prisons (NE), 1866(3715), XXXVII.233.
Thirty-second Report of the Inspectors of Prisons (NE), 1867–8(4029), XXXIV.1.
Thirty-fourth Report of the Inspectors of Prisons (NE), 1871(C.259), XXIX.1.

Report on the Discipline and Management of Convict Prisons, 1851(1419), XXVIII.213.
Report on the Discipline and Management of Convict Prisons, 1852–3(1572), LI.1.
Report on the Discipline and Management of Convict Prisons, 1852–3(1659), LI.247.
Report on the Discipline and Management of Convict Prisons, 1854(1846), XXXIII.1.
Report on the Discipline and Management of Convict Prisons, 1854–5(2004), XXV.433.
Report on the Discipline and Management of Convict Prisons, 1857–8(2414), XXIX.285.

Report of the Directors of Convict Prisons, 1851(1409), XXVIII.1.
Report of the Directors of Convict Prisons, 1852(1524), XXIV.197.
Report of the Directors of Convict Prisons, 1852–3(1656), LI.385.
Report of the Directors of Convict Prisons, 1854(1825), XXXIII.181.
Report of the Directors of Convict Prisons, 1854–5(1986), XXV.33.
Report of the Directors of Convict Prisons, 1856(2126), XXXV.1.
Report of the Directors of Convict Prisons, 1857 S.2(2263), XXIII.65.
Report of the Directors of Convict Prisons, 1857–8(2423), XXIX.483.
Report of the Directors of Convict Prisons, 1859 S.2(2556), XIII, Pt.1.191.
Report of the Directors of Convict Prisons, 1860(2713), XXXV.429.
Report of the Directors of Convict Prisons, 1861(2879), XXX.237.
Report of the Directors of Convict Prisons, 1862(3011), XXV.331.
Report of the Directors of Convict Prisons, 1863(3208), XXIV.1.
Report of the Directors of Convict Prisons, 1864(3388), XXVI.209.
Report of the Directors of Convict Prisons, 1865(3573), XXV.1.
Report of the Directors of Convict Prisons, 1866(3732), XXXVIII.1.
Report of the Directors of Convict Prisons, 1867(3928), XXXVI.1.
Report of the Directors of Convict Prisons, 1867–8(4083), XXXIV.519.
Report of the Directors of Convict Prisons, 1868–9(4212), XXX.1.
Report of the Directors of Convict Prisons, 1870(C.204), XXXVIII.1.
Report of the Directors of Convict Prisons, 1871(C.449), XXXI.1.
Report of the Directors of Convict Prisons, 1872(C.649), XXXI.385.
Report of the Directors of Convict Prisons, 1873(C.850), XXXIV.1.
Report of the Directors of Convict Prisons, 1874(C.1089), XXX.55.

Report of the Directors of Convict Prisons, 1875(C.1346), XXXIX.1.
Report of the Directors of Convict Prisons, 1876(C.1596), XXXVII.1.
Report of the Directors of Convict Prisons, 1877(C.1845), XLV.1.
Report of the Directors of Convict Prisons, 1878(C.2175), XLIII.1.
Report of the Directors of Convict Prisons, 1878–9(C.2446), XXXV.1.
Report of the Directors of Convict Prisons, 1880(C.2694), XXXVI.1.
Report of the Directors of Convict Prisons, 1881(C.3073), LII.1.
Report of the Directors of Convict Prisons, 1882(C.3374), XXXIV.1.
Report of the Directors of Convict Prisons, 1883(C.3828), XXXIII.1.
Report of the Directors of Convict Prisons, 1884(C.4178), XLIII.1.
Report of the Directors of Convict Prisons, 1884–5(C.4568), XXXIX.1.
Report of the Directors of Convict Prisons, 1886(C.4833), XXXV.457.
Report of the Directors of Convict Prisons, 1887(C.5205), XLI.725.
Report of the Directors of Convict Prisons, 1888(C.5551), LVIII.615.
Report of the Directors of Convict Prisons, 1889(C.5880), XLI.657.
Report of the Directors of Convict Prisons, 1890(C.6190), XXXVII.515.
Report of the Directors of Convict Prisons, 1890–1(C.6471), XLIII.449.
Report of the Directors of Convict Prisons, 1892(C.6737), XLII.467.
Report of the Directors of Convict Prisons, 1893–4(C.7184), XLVII.427.
Report of the Directors of Convict Prisons, 1894(C.7508), XLIV.491.
Report of the Directors of Convict Prisons, 1895(C.7872), LVI.1177.

First Report of the Commissioners of Prisoners, 1878(C.2174), XLII.1.
Second Report of the Commissioners of Prisoners, 1878–9(C.2442), XXXIV.1.
Third Report of the Commissioners of Prisoners, 1880(C.2733), XXXV.1.
Fourth Report of the Commissioners of Prisoners, 1881(C.3072), LI.441.
Fifth Report of the Commissioners of Prisoners, 1882(C.3373), XXXIII.443.
Sixth Report of the Commissioners of Prisoners, 1883(C.3807), XXXI.445.
Seventh Report of the Commissioners of Prisoners, 1884(C.4180), XLII.461.
Eighth Report of the Commissioners of Prisoners, 1884–5(C.4567), XXXVII.
  527.
Ninth Report of the Commissioners of Prisoners, 1886(C.4834), XXXVI.1.
Tenth Report of the Commissioners of Prisoners, 1887(C.5215), XLI.203.
Eleventh Report of the Commissioners of Prisoners, 1888(C.5552), LVIII.1.
Twelfth Report of the Commissioners of Prisoners, 1889(C.5881), XLI.1.
Thirteenth Report of the Commissioners of Prisoners, 1890(C.6191), XXXVII.1.
Fourteenth Report of the Commissioners of Prisoners, 1890–1(C.6470), XLIII.1.
Fifteenth Report of the Commissioners of Prisoners, 1893(C.6738), XLII.1.
Sixteenth Report of the Commissioners of Prisoners, 1893–4(C.7197), XLVII.1.
Seventeenth Report of the Commissioners of Prisoners, 1894(C.7509), XLIV.1.
Eighteenth Report of the Commissioners of Prisoners, 1895(C.7880), LVI.727.

Report of Commissioners of Prisons and Directors of Convict Prisons,
  1896(C.8200), XLIV.235.

Report of Commissioners of Prisons and Directors of Convict Prisons, 1897 (C.8590), XL.105.

Report of Commissioners of Prisons and Directors of Convict Prisons, 1898 (C.8998), XLVII.23.

Report of Commissioners of Prisons and Directors of Convict Prisons, 1899 (C.9452), XLIII.65.

Report of Commissioners of Prisons and Directors of Convict Prisons, 1900 (Cd.380), XLI.1.

Report of Commissioners of Prisons and Directors of Convict Prisons, 1902 (Cd.804), XLV.1.

Report of Commissioners of Prisons and Directors of Convict Prisons, 1902 (Cd.1278), XLVI.1.

Report of Commissioners of Prisons and Directors of Convict Prisons, 1904 (Cd.1800), XXXV.1.

Report of Commissioners of Prisons and Directors of Convict Prisons, 1905 (Cd.2273), XXXVII.1.

Report of Commissioners of Prisons and Directors of Convict Prisons, 1906 (Cd.2723), L.1.

Report of Commissioners of Prisons and Directors of Convict Prisons, 1906 (Cd.3169), L.587.

Report of Commissioners of Prisons and Directors of Convict Prisons, 1908 (Cd.3738), LII.1.

Report of Commissioners of Prisons and Directors of Convict Prisons, 1908 (Cd.4300), LII.447.

Report of Commissioners of Prisons and Directors of Convict Prisons, 1909 (Cd.4847), XLV.133 & 277.

Report of Commissioners of Prisons and Directors of Convict Prisons, 1910 (Cd.5360)), XLV.277.

Report of Commissioners of Prisons and Directors of Convict Prisons, 1911 (Cd.5891), XXXIX.243.

Report of Commissioners of Prisons and Directors of Convict Prisons, 1912–13 (Cd.6406), XLIII.345.

Report of Commissioners of Prisons and Directors of Convict Prisons, 1914 (Cd.7092), XLV.1.

Report of Commissioners of Prisons and Directors of Convict Prisons, 1914 (Cd.7601), XLV.361.

Report of Commissioners of Prisons and Directors of Convict Prisons, 1914–16 (Cd.7837), XXXIII.1.

Report of Commissioners of Prisons and Directors of Convict Prisons, 1916 (Cd.8342), XV.75.

Report of Commissioners of Prisons and Directors of Convict Prisons, 1917–18 (Cd.8764), XVIII.109.

Report of Commissioners of Prisons and Directors of Convict Prisons, 1918 (Cd.9174), XII.587.

Report of Commissioners of Prisons and Directors of Convict Prisons, 1919 (Cmd.374), XXVII.759.

Report of Commissioners of Prisons and Directors of Convict Prisons, 1920 (Cmd.972), XXIII.1.

Reports of Royal Commissions, Select Committees and Departmental Committees

Select Committee of House of Lords on Gaols and Houses of Correction in England and Wales, 1835(438), XI.1.

Select Committee on Prison Discipline, 1850(632), XVII.1.

Royal Commission to inquire into Condition and Treatment of Prisoners in Birmingham Borough Prison, 1854(1809), XXXI.1.

Royal Commission to inquire into Condition and Treatment of Prisoners in Leicester County Gaol and House of Correction, 1854(1808), XXXIV.197.

Royal Commission to Inquire into the Operation of the Acts Relating to Transportation and Penal Servitude, 1863(3190), XXI.1.

Select Committee of the House of Lords on Gaol Discipline, 1863(499), IX.1.

Reports of Committee to inquire into Dietaries of Convict Prisons, 1864(467), XLIX.9.

Commission to inquire into Treatment of Treason-Felony Convicts in English Prisons, 1871(C.319), XXXII.1.

Report of Committee to inquire into Dietaries of Prisons in England and Wales, 1878(95), XLII.53.

Royal Commission to inquire into Working of Penal Servitude Acts, 1878–9(C.2368), XXXVII.1.

Committee of Inquiry as to Rules concerning Wearing of Prison Dress, 1889(C.5759), LXI.269.

Report as to Treatment of Prisoners convicted of Treason-Felony, 1890(C.6016), XXXVII.629.

Departmental Committee on Prisons, 1895(C.7702), LVI.1.

Observations of Prison Commissioners on Recommendations of Departmental Committee on Prisons, 1896(C.7995), XLIV.185.

Statement by Prison Commissioners of Steps taken to carry out Recommendations in Report of Departmental Committee on Prisons, 1896(C.7996), XLIV.177, 1898(C.8790), XLVII.1.

Report of Departmental Committee on Prison Dietaries, 1899(C.9166), XLIII.1.

Return of Judicial Statistics of England and Wales

1861(2860), LX.477.

1862(3025), LVI.491.

1863(3181), LXV.437.
1864(3370), LVII.445.
1865(3534), LII.445.
1866(3726), LXVIII.485.
1867(3919), LXVI.523.
1867–8(4062), LXVII.519.
1868–9(4196), LVIII.513.
1870(C.195), LXIII.525.
1871(C.442), LXIV.1.

Miscellaneous Parliamentary Papers

Return from Each Gaol and House of Correction in the United Kingdom Relating to Prisoners for Libel, 1840(438), XXXVIII.241.

A Copy of Correspondence between Her Majesty's Secretary of State for the Home Department, and the Visiting Magistrates of York Castle respecting the Treatment of Mr Feargus O'Connor, 1840(395), XXXVIII.615.

Surveyor General of Prisons
  Second Report, 1847(867), XXIX.1.
  General Report, 1862(3055), XXV.687.

Returns relating to the recent Convict Disturbances at Chatham Convict Prison, 1861(125), LII.3.

Copy of all reports made by any of the Warders to the Governor of the Convict Establishment at Portsmouth, relative to the Attack made upon Mr George Dean, a Warder of that Establishment, by a Convict of the name of Lewis Francis, 1863(114), XLVIII.381.

Correspondence relating to a Report on Prison Discipline, 1864(313), XLIX.543.

Report of Commission on Treatment of Treason-Felony Convicts in English Convict Prisons, 1867(3880), XXXV.673.

Copy of all Affidavits used in the Court of Queen's Bench on Application of D. Reddin against Dr. Burns, Medical Officer of Chatham Convict Prison, 1873(366), LIV.287.

Copies of Evidence given before the Jury at the Inquest held recently in Portland Prisons on the Death of a Convict, 1875(302), LXII. 286.

Inquiry as to alleged Ill-treatment of Convict C. McCarthy in Chatham Convict Prison, 1878(C.1978), LXIII.769.

Depositions before Coroner at Inquest on Body of J. Nolan [Prisoner in Clerkenwell Prison], 1878–9(61), LIX.539.

Report and Evidence from Commission of Inquiry into Circumstances of Death of J. Nolan in Clerkenwell Prison, 1878–9(79), LIX, 501.

Report on an Inquiry into Allegations made against Acting Governor of Wandsworth Prison concerning his Action against certain Disorderly Prisoners, 1919(Cmd.131), XXVII.1.

Books and journal articles

Adams, R. *Prison Riots in Britain and the USA*. London: Macmillan, 1994.

Addison, P. *Churchill on the Home Front: 1900–1955*. London: Jonathan Cape, 1992.

Andenaes, J. *Punishment and Deterrence*. Michigan: University of Michigan Press, 1974.

Anon. (H.W. Holland and F. Greenwood) 'Revelations of Prison Life', *The Cornhill Magazine*, 7 (January–June 1863), pp. 638–48.

Anon. (H. Martineau) 'Life in the Criminal Class', *The Edinburgh Review*, 122 (July–October 1865), pp. 337–70.

Anon. (S. Roe) 'A Convict's Views of Penal Discipline', *The Cornhill Magazine*, 10 (July–December 1864), pp. 722–33.

Atkinson, A. 'Four Patterns of Convict Protest', *Labour History*, 37 (November 1979), pp. 28–51.

Bailey, V. 'Churchill as Home Secretary: Prison Reform', *History Today*, 35 (March 1985), pp. 10–13.

—— 'English Prisons, Penal Culture, and the Abatement of Imprisonment, 1895–1922', *Journal of British Studies*, 36 (July 1997), pp. 285–324.

—— 'Salvation Army Riots, The "Skeleton Army" and Legal Authority in the Provincial Town', in *Social Control in Nineteenth Century Britain*. ed. A.P. Donajgrodzki. London: Croom Helm, 1977.

Balfour, J.S. *My Prison Life*. London: Chapman and Hall, 1907.

Bartrip, P.W.J. 'Public Opinion and Law Enforcement: The Ticket-of-Leave Scares in Mid-Victorian Britain', in *Policing and Punishment in Nineteenth Century Britain*, ed. V. Bailey. London: Croom Helm, 1981.

—— 'State Intervention in Mid-Nineteenth Century Britain: Fact or Fiction?' *Journal of British Studies*, 23, No. 1 (Fall 1983), pp. 63–83.

Beccaria, C. *On Crimes and Punishments*, translated by H. Paolucci. Indianapolis: Bobbs-Merrill, 1963.

Beetham, D. 'In Defence of Legitimacy', *Political Studies*, 41 (1993), pp. 488–91.

—— *The Legitimation of Power*. London: Macmillan, 1991.

Bentley, R. *Five Years' Penal Servitude by One Who Has Endured It*. London, 1877.

Bird, J.C. *Control of Enemy Alien Civilians in Great Britain 1914–1918*. New York: Garland Publishing, 1986.

Blake, W. *Quod*. London: Hodder & Stoughton, 1927.

Blom-Cooper, L.J. 'The Centralization of Governmental Control of National Prison Services, with Special Reference to the Prison Act 1877', in *Prisons, Past and Future*, ed. J.C. Freeman. London: Heinemann, 1978.

Borland, J., R.D. King, and K. McDermott. 'The Irish in Prison: a tighter nick for "the Micks"?' *British Journal of Sociology*, 46 (1995), pp. 372–94.

Bottomley, A.K. 'What is Special about Special Units', *Prison Service Journal*, 92 (March 1992), pp. 2–5.

Brewer, J., and J. Styles 'Popular Attitudes to the Law in the Eighteenth Century', in *Crime and Society, Readings in History and Theory*, compiled by M. Fitzgerald, G. McLennon and J. Pawson. London: Open University Press, 1981.

Brockway, A. Fenner. *Inside the Left: Thirty Years of Platform, Press, Prison and Parliament*. London: George Allen & Unwin, 1947.

Brown, A. 'Conflicting Objectives: Suffragette Prisoners and Female Prison Staff in Edwardian England', *Women's Studies: An Interdisciplinary Journal* 31, No. 5, (2002), pp. 627–44.

—— 'A Disciplined Environment: Penal Reform in the East Riding House of Correction', *Family and Community History* 4, No. 2 (2001), pp. 99–110.

—— '"Doing Time": The Extended Present of the Long-term Prisoner', *Time and Society* 7, No. 1 (1998), pp. 93–102.

—— 'Hull Prison and its Inmates', in *Aspects of Hull*. Bradford: Warncliffe Publications, 1999.

—— 'Legitimacy in the Evolution of the Prison: The Chatham Convict Prison Outbreak 1861', *Criminal Justice History* 18 (2003).

Campbell, J. *Thirty Years' Experience of a Medical Officer in the English Convict Service*. London: T. Nelson and Sons, 1884.

Carlen, P (ed.) with J. Hicks, J. O'Dwyer, D. Christina and C. Tchaikovsky. *Criminal Women: Autobiographical Accounts*. Cambridge: Polity Press, 1985.

Cashman, D.B. *The Life of Michael Davitt*. Glasgow: Cameron, Fergusson, n.d.

Cavadino, M. 'Explaining the Penal Crisis', *Prison Service Journal* 87 (1984), pp. 2–12.

Cavadino, M., and J. Dignan. *The Penal System: An Introduction*, 3rd edn. London: Sage Publications, 2002.

Chamberlain, W.J. *Fighting for Peace: The Story of the War Resistance Movement*. London: No More War Movement, 1928.

Clarke, J., S. Hall, T. Jefferson and B. Roberts, 'Subcultures, Cultures and Class: A Theoretical Overview', in *Resistance through Rituals: Youth Subcultures in Post-War Britain*, ed. S. Hall and T. Jefferson. London: Hutchinson, 1976.

Clarke, T. *Glimpses of an Irish Felon's Prison Life*. Dublin/London, 1922.

Clay, W.L. *The Prison Chaplain: A Memoir of the Rev. John Clay, B.D. Late Chaplain of the Preston Gaol*. London: Macmillan, 1861.

Clemmer, D. *The Prison Community*. New York: Holt, Rinehart and Winston, 1958.

Cloward, R.A., and G.H. Grosser, eds. *Theoretical Studies in Social Organisation of the Prison*. New York: Social Science Research Council, 1960.

Cohen, A.K. *Prison Violence*, ed. A.K. Cohen, G.F. Cole and R.G. Bailey. Lexington, Mass.: D.C. Heath, 1976.

Cohen, C. *Civil Disobedience, Conscience, Tactics and the Law*. New York: Columbia University Press, 1971.

Cohen, E.A. *Human Behaviour in the Concentration Camp*. London: Jonathan Cape, 1954.

Cohen, S., and L. Taylor. *Psychological Survival: The Experience of Long-Term Imprisonment*. Harmondsworth: Penguin, 1972.

Cole, Gilbert. C. *The Objectors to Conscription and War*. Manchester: Co-operative Printing Society, 1936.

Collins, W.J. 'The Treatment of Inebriates, Municipal Reformers and the Farm Field Reformatory', *The Nineteenth Century and After* 74 (October 1913), pp. 764–73.

Colum, P. *Arthur Griffith*. Dublin: Gill & Macmillan, 1959.

Connolly, W. *Legitimacy and the State*. Oxford: Basil Blackwell, 1984.

Connolly, W.E. 'Beyond Good and Evil: The Ethical Sensibility of Michel Foucault', *Political Theory* 21, No. 3 (Aug 1993), pp. 365–89.

Coogan, T.P. *On The Blanket: The H-Block Story*. Dublin: Ward River Press, 1980.

Cook, A. *Our Prison System*. London: Drane, 1914.

Cornish, W.R., J. Hart, A.H. Manchester and J. Stevenson. *Crime and the Law in Nineteenth Century Britain*. Dublin: Irish Academic Press, 1978.

Cross, G. *A Quest for Time: The Reduction of Work in Britain and France, 1840–1940*. Los Angeles/London: California Press, 1989.

Cross, R. *Punishment, Prison and the Public: An Assessment of Penal Reform in Twentieth Century England by an Armchair Penologist*. London: Stevens, 1971.

Dangerfield, G. *The Strange Death of Liberal England*. London: Macgibbon & Kee, 1966.

Davis, J. 'The London Garotting Panic of 1862: A Moral Panic and the Creation of a Criminal Class in Mid-Victorian England', in *Crime and the Law: The Social History of Crime in Western Europe since 1500*, ed. V.A.C. Gatrell, B. Lenman and G. Parker. London: Europa Publications, 1980.

Davitt, M. 'Criminal and Prison Reform', *The Nineteenth Century*, 36 (December 1894), pp. 875–89.

—— *Leaves from a Prison Diary, or Lectures to a 'Solitary' Audience*, introduced by T.W. Moody, Shannon: Irish University Press, 1972.

—— 'The Punishment of Penal Servitude', *The Contemporary Review*, 44 (Aug 1883): pp. 169–82.

De Berker, P. 'The Sociology of Change', in *Changing Concepts of Crime and its Treatment*, ed. H.J. Klare. Oxford: Pergamon Press, 1966.

De Lacy, M. 'Grinding Men Good? Lancashire's Prisons at Mid-Century', in *Policing and Punishment in Nineteenth Century Britain*, ed. V. Bailey. London: Croom Helm, 1981.

—— *Prison Reform in Lancashire 1700–1850: A Study in Local Administration*. Manchester: Manchester University Press, 1986.

Devoy, J. *Recollections of an Irish Rebel*, 2nd edn, introduction by S.O. Luing. Dublin: Irish University Press, 1969.

Du Cane, E.F. *An Account of the Manner in which Sentences of Penal Servitude are Carried out in England*. London: HMSO, 1872.

—— 'The Decrease in Crime', *The Nineteenth Century* 33 (March 1893), pp. 480–92.

—— 'Experiments in Punishment', *The Nineteenth Century* 6 (November 1879), pp. 869–92.

—— 'The Prison Committee Report', *The Nineteenth Century* 38 (August 1895), pp. 278–94.

—— 'The Prisons Bill and its Progress in Criminal Treatment', *The Nineteenth Century* 43 (May 1898), pp. 809–21.

—— *The Punishment and Prevention of Crime*. London: Macmillan, 1885.

—— 'The Unavoidable Uselessness of Prison Labour', *The Nineteenth Century*, 40 (October 1896), pp. 632–42.

Duckers, J.S. *'Handed Over': The Prison Experiences of Mr. J. Scott Duckers, Solicitor, of Chancery Lane, under the Military Service Act*. London: Daniel, 1917.

Evans, R. *The Fabrication of Virtue: English Prison Architecture 1750–1840*. Cambridge: Cambridge University Press, 1982.

Figgis, D. *A Second Chronicle of Jails*, Dublin: Talbot Press, 1919.

Finkelstein, E. *Prison Culture: An Inside View*. Aldershot: Avebury, 1993.

Fitzgerald, M. *Prisoners in Revolt*. London: Penguin, 1977.

Fitzgerald, M., and J. Sim. *British Prisons*. Oxford: Basil Blackwell, 1982.

Fletcher, I.C. '"A Star Chamber of the Twentieth Century": Suffragettes, Liberals and the 1908 "Rush the Commons" Case', *Journal of British Studies* 35 (October 1996), pp. 504–530.

Fletcher, S. Willis. *Twelve Months in an English Prison*. Boston: Lee & Shepherd, 1884.

Forsythe, W.J. 'The Aims and Methods of the Separate System', *Social Policy and Administration* 14, No. 3 (1980), pp. 249–56.

—— 'Centralisation and Local Autonomy: The Experience of English Prison 1820–1877', *Journal of Historical Sociology* 4, No. 3 (September 1991), pp. 317–45.

—— 'The Garland Thesis and the Origins of Modern English Prison Discipline', *Howard Journal of Criminal Justice* 34, No. 3 (Aug 1995), pp. 259–73.

—— 'National Socialists and the English Prison Commission: The Berlin Penitentiary Congress of 1935', *International Journal of the Sociology of Law* 17, No. 2 (1989), pp. 131–45.

—— *Penal Discipline, Reformatory Projects and the English Prison Commission, 1895–1939*. Exeter: University of Exeter Press, 1991.

—— 'Prisons and Panopticons', *Social Policy and Administration*, 18, No. 1 (Spring 1984), pp. 68–88.

—— *The Reform of Prisoners 1830–1900*. London: Croom Helm, 1987.

—— 'Relaxation and Reformation in English Prisons 1895–1939', *Social Policy and Administration* 23, No. 2 (July 1989), pp. 161–70.

—— A System of Discipline: Exeter Borough Prison 1819–1863. Exeter: Exeter University Press, 1983.

—— 'Women Prisoners and Women Penal Officials 1840–1921', British Journal of Criminology 33, No. 4 (Autumn 1993), pp. 525–40.

Foucault, M. Discipline and Punish: The Birth of the Prison. Harmondsworth: Penguin, 1979.

—— The Foucault Reader: An Introduction to Foucault's Thought, ed. P. Rabinow. London: Penguin, 1991.

—— 'Prison Talk', Michel Foucault: Power/Knowledge, Selected Interviews and Other Writings, ed. C. Gordon. Brighton: Harvester Press, 1980.

—— 'Two Lectures', Michel Foucault: Power/Knowledge, Selected Interviews and Other Writings, ed. C. Gordon. Brighton: Harvester Press, 1980.

Garland, D. Punishment and Modern Society: A Study in Social Theory. Oxford: Clarendon Press, 1990.

—— Punishment and Welfare: A History of Penal Strategies. Aldershot: Gower, 1985.

Gatrell, V.A.C. 'The Decline of Theft and Violence in Victorian and Edwardian England', in Crime and the Law: The Social History of Crime in Western Europe since 1500, ed. V.A.C. Gatrell, B. Lenman and G. Parker. London: Europa Publications, 1980.

Gatrell, V.A.C., and T.B. Hadden. 'Criminal Statistics and their Interpretation', in Nineteenth Century Society, ed. E.A. Wrigley. Cambridge: Cambridge University Press, 1972.

Glennie, P., and N. Thrift. 'Reworking E.P. Thompson, Work-discipline and Industrial Capitalism', Time and Society 5, No. 3 (1996), pp. 275–99.

Godfrey, C. 'The Chartist Prisoners, 1839–41', International Review of Social History 24 (1979), pp. 189–228.

Godfrey, C., and J. Epstien. 'Notes on Sources, HO 20/10: Interviews of Chartist Prisoners 1840–1', Society for the Study of Labour History Bulletin 34 (Spring 1977), pp. 27–34.

Goffman, E. 'On the Characteristics of Total Institutions: The Inmate World', in The Prison: Studies in Institutional Organization and Change. New York: Holt, Rinehart and Winston, 1966.

Gordon, M. Penal Discipline. London: Routledge and Sons, 1922.

Griffiths, A. Fifty Years of Public Service. London: Cassell, 1904.

—— Secrets of the Prison-House or Gaol Studies and Sketches, Vols I and II. London: Chapman and Hall, 1894.

Harding, C. 'The Inevitable End of a Discredited System? The Origins of the Gladstone Committee Report on Prisons', Historical Journal 31 (1988), pp. 591–608.

Harding, C., B. Hines and R. Ireland. Imprisonment in England and Wales: A Concise History. London: Croom Helm, 1985.

Hart, H.L.A. 'Principles of Punishment', in Philosophical Perspectives on Punishment, ed. G. Ezorsky. Albany, NY: University of New York Press, 1972.

Hartley, S. *The Irish Question as a Problem in British Foreign Policy 1914–1918*. London: Macmillan Press, 1987.

Hay, D. 'Property, Authority and the Law', in *Albion's Fatal Tree: Crime and Society in Eighteenth Century England*, ed. P. Linbaugh, J. Rule and E.P. Thompson. New York: Pantheon, 1975.

Heather Tomlinson, M. '"Not an Instrument of Punishment": Prison Diet in the Mid-Nineteenth Century', *Journal of Consumer Studies and Home Economics* 2 (1978), pp. 15–26.

—— 'Penal Servitude 1846–1865. A System in Evolution', in *Policing and Punishment in Nineteenth Century Britain*, ed. V. Bailey. London: Croom Helm, 1981.

—— '"Prison Palaces": A Re-appraisal of Early Victorian Prisons, 1835–1877', *Bulletin of the Institute of Historical Research* 51 (1978), pp. 60–71.

Henderson, C.R. *Modern Prison Systems: Their Organization and Regulation in Various Countries of Europe and America*. Washington: Government Printing Office, 1903.

Hennock, E.P. 'Central/Local Government Relations in England: An Outline 1800–1950', *Urban History Yearbook* (1982), pp. 38–49.

Henriques, U.R.Q. 'The Rise and Decline of the Separate System of Prison Discipline', *Past and Present* 54 (1972), pp. 61–93.

Heritage, I. 'The Politics of Rule 43', *Prison Service Journal* 94 (July 1994), pp. 14–19.

Hobhouse, Mrs. H. *I Appeal unto Caesar*. London, 1917.

Hobhouse, S. 'An English Prison from Within', *The Quarterly Review* 230 (July 1918), pp. 21–37.

Hobhouse, S., and A. Fenner Brockway. *English Prisons Today*. London: Longman, Green & Co., 1922.

Holton, S.S. 'In Sorrowful Wrath: Suffragette Militancy and the Romantic Feminism of Emmeline Pankhurst', in *British Feminism in the Twentieth Century*, ed. H.L. Smith. Aldershot: Elgar, 1990.

Ignatieff, M. 'The Ideological Origins of the Penitentiary', in *Crime and Theory: Readings in History and Theory*, ed. M. Fitzgerald, G. McLennon and J. Pawson. London: Routledge, 1981.

—— 'State, Civil Society and Total Institutions: A Critique of Recent Social Histories of Punishment', in *Social Control and the State*, ed. S. Cohen and A. Scull. Oxford: Robertson, 1983.

—— *A Just Measure of Pain: The Penitentiary in the Industrial Revolution 1750–1850*. London: Macmillan, 1978.

Jackson, J. *A Peep into the Prison House*. Hull, 1833.

James, A. and K. Bottomly, 'Prison Privatisation and the Remand Population: Principle Versus Pragmatism?', *Howard Journal of Criminal Justice* 37, No. 3 (1998), pp. 223–33.

Jebb, Major-General Sir Joshua. 'Prison Discipline', *Transactions of the National Association for the Promotion of Social Science* (1862), pp. 425–36.

Jones, D. *Crime, Protest, Community and Police in Nineteenth Century Britain*. London: Routledge & Kegan Paul, 1982.

Kennedy, T.C. 'Public Opinion and the Conscientious Objector, 1915–1919', *Journal of British Studies* 12, No. 2 (May 1973), pp. 105–19.

Lacey, N. *State Punishments, Political Principles and Community Values*. London: Routledge, 1988.

Lacombe, D. 'Reforming Foucault', *British Journal of Sociology* 2 (June 1996), pp. 332–52.

Laffan, M. 'The Unification of Sinn Fein in 1917', *Irish Historical Studies* 17 (1970–1), pp. 353–79.

Lee, J. *Ireland 1912–1985, Politics and Society*. Cambridge: Cambridge University Press, 1989.

—— *The Modernisation of Irish Society 1848–1918*. Dublin: Gill & Macmillan Ltd, 1973.

Leibling, A., G. Muit, G. Rose and A. Bottoms, *Incentives and Earned Privileges for Prisoners – An Evaluation*, Home Office Research Findings No. 87. London: Home Office Research and Statistics Directorate, 1999.

Leslie, S. 'Sir Evelyn Ruggles-Brise and Prison Reform', *The Nineteenth Century* 123 (January 1938), pp. 65–77.

Liddle, H. Gordon. *The Prisoner: An Experience of Forcible Feeding by a Suffragette*. Letchworth: Garden City Press, 1911.

Luckin, B. 'Towards a Social History of Institutionalization', *Social History* 8, No. 1 (January 1983), pp. 87–94.

Lyons, F.S.L. *Ireland Since the Famine*. London: Weidenfeld and Nicolson, 1971.

Lytton, C. *Prisons and Prisoners*. London: Heinemann, 1914.

Macartney, W. *Walls Have Mouths: A Record of Ten Years' Penal Servitude*. London: Gollancz, 1936.

McConville, S. *English Local Prisons 1860–1900: Next Only to Death*. London: Routledge , 1995.

—— *A History of English Prison Administration, Vol. 1 1750–1877*. London: Routledge & Kegan Paul, 1981.

—— 'The Victorian Prison: England, 1865–1965', in *The Oxford History of the Prison: The Practice of Punishment in Western Society*, ed. N. Morris and D.J. Rothman. New York and London: Oxford University Press, 1995.

McCord, N. 'The Fenians and Public Opinion in Great Britain', in *Fenians and Fenianism*, ed. M. Harmon. Dublin: Scepter Books, 1970.

McEwan, J.M. 'The Liberal Party and the Irish Question During the First World War', *Journal of British Studies* 12, No. 2 (May 1973), pp. 109–31.

McGowen, R. 'The Well-Ordered Prison, England 1780–1865', in *The Oxford History of the Prison: The Practice of Punishment in Western Society*, ed. N. Morris and D.J. Rothman. New York and Oxford: Oxford University Press, 1995.

MacLeod, R.M. 'Law, Medicine and Public Opinion: The Resistance to

Compulsory Health Legislation 1870–1907', Part I and Part II, *Public Law* (Summer–Autumn 1967), pp. 107–28 and 189–211.

Maier, C. 'The Politics of Time: Changing Paradigms of Collective Time and Private Time in the Modern Era', in *Changing Boundaries of the Political: Essays on the Evolving Balance Between the State and Society, Public and Private in Europe*, ed. C. Maier. Cambridge: Cambridge University Press, 1987.

Manton, J. *Mary Carpenter and the Children of the Streets*. London: Heinemann, 1976.

Mason, E.W. *Made Free in Prison*. London: George Allen and Unwin, 1918.

Mathiesen, T. 'The Viewer Society, Michael Foucault's "Panopticon" Revisited', *Theoretical Criminology* 1, No. 2 (1997), pp. 216–34.

Matthews, R. *Doing Time: An Introduction to the Sociology of Imprisonment*. London: Macmillan, 1999.

Maybrick, F. *My Fifteen Years Lost*. New York/London, 1905.

Mayhew, H., and J. Binney. *The Criminal Prisons of London and Scenes of London Life*. Bohn: L. Griffin, 1862; reprinted Frank Cass, 1968.

Monaghan, R. '"Votes for Women": An Analysis of the Militant Campaign', *Terrorism and Political Violence* 9, No. 2 (Summer 1997), pp. 65–78.

Morgan, S. 'Prison Lives: Critical Issues in Reading Prisoner Autobiography', *Howard Journal* 38 (3) (1999), pp. 328–40.

Morris, T. and P. Morris. *Pentonville: A Sociological Study of an English Prison*. London: Routledge & Kegan Paul, 1963.

Morrison, W.D. 'Are Our Prisons a Failure?', *The Fortnightly Review* 61 (April 1894), pp. 459–69.

—— 'The Increase in Crime', *The Nineteenth Century* 31 (June 1892), pp. 950–57.

—— 'Prison Reform', *The Fortnightly Review* 69 (May 1898), pp. 781–9.

—— 'Prisons and Prisoners', *The Fortnightly Review* 69 (May 1898), pp. 789–98.

Mountbatten, Earl of Burma. *Report of the Inquiry into Prison Escapes and Security*, Cmnd 3175. London: HMSO, 1966.

Neier, A. 'Confining Dissent: The Political Prisoner', in *The Oxford History of the Prison: The Practice of Punishment in Western Society*, ed. N. Morris and D.J. Rothman. New York and Oxford: Oxford University Press, 1995.

Nellis, M. 'John Galsworthy's *Justice*', *British Journal of Criminology* 36, No. 1 (Winter 1996), pp. 61–84.

Nicolson, D. 'Feigned Attempts at Suicide', *Journal of Medical Science* 17 (January 1872), pp. 484–99.

Nield, K. *Prostitution in the Victorian Age*. Farnborough: Gregg, 1973.

'No. 7'. *Twenty-Five Years in Seventeen Prisons: The Life Story of an Ex-Convict*. London: F.E. Robinson & Co., 1903.

O'Brien, P. 'Crime and Punishment as Historical Problem', *Journal of Social History* 4 (Summer 1978), pp. 508–17.

—— 'The Prison on the Continent: Europe, 1865–1965', in *The Oxford History of the Prison: The Practice of Punishment in Western Society*, ed. N. Morris and D.J. Rothman. New York and London: Oxford University Press, 1995.

O'Brien, W., and D. Ryan, eds. *Devoy's Post Bag 1871–1928, Vols I and II*, introduction by P.S. O'Hegarty. Dublin: J.C. Fallon, 1948 and 1953.

O'Donnell, F.H. 'Fenianism – Past and Present', *The Contemporary Review* 43 (May 1883), pp. 747–66.

O'Donovan Rossa, J. *Irish Rebels in English Prisons*. New York: Sadleir, 1991.

O'Kane, R.H.T. 'Against Legitimacy', *Political Studies* 41 (1993), pp. 471–87.

O'Sullivan, N. *Terrorism, Ideology and Revolution*. Sussex: Wheatsheaf Books, 1986.

Peddie, R. *The Dungeon Harp*. Edinburgh, 1844.

Peek, F. 'Official Optimism', *The Contemporary Review* 46 (July 1884), pp. 72–86.

Phillips, D. *Crime and Authority in Victorian England: The Black Country 1835–60*. London: Croom Helm, 1977.

Phillips, D. 'A Just Measure of Crime, Authority, Hunters and Blue Locusts': The "Revisionist" Social History of Crime and the Law in Britain, 1750–1850', in *Social Control and the State*, ed. S. Cohen and A. Scull. Oxford: Robertson, 1983.

Pollard, S. 'Factory Discipline in the Industrial Revolution', *Economic History Review* 16, Sr 2 (1963–4), pp. 254–71.

Pope Hennessy, J. 'The Treatment of Political Prisoners', *Transactions of the National Association for the Promotion of Social Science* (1867), pp. 295–8.

Priestly, P. *Jail Journeys: The English Prison Experience since 1918, Modern Prison Writings*. London: Routledge, 1989.

—— *Victorian Prison Lives: English Prison Biography 1830–1914*, London: Methuen, 1985.

Prison Matron (Frederick William Robinson). *Female Life in Prison*, 2 vols. London: Hurst & Blackett, 1862.

Purvis, J. 'Doing Feminist Women's History: Researching the Lives of Women in the Suffragette Movement in Edwardian England', in *Researching Women's Lives from a Feminist Perspective*, ed. M. Maynard and J. Purvis. London: Taylor & Francis, 1994.

—— 'The Prison Experiences of Suffragettes in Edwardian England', *Women's History Review* 4, No. 1 (1995), pp. 103–33.

Quin, P. 'Managing Prisons in a Time of Change', *Prison Service Journal* 94 (July 1994), pp. 2–10.

Quinlivan, P., and P. Rose. *The Fenians in England 1865–1872: A Sense of Security*. London: John Calder, 1982.

Quinton, R.F. *Crime and Criminals 1876–1910*. London: Longman, Green & Co., 1910.

Radzinowicz, L., and R. Hood. *A History of English Criminal Law, Vol. 5 The Emergence of Penal Policy*. London: Stevens & Sons, 1986.

—— *Ideology and Crime: A Study of Crime in its Social and Historical Context*. London: Heinemann, 1966.

—— 'The Status of Political Prisoners in England: The Struggle for Recognition', *Virginia Law Review* 65, No. 8 (1979), pp. 1421–81.

Rae, J. *Conscience and Politics: The British Government and the Conscientious Objector to Military Service 1916–1919*. London: Oxford University Press, 1970.

Rawls, J. 'Justice as Fairness', *Philosophical Review* 67, No. 2 (April 1958), pp. 164–94.

Reid, A.J. *Social Classes and Social Relations in Britain, 1850–1914*. London: Macmillan, 1992.

Reid, D.A. 'The Decline of Saint Monday, 1766–1876', in *Essays in Social History, Vol. 2*, ed. P. Thane and A. Sutcliffe. Oxford: Oxford University Press, 1986.

Rickards, Rev. C. *A Prison Chaplain on Dartmoor*. London: Edward Arnold, 1920.

Roberts, D. 'The Scandal at Birmingham Borough Gaol 1853: A Case for Penal Reform', *Journal of Legal History* 7 (1986), pp. 315–40.

Rothman, D. *Conscience and Convenience: The Asylum and its Alternatives in Progressive America*. Boston and Toronto: Little, Brown, 1980.

—— *The Discovery of the Asylum: Social Order and Disorder in the New Republic*. Boston and Toronto: Little, Brown, 1971.

Ruggles-Brise, E. *The English Prison System*. London: Macmillan, 1921.

Runciman, W.G. *Relative Deprivation and Social Justice. A Study of Attitudes to Social Inequality in the Twentieth Century*. London: Routledge & Kegan Paul, 1972.

Scott, J.C. *Weapons of the Weak: Everyday Forms of Peasant Resistance*. New Haven: Yale University Press, 1985.

Scott, S. *The Human Side of Crook and Convict Life*. London: Hurst & Blackett Ltd, 1924.

Semple, J. *Bentham's Prison: A Study of the Panopticon Penitentiary*. Oxford: Clarendon Press, 1993.

Sheehan, W.J. 'Finding Solace in Eighteenth-Century Newgate', *Crime in England 1550–1800*, ed. J.S. Cockburn. London: Methuen, 1977.

Short, K.R.M. *The Dynamite War: Irish-American Bombers in Victorian Britain*. Dublin: Gill & Macmillan, 1979.

Sigerson, G. *"Custodia Honesta": Treatment of Political Prisoners in Great Britain*, introduced by H.W. Nevison. Liberal Women's Press, 1913.

Sim, J. *Medical Power in Prisons: The Prison Medical Service in England 1774–1989*. Milton Keynes: Open University Press, 1990.

Sinn Fein Rebellion Handbook, compiled by the *Weekly Irish Times*, 1916.

Smith, B.A. 'Irish Prison Doctors – Men in the Middle, 1865–90', *Medical History*, 26 (1982), pp. 371–94.

Sorokin, P., and R. Merton. 'Social-time: A Methodological and Functional Analysis', in *The Sociology of Time*, ed. J. Hassard. London: Macmillan, 1990.

Sparks, R. 'Can Prisons be Legitimate', *British Journal of Criminology* 34 (Special Issue 1994), pp. 14–28.

Sparks, R., and A. Bottoms. 'Legitimacy and Order in Prisons', *British Journal of Sociology* 46, No. 1 (March 1995), pp. 45–62.

Sparks, R., A. Bottoms and W. Hay. *Prisons and the Problem of Order*. Oxford: Clarendon Press, 1996.

Stern, V. 'An Open Letter to Lord Justice Wolf', *Prison Service Journal* 77 (1990), pp. 11–12.

Stockdale, E. 'The Rise of Joshua Jebb, 1837–1850', *British Journal of Criminology* 16, No. 2 (April 1976), pp. 164–70.

—— 'A Short History of Prison Inspection in England', *British Journal of Criminology* 23 (1983), pp. 209–28.

—— *A Study of Bedford Prison 1660–1877*. London: Phillimore, 1977.

Sykes, G.M. *Society of Captives: The Study of a Maximum Security Prison*. Princeton: Princeton University Press, 1958.

Taylor, C. 'Foucault on Freedom and Truth', *Political Theory* 12, No. 2 (May 1984), pp. 152–83.

Taylor, I., P. Walton and J. Young. *The New Criminology: For a Theory of Deviance*, International Library of Sociology, ed. J. Rex. London: Routledge & Kegan Paul, 1973.

Thomas, J., and R. Pooley. *The Exploding Prison: Prison Riots and the Case of Hull*. London: Junction Books, 1980.

Thomas, J.E. *The English Prison Officer since 1850: A Study in Conflict*. London: Routledge & Kegan Paul, 1972.

—— 'Killed on Duty', *Prison Service Journal* (July 1972), pp. 9–10.

Thompson, A.S. 'A Review of Prison Diet in England and Wales', *Prison Service Journal* 68 (October 1987), pp. 19–22.

Thompson, E.P. 'Time, Work Discipline and Industrial Capitalism', *Past and Present* 38 (1967): pp. 56–97.

Thomson, B. *The Story of Dartmoor Prison*. London: William Heinemann, 1907.

Tibber, P. 'Edmund Du Cane and the Prison Act 1877', *Howard Journal* 19 (1980), pp. 9–16.

Tomes, N. 'A "Torrent of Abuse": Crimes of Violence between Working-Class Men and Women in London, 1840–1875', *Journal of Social History* 11 (1978), pp. 328–45.

Tumin, S. *Doing Time or Using Time – Report of a Review by Her Majesty's Chief Inspector of Prisons for England and Wales of Regimes in Prison Service Establishments in England and Wales Cm.2128*. London: HMSO, 1993.

Walker, N. *Punishment, Danger and Stigma: The Morality of Criminal Justice*. Oxford: Blackwell, 1980.

Webb, S., and B. Webb. *English Prisons Under Local Government*. London: Longman, Green & Co., 1932.

Welldon, J.E.C. 'Conscience and the Conscientious Objector', *The Nineteenth Century and After* 79 (May 1916), pp. 977–87.

Wheatly, P. 'Riots and Serious Mass Disorder', *Prison Service Journal* 44 (1981), pp. 1–4.

Wiener, M.J. *Reconstructing the Criminal: Culture, Law and Policy in England, 1830–1914*. Cambridge: Cambridge University Press, 1990.

Williamson Mason, E. *Made Free in Prison*. London: George Allen & Unwin, 1918.

Wilsnack, R.W. 'Explaining Collective Violence in Prisons: Problems and Possibilities', in *Prison Violence*, ed A.K. Cohen, G.F. Cole and R.G. Bailey. Lexington, Mass.: D.C. Heath, 1976.

Wolfgang, M.E., and F. Ferracuti. *The Subculture of Violence: Towards an Integrated theory in Criminology*. London: Tavistock, 1967.

Woolf, H., and S. Tumin. *Prison Disturbances April 1990*, Cm.1456. London: HMSO, 1991.

Zedner, L. *Women, Crime, and Custody in Victorian England*. Oxford: Clarendon Press, 1991.

Zimring, F.E., and G.J. Hawkins. *Deterrence: The Legal Threat in Crime Control*. Chicago and London: University of Chicago Press, 1973.

Unpublished material

Carrabine, E. 'The State of Power: Taking the "New-Old Penology", Seriously in Understanding Prison Riots', paper presented to the British Criminology Conference, July 1995.

Frouxides, S.G. 'The English Prison Inspectorate 1835–77: Its Role and Effectiveness', Ph.D. thesis, University of London, 1983.

Saunders, J.F. 'Institutionalised Offenders: A Study of the Victorian Institution and its Inmates with Special Reference to Late Nineteenth Century Warwickshire', Ph.D. thesis, University of Warwick, 1983.

Contemporary journals and newspapers

Blackwood's Edinburgh Magazine
The Chatham News
The Contemporary Review
The Cornhill Magazine
The Edinburgh Review
The Evening News
The Fortnightly Review
Hansard's Parliamentary Debates

The Hull Advertiser
The Hull Daily Mail
The Nineteenth Century (and After)
The Saturday Review
The Times
Transactions of the the National Association for the Promotion of Social Sciences

Index

Lightning Source UK Ltd.
Milton Keynes UK
UKOW021319040212

186650UK00001B/43/P